Women of Belize

Women of Belize

Gender and Change in Central America

Irma McClaurin

Rutgers University Press
New Brunswick, New Jersey, and London

Second paperback printing, 2000

Library of Congress Cataloging-in-Publication Data

McClaurin, Irma.
    Women of Belize : gender and change in Central America / Irma
    McClaurin.
        p.   cm.
    Includes bibliographical references and index.
    ISBN 0-8135-2307-9 (cloth: alk. paper).—ISBN 0-8135-2308-7
    (pbk. : alk. paper)
    1. Women—Belize—Social conditions.   I. Title.
HQ1470.5.M33   1996
305.4'097282—dc20   95-52269
                                                              CIP

British Cataloging-in-Publication information available

Published by Rutgers University Press, New Brunswick, New Jersey

For my children, Antonio Maceo and Zena Carlota Pearl

Contents

Acknowledgments

This book is dedicated especially to the memories of two women: Sylvia Helen Forman, whose insights, tough love, and rigorous standards of excellence enabled me to negotiate the tricky terrain of anthropology, and Bernice Yorke, whose Belizean hospitality and wisdom were unmatched; to my Belizean sisters (Zee Edgell, Santiago Espat, Barbara Fernandez, Eva Middleton, Therese Paulino, Wilma Wright, Ida Westby, Rita Wagner, Denyse Barrows, and many others whose paths I crossed), without whose friendship, support, and cultural guidance the research for this work could not have been completed; to the Belizean women's groups and nongovernmental organizations who unsparingly contributed their time and experiences; to my children, Zena Carlota Pearl Allen and Antonio Maceo McClaurin Allen, who I hope will accept this book as an equal exchange for the sacrifices they had to make of my time and attention, though never my love; and finally to "Evelyn," "Rose," "Zola," and the other women and men who wished to remain nameless, without whose life experiences this book would not have been possible.

Although the act of putting pen to paper may be a solitary venture, the process of completing a book is collective. Thus while I take full responsibility for the ideas contained in these pages, I owe its completion to more people than I can ever thank. Along the way I was supported in my efforts by various individuals who gave me suggestions, encouragement, love and whose general good spirits sustained me through a communal reservoir of strength and determination as I struggled to finish the last page, the last word. I am forever indebted to my mother, Bennie Pearl Brown, and her husband, Navy Brown, for all the comforts of home they provided me whenever I needed nurturing; to my sister, Reece René Bell, and her family, who resurrected the meaning of extended family; to Cecila Gross, who fed me with food and friendship; to Tom McBee and Carlie and Gary Tartakov who gave me sanctuary amid the isolation of Iowa; to Lou, whose friendship and love were a gift in the early stages; to Johnnetta Betsch Cole, whose ability to combine scholarship and social responsibility with anthropology first inspired me; to William Darity and Esther and Eugene Terry, who always showered me with words of kindness and support; to Kesho Scott, whose friendship, vision, and love were constant and whose own writings were a source of inspiration; to Ralph Faulkingham and Robert Paynter, professors and mentors, who encouraged me to be creative in writing anthropology; and the many others—including Helan Page, Martin Wobst, Carlene Edie, Sue Hyatt, Maki Mandela, and Tom McGuire—who supplied me with friendship and support en route to the completion of this work.

In Belize, I was fortunate to find my path unobstructed. I wish to thank the governmental agencies and individuals who supported the research on which this ethnography is based: the Department of Archaeological Services; the Ministry of Natural Resources; the staff of the Central Statistical Office; Ruby Beiber and Anita Zetina, former and current directors, respectively, of the Department of Women's Affairs; and the Social Service Staff of the Toledo District. Others who gave generously of their time and knowledge were Joseph Palacio of the University of the West Indies, School of Continuing Studies; the Honorable Kathy Esquivel; Al and Zee Edgell; the staff of the Toledo Small Farmer Association; the staff of the Society for the Promotion of Education and Research; Jewel Quallo, director of the Belize Family Life Association; Belize Women Against Violence; Eva Middleton, director of Breast Is Best; Lucia Engleton, former director of the Belize Rural Women's Association; the Belize Public Library; and the Belize Archives.

The research for this book would not have been possible without the support of a National Science Foundation Minority Pre-doctoral Fellowship, a National Science Foundation Travel Grant, and a Sigma Xi Research Grant. Various phases of the writing were completed under the auspices of a University of Massachusetts at Amherst Graduate Fellowship, a Grinnell College Consortium for a Stronger Minority Presence (CSMP) Dissertation Fellowship, and several Grinnell College faculty grants. To Karen Groves, secretary at Grinnell College, I give my unabashed appreciation for her attention to the tedious but necessary details during the final stages of manuscript preparation and to Kevin Engel, Grinnell College reference librarian, my gratitude for all his support.

Women of Belize

Prologue

Sitting here at Chaa Creek, staring out at the Maya Mountains, I am awed by the events that have brought me to this country. On September 9, 1990, I first traveled to Belize, Central America. Almost four years later I have arrived again, this time to finish a book. As I stare out at an expanse of verdant mounds cascading the sky I am elated over being here; I feel as if I am sitting in the palm of some great being, looking upward into eternity. Yet I am saddened by the knowledge that the next time I return to Belize, to this "diamond in the rough," another human dent will have been made somewhere. Already I can see land being cleared down below me—whether for planting or a road, I don't know, but the imprint is visible and seemingly permanent.

On the days that I tramp through Terra Nova, a national land reserve set aside to preserve the plants and trees used by traditional healers in Belize, or Monkey Bay, a private land reserve, I am acutely aware that my footprints are indelible. Even as I work with a crew of scientists and student apprentices to map and tag the forest growth and, we hope, preserve this last precious resource, I know that I have unwittingly stepped on a plant, smashed a seed, and possibly destroyed the very things we set out to save. This is the dual-edged sword of human existence: creativity and destruction.

Change, welcomed or not, is inevitable. I know this from the fact that since my first site visit to Belize in 1990, and since my extended stay in 1991 to do fieldwork, so much has happened here. The country has grown by over forty thousand people since the census of 1980, with a number of Central American immigrants still uncounted.[1]

It is raining people in Belize. Spanish-speaking refugees seek serenity from the political and economic turmoil of their native Guatemala and El Salvador that threatens to annihilate them. They escape to sanctuary in Belize. One refugee camp has sprung up outside of Belmopan, the capital. It is called the Valley of Peace. But all is not peaceful in Belize.

And yet, despite the growing number of Spanish-speaking immigrants, the Caribbean influence is strongly imprinted onto the country. Prior to the 1991 census, Creoles dominated the population. Although occasionally a person of any racial background that includes Black ancestry will use the term "Creole" to indicate a mixed heritage, the word most frequently refers to both people and cultural elements that are a mélange of African, West Indian, and Afro-British traits. Historically, Creoles have resided in Belize City and dominated civil service jobs. Unlike in the United States, where people are essentially viewed through a lens of skin color (combined with known ancestry) and classified accordingly, in Belize ethnicity is highly nuanced. While to my Americanized eyes, Creoles and Garifuna, another ethnic group descended from a fusion of escaped slaves and Carib Indians, are both "Afro-Belizeans," linked by their African ancestry, Creoles take pains to distinguish themselves from Garifuna. When I lapse into my cultural habit of lumping all people of African ancestry together, I am reminded that I stand in a different cultural context in Belize. Creole parents, I am told, caution their children about ethnic differences early on: "We da Creole and deh da Garifuna; we da no one." (We are Creole and they are Garifuna; we are not the same.)

There is an ongoing debate in Belize today over whether Creole is an "authentic" culture. Rather than Creole culture being taken as another example of cultural diffusion, innovation and transculturation in the Americas, the lingering evidence of British tastes in food, manners, daily routines (like tea time), and education are viewed as a colonial hangover (and hence inauthentic), which adds fuel to the debate. The discussion, while fascinating, may be impossible to resolve. Much depends on the definition of culture and authenticity that is applied, and even anthropologists are not always able to agree. In the meantime, though Creoles no longer constitute the majority, their influence is strong. The Creole language continues to serve as the lingua franca of daily life and is indispensable.

Any attempt to neatly categorize people, towns, or political alliances in Belize immediately falls apart. This is a country of paradoxes and malleability. Moving about, one inevitably encounters Creoles living in the northern and western districts of Corozal, Cayo, and Orange Walk who speak Spanish and reside comfortably within the Mestizo cultural milieu and Mestizos who reside in Belize City, speak only Creole, and have little to do with Spanish culture. One can also find within a matter of miles, minutes, or hours East Indians, Garifuna or Garinagu, Chinese, and Whites (mostly German-speaking Mennonites and a small but growing number of American, Canadian, and British expatriates) as well as Creoles, Mestizos, and Maya, all coexisting fairly harmoniously. Belize has no ethnic voting blocs, because neither of the two political parties could prevail without the support of many different ethnic groups. In this country, "difference" sometimes seems to make very little difference.

Other changes in Belize have a more personal meaning. Several people are now gone who were crucial to my acquiring some understanding of Belize, its people, and its cultures. One such person who has passed on is Mrs. Bernice Yorke, my proverbial guardian angel. A "proper" Creole woman, Mrs. Yorke was noted for her role as an educator in the community—the private school she started continues to operate on a minimal budget but with an impeccable reputation. By way of the school, her Bahai faith, and her social standing, Mrs. Yorke knew virtually everyone in Belize and presented me to officials and acquaintances alike as if I were kin. No matter to which district I traveled, Mrs. Yorke always found me a host. After her sudden death, her unexpected burial in Guatemala rather than Belize for religious reasons was taken by some Belizeans as a national tragedy. Yet others, like myself, see it as perhaps a sign, an omen. I remember that Mrs. Yorke had a sharp sense of humor, marked by double-entendre jokes, and was not afraid to stir up controversy. I am not beyond thinking that perhaps this was her way, inadvertently, of fostering international relations. In death, she may have found a means to ease the ongoing territorial dispute between her beloved Belize and its nemesis Guatemala.[2] After all, what Belizeans can hate a country in which one of their beloved kinspersons is buried?

Change in Belize is ever-present, and in some instances the question of whether it is good or bad seems irrelevant and indiscernible. Except for those rare moments of natural or political disasters, most change is slow and can only be disclosed by time. One of our tasks as scholars is to examine the degree or rate of change and analyze and document its impact. Thus, even as I think about the Belize I have come to know and love, it is undergoing this process. The same is true of the research I conducted for this book. Some of the conditions that compelled me to document women's lives may no longer obtain, at least according to one "cultural consultant" who hesitated to give me permission to quote her because she feared that people might believe that the Belize of today is exactly as I describe the Belize of 1991.[3] Other consultants argue that there are a few changes, but the major problems of economic uncertainty, domestic violence, and lack of self-esteem still characterize many Belizean women's lives. Moreover, there is no telling what effect the presence of so many new immigrant women from cultures characterized by *machismo* will have on Belize's cultural practices. Thus the overarching issues seem almost eternal. This book stands as a kind of testimonial, a form of "witnessing," for the women whose stories are not included but who face these issues daily in their lives.

At the time I began writing, women feared talking about what I would call "women's issues."[4] The lives of some of the women I met seemed held together by a thinly woven mat of silence. Yet like the sap that suddenly emerges each time you snap a leaf or scrape the bark of certain trees, I often encountered spontaneous bursts of revelations and confidences. One moment a rushing of words, then suddenly gone, dried up like the sap, though we all knew that underneath the women's fears, their worries, their dreams were ever present.

The changes that most affect women's lives in Belize today are apparent both at the individual and at the broader structural and institutional level. The Belize Organization for Women and Development launched a minimum wage campaign in 1992 on behalf of domestic workers.[5] They were able to reverse a minimum wage law that would have further entrenched unequal wages and privileged those jobs dominated by men over those held traditionally by women. Another triumph and change for Belizean women was the passage of the Domestic Violence Bill in 1993. Whether women actually take advantage of the protection promised under the law remains to be seen. This is an area in need of attention, since violent crimes against women (deaths and disfigurements from mutilations, burnings, and beatings) are still prevalent.

It does not seem too ambitious to say that today Belizean women appear more aware of their rights as women. The proof of this is in the crowds that form weekly inside Family Court in the Parslow Building on North Front Street upstairs from the post office.[6] Women go alone or with friends as they enlist the aid of the legal system either to collect child support or to file the documents needed to require a man to maintain his children. The payments they receive are small, but for some they are the difference between starvation and survival. The face of the government is changing too: there are more women today in positions of power (heads of departments, permanent secretaries, and so on) than there were a decade ago.[7] And within political parties, women's issues are gaining greater visibility as part of the political agendas; whether this translates into real political capital for women remains to be seen. On a different front, Women Against Violence, the organizational catalyst on domestic violence issues, has begun work on a sexual harassment bill.

The specific women I interviewed are at different stages in their continuing search for meaning in the events and experiences of their lives. Their ability to do something about their circumstances is largely determined by the economic, social, and personal resources open to them. When I ask them how things are with them, their common response is "not bad, surviving." Surviving! They still struggle to make do in a world of increasingly limited resources, trying to make meaningful decisions that create greater opportunities for themselves and their families.

Ironically, "development" or "modernization" in the form of technology is still touted by foreign aid agencies as the panacea of developing countries. Yet it seems to have had little substantive effect on women's lives. Although technology has brought to Belize cable television, computers, and a growing tourist industry, I still observe women and children in Belize City carrying water in plastic jugs from faucets that are blocks away, because they cannot afford indoor plumbing or the high price of water. Kerosene sales are stable because many are unable to afford electricity. Whatever benefits are reaped by the government from development projects, few trickle down.

Those at the lowest rung of the economic ladder in this developing country are the women and their children. Many of Belize's women who might desire to work are either unemployed or underemployed. In the 1991 census, of the women surveyed, most listed their "occupation" as "home duties," work that we know is labor intensive, unpaid, and undervalued.

For now, it seems necessary to offer one caveat: because of all the changes I have described and owing to my belief that human beings are predictably different at any given point in their lives, future researchers who go to Belize with the intent of trying to reconstruct this project or those travelers in search of the Belize I have captured here will undoubtedly find "dis heah time no stand like befo time"; the present is not like the past. This work stands then mostly as a record of one small segment of the "befo time."

Chapter 1　*Women of Belize*

This book is about the women of Belize, Central America, and how a few of them are working to change the gender rules, ideas, attitudes, and behaviors that govern the meaning of what it is to be a woman in their communities and country. Others, at a different stage, are in the process of figuring out how to do the same. Everyday around the world, in India, Africa, Latin America, Europe, and the United States, women confront the power and control of gender. They face personal and social constraints that are generally communicated through words, cultural symbols and practices, individual deeds, and institutional policies. In response, some women have moved to set limits on the degree to which these cultural elements determine their lives.

Setting Limits on Traditional Gender Roles

All of us know when we have reached our limit—whether physical or emotional. We all know when what is being demanded of us is too great for the meager reward, if any, that we might receive. This book is about how women find courage and awareness in the events of their lives and through collective action to dare to challenge the power of gender in their country. They are now the ones who set limits.

The decisions these women of Belize make, as they strive toward personal and social change, directly affect whether they will participate in gender roles, by which I mean the "tasks and activities that a culture assigns to the sexes"; whether they will behave according to gender stereotypes, which are "oversimplified but strongly held ideas about the characteristics of males and females"; and whether they will accept gender stratification, which refers to an "unequal distribution of rewards," especially the resources, power, prestige, and personal freedoms that are socially valued.[1] By taking action, by becoming agents in their own lives, some women in this small Central American country have acquired a greater understanding and appreciation of themselves as individuals. Other women have come to recognize that together women may grow into a social and political force to be reckoned with—a force that has the potential to transform how gender is understood, practiced, and lived. Every one of these women, regardless of the level of their commitment to collective action, seems to have experienced greater self-awareness and introspection.

This ethnography stands as an exploration of the varied individual strategies used by women to achieve personal, community, and institutional change. The study grew out of my interactions with women in various organizations and a survey I conducted in the small town of "Lemongrass" on women's participation in such groups.[2] I spoke with fifty-seven women, of whom twenty-three identified themselves as active members of women's groups and twenty-four said they were not members of such groups. In addition to these two segments, I also interviewed seven Maya women who lived in the rural part of Toledo District, where Lemongrass is located.

As I collected my data for the survey, a few women's voices stood out. They seemed able to speak frankly about their lives, the problems they faced, and the strategies they had devised or hoped to create to resolve some of the issues affecting their lives. Of the fifty-seven women who completed the survey, I interviewed five women about their lives. Three of their narratives form the core of this work. I do not think it accidental that the three most articulate were also members of women's organizations. My reasons for reaching this conclusion will become more apparent later, when I discuss the impact of women's groups on the lives of their members. This ethnography is thus biased toward women who are activists.

Women's groups do not operate in isolation, of course. Although the presence of women's groups may help to create a climate amenable to change, Helen Safa has suggested that multiple variables such as land ownership, increased educational levels, expanded participation in the labor force, and migration may be much more significant in accounting for women's achievement of increased economic autonomy and their efforts to gain empowerment in the sociocultural spheres of daily life.[3]

The survey I conducted not only focused on specific issues related to the efficacy of women's groups in individual lives, but also tried to gauge women's awareness about relevant laws and other public matters. The interviews, however, were much broader in scope. My aim in collecting these narratives was to present the meaning women themselves attach to the events of their lives and to analyze the way in which they are sometimes able to translate this understanding into specific actions. This process of change, this experience of agency, is best articulated by the women themselves. The ethnography is built around their voices primarily, with my own voice as the anthropological "interlocutor," whose role is to reveal the linkages that exist between the women's personal understanding of the power of gender (evident in the roles, stereotypes, and structures of stratification) and larger social processes.

Toward this end, I have sought to describe the beliefs, values, and behaviors that make up Belize's culture of gender. By focusing on women as the unit of analysis, I hope to reveal the specific ways in which they are enculturated and the strategies they deploy to negotiate, modify, and challenge gender. I also hope to disclose the way in which they sometimes unintentionally modify and challenge their culture and society. Collectively the women's narratives provide personal insights into important aspects of Belize's culture of gender, which include, but are not limited to, the cultural view of women as minors and property; the reasons for the economic-sexual dynamics that underlie many heterosexual relationships in Belize; the degree to which the physical and mental abuse of women by men reveals strategies to elicit the former's compliance; the process of gender enculturation for women; and the role of women's groups in changing attitudes and behaviors in various communities.

In this chapter I discuss some of the critical stances in anthropology (gender, reflexivity, dialogic process) that have shaped my own thinking and guided this work. One important dimension is the relationship between my personal experiences as an African American woman anthropologist in the field to the evolution of my research. I also explain my approach to the use of oral narratives in the ethnographic process. In chapter 2, I look at some of the social and demographic features that influence Belize's culture of gender. These include ethnicity and ethnic relations, immigration and migration patterns, the origins of its people, the formation of a national identity, and the impact of changing population patterns. Chapter 3 focuses on the sites of my fieldwork: the market in Belize City and the town of Lemongrass. Chapters 4, 6, and 8 are the oral narratives. Fashioned from in-depth interviews (edited for length), field notes, observations, and my own recollections and interpretations of my interactions with the women who tell the stories of their lives, these chapters literally speak for themselves. Though of varying lengths, the three narratives reflect the individuality of the women who speak them. The chapters stand as testimonies about physical and/or emotional abuse, personal frustrations, and the women's involvement in women's groups that seem to transcend boundaries of ethnicity, religion, politics, and education. The commonalities that resonate through these narratives speak strongly for the potential that Belizean women have to organize in order to change specific aspects of their lives.

Chapters 5 and 7 shift away from the microperspective; both take up general themes introduced by the individual narratives and elaborate upon their significance within the larger societal context. Chapter 5 looks at the process of gender enculturation—that is, how young girls learn their social roles. I also analyze some of the behaviors and attitudes that shape women's sexuality and become part of the mechanisms that help to form the social category of "woman" in the context of Belize. Chapter 7 is a macroanalysis of the structural elements and institutions (political, economic, and religious) in the society that conspire with cultural beliefs and practices to produce and reinforce women's subordination.

Chapter 9 explores the way in which women negotiate the culture of gender and challenge the constraints of the gender system by participating in women's groups. Using the case study method, I examine the membership composition and range of activities of two groups and evaluate their relative success and failure. National women's groups are also assessed in terms of their potential (or lack of potential) to foster a mass women's movement in the country. Little has been written about Belizean women's involvement in party politics despite the importance of political party affiliations in individuals' and groups' access to resources through patron-client relationships.[4] My discussion of women and politics in Belize, as part of a larger description of women's agency, affirms their enormous contributions to Belize's struggle for self-rule and independence. Finally, chapter 10 picks up all the filaments of ideology, theory, cultural meaning and practices, history, and personal experience and weaves them into a commentary on the study of gender in Belize.

As I wrote this book, I consciously sought to distance myself from traditional ethnographic writings that focus primarily on the analysis of structures and systems. This ethnography is not an elaborate study of kinship, political institutions, systems of reciprocity, or the exotic "Other." I have chosen to focus on the individual lives of a few Belizean women. My conclusions emerge from their voices, their experiences, and the sense that they make out of how the culture of gender in Belize is both constructed and lived. In keeping with the aims of what Lila Abu-Lughod calls the "ethnography of the particular," I use the specific words and world view of a few select women.[5] Doing so enables me to describe some, though certainly by no means all, Belizean women's experiences. As I moved toward the completion of this work, I was encouraged by the women themselves to share their stories because they are "real, not made up."

Finding Stories: Deciphering Women's Narratives

Life history informants are not just found, they are made. In the engagement between interviewer and interviewee, something clicks. In the process of asking survey questions I looked for a level of self-reflection and thoughtfulness. Even if the informant has little schooling, you can tell that they've given thought to their lives. It is "awareness," "consciousness" if you will, that lets you know intuitively that there is a story.   —*Field notes, 1991*

I began my research with the aim of studying women's grass-roots organizations; I visited national organizations in Belize City and from them obtained information about local women's groups. But I often found that women's grass-roots organizations were more real in name than in any formal sense. Structured organizational meetings rarely occurred. Women met when they could. Indeed, leadership and authority were often shared, and a real effort was made to cast the net of participation as broadly as possible. Some groups organized around particular objectives—breast feeding, family planning—others based their agenda on events in the community or concerned themselves with specific issues that emerged in individual members' lives. The absence of structured organizational forms that corresponded to those found among women's groups in the United States forced me to redirect my attention. A year after I left the field, as I sought to understand what I had observed, I realized that a more general description and analysis of women's experiences and status in the broader social context were needed before I could understand the lives of the members of these women's groups. Thus my emphasis shifted from a narrow focus on women's groups to the larger economic, sociocultural, and political contexts of women's lives in Belize.

In retrospect I realize how much I would have missed had I followed my original research design. Conversations with women directed me toward understanding how various beliefs and behaviors related to gender operated in their lives and how these shaped the attitudes that prevailed in their communities. I also wanted to find out how women maneuvered their lives and negotiated strategies around what they had defined as "women's issues." For data on these aspects of daily life, I turned to the women themselves.

The voices in this work were recorded in a variety of settings and through a multiplicity of mediums. Upon my first entrance to the field, I used the standard ethnographic method of participant observation. This was later augmented by a survey I conducted on women's groups and women's issues, analysis and interpretation of census data, reading local newspapers, listening to radio and television talk shows on issues pertaining to women, and conducting both informal and formal interviews. Some of the information and perspectives that appear in this work were derived from my more formal discussions with people as I sat on their verandas, in their kitchens, or as they gathered in stores. Other data emerged from the responses women gave to my survey; still other data grew out of spontaneous conversations that I held with various women as we walked home in the encroaching dusk or lingered to speak in the market. The specific information that I needed to understand the community context for Belizean women's lives came not only from the survey responses or from interviews but from gossip, "kitchen-talk," confessions, and the like. "Cultural experts" on the problems women faced were in abundance. Every woman I met was a potential authority in this area. I learned to accept the acts of "making self" that I encountered in some of my interviews. In doing so what I observed and heard were not just women concerned with providing me with a chronology of life events but individuals formulating an identity through the conveyance of their stories.

Sherna Berger Gluck and Daphne Patai remind us in their work on women's oral history that "narrators frequently shape their narratives according to their own sense of direction, often in the face of considerable interference from single-minded interviewers." [6] As narrators attend to the details they are telling, they arrive at an understanding they did not have at the beginning. An epiphany of self emerges as they seek to explain the meaning of various experiences and events in their lives. These are also moments of consciousness and empowerment within which oral narratives not only "empower" but, in Gluck and Patai's words, also serve to validate the "importance of the speaker's life experience."

Of equal significance to the content of oral narratives is their form. It is through the form of women's testimonies that we glimpse patterns of how they think and reflect on their lives. Although it is true, as Gluck and Patai assert, that in the editing of oral narratives appropriation can occur under the guise of empowerment, I have tried to maintain the authenticity and accuracy of the women's narratives. They were edited for length, where needed, but I attempted to maintain the narrative sequence each woman established rather than impose my own. The narratives' movement back and forth through time may be disconcerting, for example, but it reflects how the women actually think about their lives. The women in this ethnography did not tell their stories in neat, chronological style. Rather, as they discussed present issues, these often triggered a memory about the past, and vice versa. Thus past events are just as urgent and meaningful as something that happened today.

The language the women speak is Creole. Their words have been phonetically rendered in English, because at the time of my study there was no standardized spelling for Creole, but I have kept their original syntax, repetitions, and grammatical constructions. My goal was to maintain, as much as possible, the distinctiveness of each woman's voice.

Topical subheadings serve as guides throughout each of these narratives. They are my interventions to illustrate the degree to which certain themes permeate each woman's experience. The themes reveal the commonalities of women's lives in Belize across ethnicity, across differing educational levels, across vastly different personal circumstances, and despite women's varied responses to those circumstances. They demonstrate the degree to which the sociocultural features of Belize's culture of gender have produced a kind of structural homogeneity with regard to women's political power, their economic situation, and their views of their sexuality.

Also reflected in the narratives are the social relations between the ethnographer and the consultants in the field. Often this part of the field experience gets left on the floor of the editing room so that after the first few pages of a book, the ethnographer vanishes.[7] I have kept myself a part of these textualizations to emphasize the fact that every research and interview process is framed by a negotiation of power relations. Keeping myself in the text discloses the tensions that emerged as I mediated my authoritative position in the field with my desire to break women's historic silence by sharing a power of what I would call "emvoicement," something that I would argue emerges in the collective process of talking, documenting, and writing about certain issues with my cultural consultants, who served not only as authors but also as editors and critics at virtually every stage of this work.

The results of this kind of collective, inclusive research strategy can be unpredictable; often the unusual occurs when conventions are discarded. One of the women, for example, completely appropriated the interview process for her own purposes. Zola established her own authority by ignoring my attempts to change the subject and elicit responses to specific questions; instead she focused on what she thought was important for me to know about her life.

The example of Zola and the other encounters makes the narratives seem more like conversations (and sometimes arguments) with friends rather than interviews between strangers. In this type of situation, one of the most important aspects of "data collection" was the relationship of trust and openness frequently forged between myself and the women. My experience is similar to those of Lila Abu-Lughod, Sally Cole, and Sally Price, who all speak in their ethnographies about the highly personal nature of studying women cross-culturally.[8]

Common Plight

When I traveled around Belize talking to women of different ethnic groups (mostly Creole, Garifuna, and East Indian), I believe it fair to say that some of the women viewed me as "different." I think they saw me not as better, but certainly different, because I had left my children and husband to come and do what I wanted to do. Few of them could imagine any circumstance, outside of illness or death, that would release them from their obligations as mothers and wives or give them the same degree of mobility and independence that my own circumstances symbolized. Yet these differences did not separate us. They asked my opinion on issues and problems, but I don't think they valued my insights any more than those of other women in their communities. My own problems, mainly an impending divorce, which emerged toward the end of my fieldwork, did raise questions for me, which I shared with them, about the consequences of any woman's (poor or privileged; educated or illiterate) autonomy. I discussed this issue and many others with my Belizean friends through letters and phone calls when I returned home, and again in face-to-face conversations during my return visits in 1992 and 1993. One question we all pondered, despite the differences in our personal circumstances, was whether we as women could ever acquire the requisite freedom to fulfill our own desires. This is not just a woman's question, but a human one. We all feel the pull to assert our individual desires at one time or another in our life cycle, yet as social creatures, we are always constrained by societal or community rules, obligations, and expectations. The reality of these constraints may limit our ability to fulfill our desire but in no way diminishes the desire.

At the start of my fieldwork, I often struggled with how much my western-focused, feminist-oriented perspective might interfere with my ability to gain women's confidence. The incident from my fieldwork, "A Birthday Celebration," described later in this chapter, helps illustrate how unfounded my fears were. This does not mean that Belizean women necessarily agreed with my interpretation of their circumstances. Rather, the vignette conveys the trust the women gave me and throws into sharp relief some of the ongoing questions researchers ought to have about fieldwork and ethics. The boundaries between what are true "data" and what are personal revelations disclosed in the context of intimate discussions are sometimes blurred, and I had to make sure that I specifically asked whether I could use an insight offered during an exchange of confidences. Joseph G. Jorgensen, in an early essay entitled "On Ethics and Anthropology," sees a central tension between our quest for knowledge and the "right of the individual to private personality."[9] For me in Belize, fortunately, enough trust developed that I was never denied permission, and in fact sometimes, as we sat late in Evelyn's shop waiting for the clock to strike five, I was encouraged to take notes while the women discussed the problems of men, mothers-in-law, and children. As a result of these kinds of interaction, the interview process was continuous, taking place in an atmosphere of trust.

Trust is also a crucial element in the matter of confidentiality. The way I resolved what might have been a sticking point in a town so small was to give each participant a promise of anonymity. I thus use pseudonyms for the women I quote, unless they are public figures whose identity would be impossible to hide. At the same time, I have tried to be as accurate as possible when identifying the location and sources of my data.

Although I felt it my professional responsibility to protect as much as possible the women who expressed their opinions about matters that were sensitive, taboo, or politically charged in their community, I was also guided by an ethics of friendship and the discretion it demands. Gender in Belize and in Lemongrass was and is a controversial subject. In Belize, as elsewhere, most women are under the "protection" of men, their husbands, brothers, fathers, and lovers, as well as under the protection of the state. Women who speak out about matters such as domestic violence (often viewed as "private" or "family business") incur great personal and emotional risks. I believe my promise of anonymity gave some women the courage to speak openly about their personal lives without fear of reprisal. I have done my best to protect those who wanted to remain anonymous, yet desired that their lives stand as a kind of beacon for others on the same path. I remain in awe of the trust they placed in me. I admire their honesty and their courage.

Despite tremendous differences in opportunity, nationality, ethnicity, and language that separate women in Belize from one another and that separate them from me, there is much that links us together. At any given moment in our lives, certain features of our social reality as women bind us in a common plight, regardless of our age group and regardless of whether we live in villages, towns, or cities, regardless of whether we speak the same languages or share the same values, and regardless of race and nationality. In this respect, studying gender in Belize resonates in my own and other women's experiences throughout the world.

Fieldwork and Self

> She had finally after all these decades made it across. The elderly Shouters in the person of the out-islanders had reached out their arms like one great arm and drawn her into their midst.   —Paule Marshall, *Praisesong for the Widow*

The bonds of trust that developed between some of the women and myself were very powerful. For me they confirmed the presence of an intangible quality in the experience of womanhood that transcended cultural boundaries. Some researchers have argued for the existence of a women's culture that permeates every society and that binds women across differences.[10] It is difficult, however, to attribute such bonds to a single cause. Rather, while I subscribe to a general belief that women may communicate with one another on the basis of common experiences arising out of shared social roles, I am not convinced that a single factor such as gender completely accounts for the development of such relationships and bonds. A multiplicity of variables enter into the equation and may explain why one researcher might be more accepted by a community of women than another.

In addition to my gender, I believe that my "race"/ethnicity was also a significant factor in my fieldwork. I am an African American woman anthropologist, still something of an anomaly in the field of anthropology, but someone who has multilayered perspectives. These dimensions of my personal and cultural identity placed me in an unusual position in the Caribbean/Latin American context of Belize. As anthropologists we are trained to deal with the duality of our status as outsiders and conditioned to anticipate an ongoing struggle to become an insider in the field setting to the extent that local custom allows. We are not trained, however, for immediate acceptance in a culture other than our own. And if that does occur (that is, "going native"), we are strongly cautioned and admonished to be on the alert for biases that our empathy may obscure. There are few occurrences of such convergence or easy assimilation mentioned in the history of the discipline, because by definition "anthropologist" has often meant white and male. The difficulty of finding a community that might allow an anthropologist to "go native" may also be attributed to the association of anthropology with colonialism.

In Belize, I was somewhere between an outsider and a "native." Although I am not Belizean by birth, my African American heritage garnered me an acceptance by most Belizeans as a kindred spirit in a way they assured me could not happen for white anthropologists, no matter how empathetic they might be. The Belizeans' feelings echoed sentiments expressed by several white colleagues prior to my departure. They also were confident that I would have an "easier" time conducting my research. Given what I now know about Belizean society, situated within both the Caribbean and the Latin American sociocultural milieus, their perceptions make sense. In Caribbean societies, and in certain Latin American countries such as Brazil and Venezuela, darker skin is integrally tied to an impoverished socioeconomic status. In the cultural contexts of these countries, variations of brown or black skin are the chief points of reference for social inequality. White skin is not only a symbol of the colonial past but also stands as a marker of elite social status or is a mechanism for achieving such status. It is to this which darker-skinned people are thought to want to aspire.[11]

In Belize, I was accepted by both Creoles and Garifunas because I was black in a country where people of African ancestry had dominated the population. Further, the rigid color/class system of countries like Jamaica is not as much in evidence in Belize. Although I was told that sometimes Mestizos (a reference to those who are a mixture of Spanish and Indian or who are simply Spanish-speaking) generally looked down upon those with darker skin color, I encountered no such hostility. Belizeans of every ethnicity treated me according to the specific ethnic/"racial" group(s) they thought I most resembled. The ascription varied depending on who was doing the categorizing.[12] Beyond the obvious psychological buoyancy this acceptance by many

Belizeans gave me, it also revealed to me the complexities of "race"/ethnicity in the country. The correlation between color and "race"/ethnicity and prestige, educational achievement, and political power is an aspect of Belize's social reality that warrants further study.[13]

I experienced a great sense of sisterhood during the six months I lived in Belize. It was a feeling produced by a combination of personal emotions and social bonds that occurred as part of the field experience, and my own personal and intellectual questions about women's status. There were times when this ability to "pass" probably ensured my personal safety in the urban landscape of Belize City. It certainly shielded me from the hostility often showered upon unsuspecting foreigners by Belizeans angry at the incursion of tourism. Although these outbursts are not always vicious or physically endangering, they can be unsettling.[14]

My greatest personal benefit came from a sense of belonging, a sense of place. People often insisted that I must have a Belizean ancestor somewhere in my past; when I denied this, they settled upon the idea that our ancestors must have come from the same area in Africa but ended up on ships with different destinations. Most ethnographers yearn for some degree of acceptance by those they study. Like them I too had hoped to become well regarded by my consultants, but I experienced more. I found an extension of solidarity based on color, common roots of oppression, and often gender.

Only those who have lived in a society such as the United States that constantly challenges one's authenticity, one's personal identity, through institutional and individual racism, and denies one a sense of place, of belonging, can know the relief that fills the body and releases the brain from the incessancy of second-guessing. It is rare, in the context of the United States, when I do not have to question whether people see nothing more in me than a racial category. This means I am immediately prejudged by most white Americans, who ignore my strengths and keep score of my limitations, which they see as further proof of what they believe is my "natural" racial inferiority. Charles A. Valentine describes the persuasiveness and insidiousness of American racism:

> Euro-American racism is not merely "institutionalized" as the now fashionable phrase has it. . . . Rather racism is a systemic condition of the society as a whole and its dominant culture. . . . [It] is not an individual problem or a psychological aberration but systematic oppression in all spheres of social relations, inherent in all aspects of the social system from its material foundations through its governmental forms to its ideological creations.[15]

In Belize I was able to shed my veil of double identity, of "double-consciousness," a form of alienation that W.E.B. Du Bois articulated nearly ninety years ago:

It is a peculiar sensation, this double-consciousness, this sense of always looking at one's self through the eyes of others, of measuring one's soul by the
tape of a world that looks on in amused contempt and pity. One ever feels his
twoness—an American, a Negro; two souls, two thoughts, two unreconciled
strivings; two warring ideals in one dark body, whose dogged strength alone
keeps it from being torn asunder.[16]

Living in the United States as a black person, as a person of African ancestry,
is to live a contradictory existence—one that is only further complicated by
class and gender as they interact with race. What this means in terms of my
social reality is that no matter how many university degrees I attain, or how
much money I accrue, it is virtually impossible for me or any other African
American to shed our dual identity, to extricate ourselves from the sense of
living always on the margin. We learn to negotiate it, accommodate it, challenge it, but we live with it—always. In Belize there was no real need for
double-consciousness: the veil was lifted. Finally, I could be at peace in the
world for a brief spell—Belize became for me a place of sanctuary.

Both my experience of double-consciousness and getting rid of my load
of alienation were among the circumstances that enabled me to see more
clearly the gender system at work in Belize. Contemporary trends in ethnography that we call reflexive, feminist, and "native" or indigenous acknowledge
the influence of identity in the process of fieldwork and the production of the
ethnographic text. Anthropologists such as Faye Harrison, Nancie Solien
González, and Tony Whitehead have written about their own field experiences and how new forms of ethnographic writing are generated when race,
class, gender, and even marital status are considered.[17] Their analyses are varied: some of the viewpoints are personal; others are more theoretical.[18] What
these works agree on is that it is nearly impossible to maintain distance and be
completely detached (that is, objective) or to assume only an etic point of view
under most field conditions.

In this work I do not pretend to be detached—I owe no allegiance to
scientific objectivity. Instead I insist that in any fieldwork experience we are
always involved, despite any posturing we may do to the contrary and whether
we actively participate in a culture or isolate ourselves from it. Soraya Altorki
and Camillia Fawzi El-Solh talk about this phenomenon from the perspective
of Arab women anthropologists studying other Arabs; John Gwaltney speaks
to the issue from the unique standpoint of an African American male anthropologist studying his own community.[19]

Although the relationships that develop between the anthropologist and
her "informant" have inspired a unique body of ethnographic writing,[20] the
actual impact of that encounter on the individuals and communities is vastly
understudied. We do affect the lives of our cultural consultants. As unobtru-

sive as we would like to think we are, our exchange of gifts, large or small; our contributions to the local economy, whether in the form of money or labor; and our participation in individual and community rituals such as birthdays or graduations, all have some bearing on the present and future of the towns and villages where we conduct fieldwork and on the individuals we come to love, dislike, or ignore.

Not all fieldwork situations are positive. I was fortunate in my experience of almost immediate bonding with some of the women I lived among. We had in common our age, our social identities as mothers and wives, and a common racial or colonial ancestry. Our differences were the degree of economic and social independence we had within the same social roles that bound us together. Some sense of this "kinship" is evident in the vignette I relate below.

A Birthday Celebration

Much of what I learned was acquired in the course of daily events. This vignette, taken from my 1991 field notes, reveals how women in Belize take the everyday lessons of their individual lives to understand and give meaning to larger social issues.

Tonight is a celebration of birthdays at one of the few restaurants in Lemongrass town.[21] I have been invited by Evelyn, whom I'd just met the day before. She is a local shopkeeper and soon to become my chief consultant. It is Elana's and my birthday. Elana is Evelyn's best friend. She is a chubby, East Indian woman who just turned 39. She is in the middle of a crisis. Her husband has requested a divorce. He is seeing a younger woman. She says though they live in the same house, he has not spoken to her for almost five months and cooks his own food. For her it is a shock. She married him when she was 14 and he was 32. He is a church minister and she says until recently has been a good husband.

The conversation turns to men. Elana thinks Evelyn is lucky in the sense that her husband has had "sweethearts" since the beginning of their marriage. Evelyn now places the trips to the United States she had told me about earlier in context. Each trip represents her walking out on her husband and each time she stayed in the U.S. longer. She just up and left the children. The last time she stayed for 2 1/2 years and her husband visited her five times to try to convince her to return.

Elana says that Evelyn is lucky because she has a skill. Evelyn corrects her. She did not just have a skill—she made a skill! The third woman with us urges Elana to become involved in community affairs. She says she is too busy to worry about what her husband is doing. She says they need a women's group so that Elana can learn she is not alone. On the other hand she is not hopeful about many women.

Elana has an idea that her situation could not happen in the United States. I correct her and point out that many women had to lobby and struggle to gain equal access and rights. Evelyn tells us that her husband swears that men have three sins: women, drink and drugs. Of these, he says, women are the most dangerous and expensive! We laugh, though perhaps for different reasons. I think about the fact that women are changing around the world.

The conversation continues with Elana's friends telling stories based on the lives of women they know. They all agree there is a double standard in Lemongrass, in Belize. A man who has two or three "sweethearts" is considered a Romeo while a woman doing the same is a whore.

They tell Elana that she must find her own value; she must recognize that her own happiness is important. These women believe that if the mother tolerates such a situation, the children suffer. Advice is exchanged; more stories are shared.

Elana is now eating and an occasional smile crosses her face (different from her earlier tears). She says to me that one thing is for sure, something must be done about the laws governing property. A woman is only entitled to one third of her husband's assets and if she wants more, she must prove that she actually worked with him and drew a salary. Elana's husband owns several businesses, so this has serious implications for her future if the divorce happens.[22] *Evelyn says she will give me a booklet that explains the laws tomorrow.*

This experience took place less than forty-eight hours after I arrived in Lemongrass. It illustrated for me, in a vivid way, the problems and issues that women face in this country and gave me insights into the ways in which the gender system in Belize is constructed and maintained by both men and women. Listening to Evelyn, Elana, and their friends, I learned that in Lemongrass women's value, either ascribed or self-attributed, comes from the degree to which they conform to social norms of a "good wife or mother"[23] and the degree to which they contribute to the society through reproduction and social reproduction.[24]

Elana's grief that night was for the loss of the familiar; she had been taught that she herself has little value except as the mother of four children. Only in this role is she viewed as a productive member of the community. As she comes to grips with the impending changes that a shift in her status from married to divorced will bring, she openly confronts the double standard that permits men license with their behavior and constrains women. Elana is afraid to go to dances and enjoy herself; she worries about what the community will think of her behavior. She must retain her respectability, which is interpreted by the community to mean that Elana must pretend her life is not miserable. The community also expects her to conduct herself as if she were still a wife in the fullest sense, though in truth, she has no husband. Confronting these issues and beliefs means that Elana must come face to face with her own sub-ordinate status as a woman in Belize society.

She is also frightened by the degree to which she must depend upon her husband's generosity to shape her economic future. She must accept the fact that her actual labor in the family business and her reproductive labor (moth-erhood) do not translate into income. I realized in listening to her fears that if this is the case for women who are legally married, then women in consen-sual (common-law or visiting) relationships have even less legitimacy or rights to property in the eyes of the law or the community. This point is made very clearly by Zola later on.

When I reflect back on that night, I recognize how much Elana's experi-ences and her responses to them conform to what I have read about women in the Caribbean and observed about women of color in the United States. Current literature on the topic concludes that men gain status when they en-gage in extra-household affairs, while women are expected to maintain the illusion of a stable relationship. If women attempt to follow this male behav-ior in any form, they are stigmatized.[25] In Belize, women place a high value on marriage as a legal recognition of the commitment between a man and a woman. Thus women tend to acquiesce and accept the male behavior de-scribed by both Elana and Evelyn in order to "save" the relationship—since the greatest fear many harbor is that of abandonment.

Susan Bourque and Kay Warren document comparable responses to this type of male behavior by Peruvian women.[26] Similar attitudes and behaviors also resonate in the experiences of African American women in the United States. Kesho Scott has described this acquiescence, this accommodation among African American women, as one of the "habits of surviving." She writes: "I use the phrase *habits of surviving* to refer to the external adjust-ments and internal adaptations that people make to economic exploitation and to racial and gender-related oppression."[27] The women I met in Belize were in different stages of adjusting to ethnic, sexual, and status oppression. We connected, I believe, because my own legacy as an African American woman involves similar "dance steps."[28] I recognized and recorded in their life histories my mother's life, the lives of many of my friends, and portions of my own life.

When I returned to Lemongrass in 1992, almost a year later, I was sad to note that Elana had progressed no further in her divorce demands. Although she had her own attorney, after some encouragement from her friends, she had not given him permission to make demands or be assertive on her behalf. She stated that if her husband gave up his affair and returned home, she would accept him back. He responded to her limited demands about property settle-ment by agreeing to give her the house she wanted, located in another district, but only if their teenage daughter's name was also on the deed. Even Elana could not miss the point he was making about his perception of her as a minor.[29] And as I listened to this in light of my own situation, I learned and empathized.

This and many other incidents I encountered in Belize make it clear, as many feminist scholars have argued, that gender is far more than an analytical construct or a structural form. Gender, far from being an abstract concept, is a pervasive set of obligations and limitations that saturate the entire being and make up one's identity.[30] Discussions and analysis of Belize's gender system are thus not academic; I have seen gender and how it affects my consultants, who are also my friends; I have seen gender and how it interacts with race and class in my own life. As a result I feel obligated to discuss gender as an active, dynamic, and contradictory system that interacts with and affects social structures and culture and is also affected by the same. It is this sense of gender as a personal, political, and dynamic phenomenon that has shaped my approach to the examination of women's lives and women's roles and position in Belize.

Studying Gender in Belize

> Theory is always simpler than reality.   —Joseph Viner

Much of my own thinking about gender is derived from the recent tradition of feminist scholarship in anthropology.[31] My theoretical orientation takes as its point of departure an examination of the systemic nature of social relations and power relations between men and women, recognizing that gender is a "cultural system of practices and symbols *implicating both women and men.*"[32] Toward this end, I am concerned with interrogating the social roles societies create around what it means to be a "man" or a "woman" and the specific behaviors, ideologies, institutions, and individual attitudes that reinforce them.

I have compiled a list of what Belizean women perceive to be the major impediments that block their progress as individuals and as a social group. These responses are based on the survey mentioned earlier, as well as on interviews and daily interactions I had with women over a three-year period (1991–1993). Simple recognition that certain areas of their lives are problematic is for some women a first and only step. For others, acknowledging that they are disadvantaged simply because of their gender marks the beginning of a journey toward redefinition and agency.

Problems Women Face
No man living in the house on a regular basis to contribute financially
Men beating women

Mental abuse by men

Not enough job opportunities for women

Women not able to finish their education

Men telling women what to do

No man living in the house on a regular basis to help with raising children

Women having too many children

Drugs and gangs

Husband/partner won't let them participate in women's group

The list discloses that "gender politics" in Belize center on role expectations for both men and women, behavior, and access to resources. Although the country has taken major steps toward national and economic development under self-rule, women are increasingly aware of the fact that they are no better off today than they were under colonialism. This understanding is reflected in the way in which women now organize former church and volunteer associations around projects that will improve women's economic position. Nongovernmental organizations focused on women's issues as well as the government's Department of Women's Affairs have been instrumental in raising women's awareness about their lack of economic and political power in the public sphere. National organizations such as Women Against Violence also educate women about their lack of power in the domestic arena. Increasingly, women in Belize have become aware as a group that changing their position and status in the society is a matter that requires attention above and beyond national development priorities established in the past. Ironically, nearly twenty years after the United Nations Decade for Women began in 1975, the global assessment of women's status in the 1994 Cairo Summit concluded that the general economic and political policies often pursued by developing countries in the name of the entire population frequently result in the further marginalization of women rather than assistance.[33]

In spite of the very real economic, political, and social constraints many women face globally and locally, they are not passive participants in their own lives or in their societies, as some feminist interpretations imply.[34] Women in Belize seem unwilling to tolerate some of the practices that have structured their lives in the past. This observation is supported by the growing membership of Women Against Violence and by the attendance of women at conferences organized by various women's groups, among other activities. Women are increasingly taking measures to alter the cultural views held of them by their partners and by society. They now seek change, both in national laws and policies—drawing on the leverage of such international documents as the "United Nations Convention for the Elimination of All Forms of Discrimination against Women" to which Belize is a signatory to support their demands—and in their personal relationships as well as in relations in their households and their communities.

They also actively organize themselves in women's groups with the objective of what they call the "upliftment of women." Many of these organizations activities are specifically aimed at ensuring or enhancing women's economic autonomy. Women's groups have become the primary vehicles in Belize that train women, publicize problems related to women's health, and advocate greater participation of women in the labor force, in politics, and in educational opportunities. Since there is no mass national women's movement, national women's groups are important to this politicizing process. Most, however, are funded by foreign aid, and sometimes their agendas seem ill matched to the needs of grassroots women. Because of this problem, women in Belize seem to mobilize most effectively at the local level. Why this is so can be related to the fact that local concerns are narrower in focus and oriented toward resolving community-based problems instead of national problems. Sometimes, however, the agendas of the national and local organizations do overlap, as with the successful passage of the Domestic Violence Bill and in working on women's health issues.

In Belize, as in the rest of the Caribbean in general, the impetus for local women's groups did not begin in an instant. Rather, it emanates from a long tradition of church and community service volunteer organizations whose members began in the mid-1970s to shift their attention to a more social/political and women-centered agenda. Although some groups undertake income-generating projects to assist women in creating their own economic autonomy while others organize around specific concerns such as women's health, breast feeding, or family planning or function as social clubs, they all tend to adhere to a common agenda—one in which the eradication of domestic violence and the development of self-esteem are priorities. They also seek to gain respect and recognition from husbands/partners, households, and communities for women on the basis of their contributions, which are generally undervalued and uncompensated.

Studying gender in Belize means being able to explain the historical, personal, cultural, and social circumstances that generate the problems women articulate. A central aim of this work is to assess the process by which individual women come to understand first that barriers exist, later how such barriers impinge upon their lives, and finally what steps are possible to eradicate them. The narratives in this work, to varying degrees, document how some women have learned negotiation, manipulation, and occasionally unmitigated rebellion.

To explain how women negotiate their culture of gender, I have focused my analysis on five critical themes that underlie Belize's gender system: (1) the representation of women as minors and property; (2) the reasons that generate the economic-sexual dynamics underlying heterosexual relationships in Belize;[35] (3) the degree to which men's physical and mental abuse of women reveals strategies to elicit compliance; (4) the process of gender enculturation for women; and (5) the historical origins of Belize's sexual division of labor.

It is possible for the structural features of a gender system in one culture to appear similar to those in another culture. Despite such similarities, anthropologists argue that the origins of these elements as well as the meaning they have for individuals and the society as a whole are the result of numerous variables. Individuals create their understanding of social phenomena like gender on the basis of personal experiences, while the meanings a society attributes to gender roles grow out of the geography, language, economic and political structures, cultural values, and beliefs of the country. Although located in Central America, Belize is far from being a typical Afro-Caribbean or Latin American state. As such, the models and explanations generally applied to women's circumstances in either of these two regions are not always applicable.[36] Belize is a unique configuration, and its culture of gender must be evaluated as a product of the country's specific historical, cultural, political, and economic development.

Chapter 2 *So Where the Hell Is Belize?*

Belize, located on the isthmus of Central America and a virtual English-speaking island in a sea of Spanish language and culture, has gone relatively unnoticed until recently.[1] A coastal country that faces the Caribbean Sea to the east, it measures 174 miles from north to south and 68 miles from east to west. Its total area is 8,866 square miles, making it roughly the size of the state of Massachusetts, slightly larger than neighboring El Salvador and twice the size of Jamaica. Belize shares borders with Mexico in the north and Guatemala in the west and south. With 240,000 people, an average of approximately 21.1 persons per square mile, Belize is the least populated of all the Central America countries.[2]

It was probably Guatemala's claim to the country as part of its territory from the 1960s to 1981—a claim that dates back to a "boundary recognition treaty of 1859"—that brought Belize to the attention of the international community.[3] Many saw it as a modern-day David, struggling to extricate itself from the colonial ties of the Goliath Great Britain and just as reluctant to be subsumed by yet another Goliath in the form of Guatemala. By the time Belize (formerly British Honduras) became independent in 1981, many of its Latin American neighbors and distant Caribbean cousins had been sovereign for at least ten years.

What we come to know about a country derives in part from its geography and in part from the myths floating about that attract us to it. Belize too is known by its geography and its mythology. The most noted of Belize's myths centers around its name, acquired in 1973. There are numerous competing and contradictory stories about the word's origins. Pronounced "Baylees" in Mayan, "Beliz" translates into "muddy waters." "Belikan," another word, means "road to the east."[4] Some say the name derives from the Spanish words "bela-isla," or beautiful island. Others attribute it to a Spanish corruption of an English name. The most popular myth is recounted by travel agents and historians alike: Wallace was a pirate believed to have established the first European settlement on the Bay of Honduras. According to legend, his name, Wallace or Wallis, was transformed into Vallis, because there is no "W" in Spanish. It was then pronounced as Balis or Belize.[5]

Like its name, the country's geography is also enmeshed in an aura of history, romance, and mystery. The landscape fits the Spanish reference to beautiful. Though not an island, Belize has the ambiance and closeness often associated with island culture. As an outsider I have felt that Belize can make one feel as if one is living in a fishbowl. Everyone seems to know everyone else, and gossip is perhaps third in popularity to football (soccer) and dominoes as a mass form of entertainment. In such an environment it is prudent to be cautious with criticism, because people who share virtually no resemblance to one another may be related. It is also wise to be circumspect in one's behavior, since most Belizeans adhere to the Creole saying "If it not so dan it nearly so," which means that even if something is not true, it might as well be, if people perceive it to be so.

Belize's landscape is just as varied as the origins of its name. A third of the country is formed by the Maya Mountains; they jut out from surrounding lowlands and rise to a plateau surface of over 3,600 feet in elevation at Victoria Peak.[6] Another distinguishing geological feature of Belize is its rivers. They run throughout the country, traceable by the lyrical names assigned over the centuries: Belize, Sibun, Monkey, Temash, and Rio Grande, to name a few. Many of the rivers pour into creeks with their own descriptive and suggestive names: Labouring Creek, Blue Creek, Mango Creek. This highway system of rivers and creeks, coupled with lagoons scattered around the country and offshore "cayes" or small islands, was once the domain of indigenous people (the Maya) as well as British pirates and buccaneers, each valuing Belize's inaccessibility and waterways for different reasons. Pirates could depend upon the swamps and mangroves to deter any who might hope to follow them after one of their forays out to sea to attack shipping lines. Conversely, the Maya and later the Garifuna depended upon the forests and swamps to keep Europeans at a distance. In this venture, they were helped by the inhospitable climate.

Belize is excessively hot and humid much of the time. Temperatures average between 73° F and 88° F with a normal low of 60° F. Occasionally the thermometer has dipped as far down as 50° F, causing Belizeans to pull out winter coats and making the country perhaps the coldest in the Caribbean. During Belize's rainy season, rainfall can reach 175 inches in the southernmost district. The country's coastal position accounts for its never-ending humidity. Easterly trade winds generally provide a welcome breeze as they drift inland off the Caribbean Sea. These same winds, however, under certain conditions produce the hurricanes that have periodically devastated Belize. The most disastrous one occurred in 1931 and claimed almost 1,000 lives. In 1961 Hurricane Hattie leveled Belize City, killing 275 people. As a result of the damage and in anticipation of future hurricanes, the capital was moved from Belize City further inland to Belmopan in 1973, barely ahead of the 1978 disaster, which caused extensive damage to the banana plantations.

Despite the shift in the location of official government business, Belize City still operates as a de facto capital. It is the country's largest urban area and its most unplanned, having been built on swampy terrain that rests two feet below sea level. It is impossible to build anything secure in the city without trucking in loads of gravel and other fill. Open canals create sanitary problems and constantly offend the nose on days when there is a heavy breeze, while the high humidity takes a toll on wooden houses and electrical appliances.[7] Although the humidity, swamps, and hurricanes were impediments to extensive European settlement in the colonial era, Belizeans still view Belize City as the heart of the country.

While no longer the capital, Belize City has a thriving nightlife on weekends and is one of the few places where it is possible to view local productions of plays, dances, and music under the auspices of the National Institute of Culture, now located at Bliss Institute.[8] In the month of September work practically ceases for a two-week period. During this time the country celebrates National Day on September 10. This is the date on which Creole Belizeans commemorate their national identity. In 1798 African slaves joined forces with British settlers to repel the Spanish in what is now called the Battle of St. George's Caye. British rule was almost assured after this final confrontation. September 21 marks the day of the country's independence from Britain. It is usually celebrated with fireworks, a presentation of arms, and the raising of the flag. The Garifuna (African and Carib Indian) celebrate their arrival in Belize on November 19, 1823, as Settlement Day; on this day each year Garifuna from other parts of Central America and the Caribbean congregate in Dangriga (Stann Creek). These holidays are official, which means that banks and businesses are usually closed; smaller local festivals are also held in various towns and communities at other times of the year. But Belize City is the center of activity all year round. It attracts an astonishing number of Belizeans traveling in from the farthest districts and newly returned "Belizean Americans." Visitors also include a growing number of tourists (200,000 annually) and researchers, all anxious to examine the numerous archaeological remains, the largely unscathed environment, and the numerous cultures that coexist in relative harmony.

To many, Belize is the last remaining paradise in the Caribbean. Natural and cultural resources include "jungle-clad mountains, navigable rivers meandering endless miles, natural forests, open savannah plains, swamp lands and lagoons that dwarf the Everglades."[9] The country has two major atolls and is the site of the second-largest barrier reef in the world. Along the marine and coastal areas, manatee and other marine life abound; in the jungle, part of which has been set aside as reserves and parks, jaguars still walk. In the same areas numerous species of hummingbirds, orchids, and black howler monkeys live relatively undisturbed.[10] Ironically, Belize's unexploited environment is the result of a combination of factors: the country's small population, the British colonial practice of benign neglect, and the historical dispute between the British and Spanish over the country. In 1763 Spain signed the Treaty of Paris, which allowed those British living in country to continue logwood extraction. This same treaty, however, limited settlement and prohibited agricultural development among the settlers. Such restrictions acted inadvertently to protect Belize's environment from the resource and agricultural exploitation that characterizes many of its Caribbean and Latin American neighbors.

It is the twin images of "paradise" and "diamond in the rough" often used to refer to Belize that accurately capture the sentiment that foreigners, especially Europeans, have for the country. Theirs is a nostalgia related not so much to the country itself but to their own wish to escape to a pastoral past where life is simpler. Such a desire, however, is rooted in a romantic and "imperialistic" world view. Tourists from developed countries who travel to Belize are entwined in the relationships of "underdevelopment." They seek refuge from a lifestyle of relative privilege and comfort; such an escape, however, is dependent upon countries like Belize retaining their state of original naiveté (euphemistically called "traditional") and technological simplicity for the material benefit of these foreign visitors.[11] This pattern of unbalanced economic development, often reinforced by political domination in the guise of "gunboat diplomacy" and "unequal treaties," characterizes the history of Belize.

Thus the country's "underdeveloped" status is not a "natural" consequence of internal processes but the specific outcome of multiple factors that are historical and modern, political, and economic. Of considerable importance was the British colonizers' reluctance to settle in the country because of its inhospitable climate as well as the general inaccessibility of the country's rich soils.[12] This practice in part accounts for Belize's stymied agricultural production.[13] More recently, Belize's "underdevelopment" has been reinforced by heavy reliance on U.S. foreign aid, a high ratio of foreign debt, general consumption patterns that privilege American and British imported goods over indigenous products, and both immigration and emigration processes, the former generating a strata of mostly refugee agricultural workers, the latter siphoning off some of the country's most skilled and semiskilled workers.

The "Ugly" Belize

A glimpse of paradise can sometimes blind us to the ugly or rough interiors that may be hidden from view. Such is the case with Belize. Those who come with eyes only for the environment may miss this side of the country. In most of the world, underdevelopment is often marked by inadequate technology and health care, inconvenient access to water supplies, improper waste disposal, a decline in agricultural self-sufficiency, and dependency upon imports from developed countries for staple food items and other necessities. In this respect, Belize is on equal footing with most of its underdeveloped neighbors. Carmen Deere expresses the sentiments of many Caribbean scholars about the consequences of underdevelopment on the region when she states, "[It] produces what it does not consume."[14] The statement accurately reflects the conditions of Belize.

Despite a condition of relative poverty (significant when compared with the United States; minimal, however, when contrasted to its Central American neighbors), Belize is still politically and economically one of the most stable countries in the region. It has two political parties, the People's United Party (PUP) and the United Democratic Party (UDP), and operates as a "parliamentary democracy based on the Westminster system."[15] It would be untrue to paint a portrait of Belize as a country completely without conflict. There are ethnic tensions that can be traced to colonial policies and practices; moreover, recent competition over jobs and other strategic resources has the potential to pit ethnic groups against one another in the future as the population struggles to survive in an atmosphere of shrinking natural resources and rising costs.

A Mosaic: "Many Cultures, One Nation"

Perhaps the most interesting aspect of Belize is its people. As one moves about the country, ethnicity is real and palatable.[16] In many respects an infant among independent nations, Belize offers a lesson to the giants that grapple with questions of cultural tolerance, equality, and ethnic civility. Though not without internal problems and operational ethnic boundaries and tensions, the country still lacks the ethnic turmoil of a Guyana or a Trinidad. Nor does the country exemplify either the structural dimensions of segregation and institutional racism that characterize the United States or the intense color caste system of Jamaica. Belize might be called truly "multicultural." The government actively seeks to construct a national identity that deemphasizes ethnic differences and builds on common national interests. Its efforts are captured in a former slogan of the People's United Party, "We all de one," and in the United Democratic Party's more recent rallying cry, "Many cultures, one nation."

One major reason for Belize's lack of stressed ethnic relations is spatial. Fredrik Barth has argued that where ethnic groups can maintain distances that allow them to create their own niches, diminishing competition for strategic resources, ethnic conflicts are minimal.[17] Spatial circumstances can be cited to explain why Belize has not experienced the extreme ethnic tensions that characterize social relations in some of the surrounding Central American countries or among some of its Caribbean neighbors. The two largest ethnic groups (Mestizos and Creoles) in Belize are geographically dispersed (see map). Mestizos live in those areas of the country bordering Mexico and Guatemala; Creoles dominate Belize City. Moreover, neither group can claim to be the "original" Belizeans, since nearly all of the country's population came from somewhere else. The ancestors of most Belizeans arrived by force from Africa and the West Indies as slaves, others came from India as indentured laborers, and still others first crossed over the borders of Belize from the Yucatan to escape the bloody turmoil during the Guerras de Casta (Caste Wars). Even many of the present-day Maya, who are the "original" people of the area according to archaeologists, also immigrated.

Travel writers and historians both assert that only a small segment of the Maya population now living in Belize can claim to be direct descendants of the people who built the ruins that so delight archaeologists and attest to the presence of a highly developed Maya civilization at one time. The majority of those living in Belize today are believed to be descendants of Maya from adjacent empires who fled from the Yucatan in the nineteenth century and of later groups of Mopan and Ketchi Maya in the south of Belize who came during the late nineteenth century to escape forced labor plantations in their native Guatemala.[18] While to the outside eye these groups are all Maya (that is, a homogeneous group), among themselves they are separated by language (Yucateco, Mopanero, and Ketchi) and different interests.[19]

Ethnic boundaries do exist in Belize among the various groups, but people who reside in close proximity interact without enmity. The consequences for marrying outside the group are generally not severe, though stories of violence against one party of an interethnic relationship do surface.

The Mestizos are the largest ethnic group in Belize today, making up 43.6 percent of the total population. This proportion is the result of changing

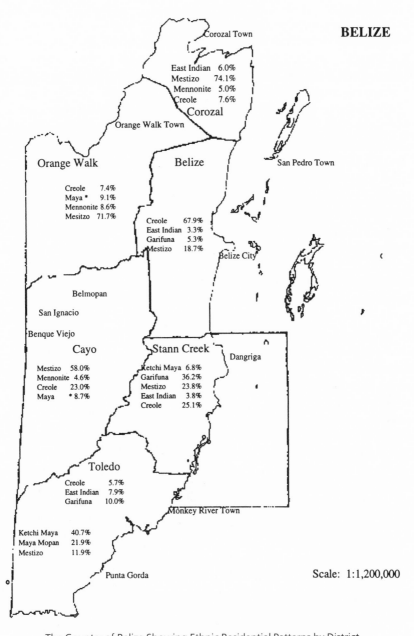

BELIZE

Corozal Town

East Indian 6.0%
Mestizo 74.1%
Mennonite 5.0%
Creole 7.6%
Corozal

Orange Walk Town

Orange Walk

Creole 7.4%
Maya * 9.1%
Mennonite 8.6%
Mesitzo 71.7%

Belize

San Pedro Town

Creole 67.9%
East Indian 3.3%
Garifuna 5.3%
Mestizo 18.7%
Belize City

Belmopan

San Ignacio

Benque Viejo

Cayo

Mestizo 58.0%
Mennonite 4.6%
Creole 23.0%
Maya * 8.7%

Stann Creek

Dangriga

Ketchi Maya 6.8%
Garifuna 36.2%
Mestizo 23.8%
East Indian 3.8%
Creole 25.1%

Toledo

Creole 5.7%
East Indian 7.9%
Garifuna 10.0%

Monkey River Town

Ketchi Maya 40.7%
Maya Mopan 21.9%
Mestizo 11.9%

Punta Gorda

Scale: 1:1,200,000

The Country of Belize Showing Ethnic Residential Patterns by District
(Figures are based on the 1991 Population Census)
*Where Ketchi Maya and Maya Mopan are less than 5% of the population, the
percentage shown is an aggregate of Ketchi Maya, Maya Mopan, and other Maya.
(Adapted from Map by Ministry of Natural Resources, Belmopan, Belize, Central America)

demographics. Like many of the Maya, much of Belize's local Mestizo population owes its origins to the Yucatan. Since that initial influx during the colonial period, this segment of the population has been enlarged by more recent Central American immigrants fleeing Guatemala, El Salvador, and the Honduras as political and economic refugees.

Whereas in the general context of Latin America, "Mestizo" refers to people of Spanish and Amerindian mixture, in Belize it is a generic designation for anyone who adheres to Spanish language and culture. Thus in Belize, regardless of national origin, Argentineans, Costa Ricans, Spaniards, and Puerto Ricans all become homogenized as "Mestizo," sometimes referred to derisively by mostly Creole Belizeans as "Spanish." Even Mestizos in Belize participate in this ritual of communality, and it is this aspect of nondistinction that has made it easy for refugees from neighboring countries to blend in. If these newcomers master the Creole language, they are indistinguishable from native-born Mestizos, a fact that has created some problems for the latter.

Creoles, as a result of their large numbers during the earliest part of the country's formation, have largely shaped much of Belizean culture. Although, according to the 1991 census, they represent only 29.8 percent of the population as compared with 39.7 percent in 1980, their language is the everyday medium of communication, and cultural preferences for reggae and soca music permeate the airways more than any other musical form. At one time Creoles dominated most of the important occupations, especially in the civil service arena. Today, though they remain part of Belize's cultural mosaic, their influence is diminishing, largely due to attrition via emigration to the United States. Their shrinking numbers and the increased presence of other groups who adhere to Spanish in language and culture has created a crisis of identity for Creole Belizeans.

Creoles now engage in debates over whether they have a culture, over whether Creole is an "authentic" language or just a denigrated form of English. Notwithstanding those who might wish to disparage it, Creole culture and identity are key aspects of Belize's general national culture, its food, language, and ambiance. Having fallen from a position of ethnic ascendancy, Creoles now find themselves increasingly at the lower end of privilege, and new tensions and antagonisms increasingly surface as they perceive newcomers as encroachers. Some Creoles hold the large influx of Central American refugees responsible for their current lowered socioeconomic position. They feel the new immigrants do not truly wish to become Belizean, but only want to take advantage of resources such as land, government-subsidized education, and other social services unavailable in their countries of origin (a view shared by other Belizean ethnic groups as well). Moreover, they feel these newcomers bring with them a lifestyle premised on violence. I have been warned by Creole friends to travel with caution. A Belizean will rob you, I am told, but the (Central American) refugees will rob you and kill you. They have grown accustomed to violence because of the conflict in their countries, or so some Belizeans believe. Whether fact or fiction, the belief shapes people's attitudes, creates stereotypes, guides behavior, and stretches taut the growing band of tension among ethnic groups today.[20]

Nowhere is this tension more noticeable than in social relations between Creoles and Asians (Chinese and newly arrived East Indians). Unlike Mestizos, who are concentrated in their own districts, Asians now reside in close proximity in Belize City to Creoles, who formerly made up the dominant segment of the urban population. The dislike between Asians and Creoles appears to be mutual, and the irrefutable divide is symbolized by the iron bars that grace many Chinese businesses in Belize City. The bars, while an obvious defense against crime, which is sometimes ethnically based, also signal an unspoken desire by many Chinese to remain aloof and separate from the rest of Belizean society. In addition, the Chinese style of interaction seems to most local Belizeans to be rude and intolerant. The tensions between East Indians and Creoles seem less strained in comparison. However, new East Indians living in the city remain fairly endogamous, speak their own language, and generally interact very little with Creoles outside of the merchant-customer dyad. Finally, many Belizeans, especially Creoles, express anger at the commercial success of Asians, who while forming a very small portion of the population dominate the retail market. Their family-oriented mode of operating excludes Belizeans who seek employment, for jobs are given to relatives, children, and spouses. Further, urban Creole entrepreneurs not only lack the initial capital but appear more individualistic in their orientation, and so do not subscribe to the ethnic solidarity that enables East Indian merchants to pool resources to purchase stock and sometimes share facilities.

Few of the newcomers to Belize bother to learn the Creole language. The failure to speak Creole introduces into what has traditionally seemed an ideal ethnic complex a new element of intercultural tensions and linguistic misunderstanding, especially with those populations that are non-Spanish speaking (most Creoles have some familiarity with Spanish, and those living in the northern, southern, or western districts possess a certain degree of proficiency). Although other ethnic groups in the country do not as a general rule adhere rigidly to endogamy (though intermarriages between Creoles and Garifuna seem rarer than between Creoles and Mestizos or Maya, or between Creoles and East Indians), the newer Asian immigrants tend to be more strict in their practices, marrying primarily within their group or importing spouses for themselves and their children. All of this contributes to a proliferation of ethnic stereotypes, exacerbates feelings of economic exclusion on the part of

Creoles, and threatens to bring closer to the surface whatever ethnic tensions may lay hidden in the recesses of Belize's past.

Both Creole and Mestizo contributions to the development of Belize's national culture are the most recognizable, but the Maya and the Garifuna have also had an impact. The Maya contributions are documented in the remains of Altun Ha, Caracol, Lamanai, Cuello, Ceros, El Pilar, Santa Rita, Teotehuquancan, Xunantunich, and the many other sites either unexcavated or under excavation. The Garifuna (or Garinagu, as they prefer to be called today) have made their mark in the areas of food, language, and music. Forcibly expelled by the British from the island of St. Vincent in the Caribbean, they took a circuitous route to Belize, by way of the Bay Islands off Honduras, the largest group arriving in 1832 to settle along the southern coastal areas of Stann Creek, now known primarily by the Garifuna name of Dangriga. The Garifuna are descendants of African slaves and Carib Indians and in Belize are considered an indigenous people like the Maya. Spanish surnames attest to their connections to the Spanish Honduras. If Creoles are prominent in the civil service, the Garifuna tend to dominate in the field of education. A more recent area of social life in which they have a strong influence is popular music. Down Albert Street, the main thoroughfare in Belize City, the "punta" sounds of Andy Palacio and Chico Ramos can be heard rocking the streets.

In different communities throughout Belize, efforts at cultural preservation are occurring—not just among the Garifuna, who have established their own cultural council and hold an annual conference on Garinagu life and culture, but also among the Maya, who attempt to transmit to their children the music, dances, foods, and lifeways that make them culturally unique. Increasingly, Creoles have joined in to preserve their own distinctive culture, especially with regard to language, food, and music. The central aim of all these ventures is to document the elements that embody Belize's cultural heritage. It is against this rich, complex, and ever-changing backdrop that the lives of Belizean women must be examined. And while national institutions and sociocultural processes exert pressures on women, local communities also play an important role in structuring women's understanding of gender. An examination of the culture of gender as it pertains to the lived experiences of women must take into account national policies and institutional barriers as well as the role of community norms, expectations, and local sanctions.

Chapter 3 *From the Marketplace to Lemongrass*

It was to this proverbial paradise, with its own catalog of myths and reservoir of social secrets, that I came in January 1991. I spent the first three months of a planned six-month stay based in Belize City while traveling around to different parts of the country. Because my initial research plan was to study women's grass-roots organizations, I began by talking to women who worked in national nongovernmental organizations such as the Belize Rural Women's Association (BRWA), the Belize Women Against Violence (BWAV), the Belize Family Life Association (BFLA), and Breast Is Best (BIB). Although most of these are heavily supported by external (foreign) funds, they are managed by local Belizean women who set local Belizean agendas based on their knowledge of the needs of women in the country. This partnership of dependency and struggling autonomy is an uneasy one for many of the Belizean directors of these agencies.

I accompanied staff from the BRWA into the field and also went with staff members from the government's Department of Women's Affairs (DWA) as they visited women in different parts of the country. In this way, I was able to observe various women working among themselves and with one another. Rarely were women excluded from joining an organization, and often the only "divisive" force organizations encountered was that of political affiliation. Although Belize is a stable democratic country, people are quite passionate about their political party alliances. The fights over whether one is red (UDP) or blue (PUP) have split families and have sometimes interfered with the ability of women's groups to attract members. In response, most women's groups represent themselves as explicitly "nonpolitical," in hopes of diffusing the matter.

On days not spent on the road, I assisted the staff in the Department of Women's Affairs or visited the Belize City market. There I encountered my

first real consultant, Auntie Barbara, a traditional healer, who was instrumental in helping broaden the focus of my research objectives.[1]

What is now called the old market is located in what looks like an iron
corrugated, dimly lit airplane hangar painted iridescent orange.[2] At the market the life of the city is in full view as people come in and out to buy herbs,
vegetables, meats, or fresh fish. Here I worked under the loving eye of Auntie
Barbara, a Creole with caramel skin and shoulder-length wavy hair who
proudly asserts her African heritage. I recorded the following description in
my journal at the time:

*Aunt Barbara (A.B.) is a plump woman of short stature, about 5"1' and in her
mid-fifties, I suspect. She has a medium brown complexion, the color of cafe
au lait or caramel. Her hair is wavy and usually caught back into a bun. She
wears glasses but the eyes behind them are active; they seem to take in everything going on about her. A.B. wears two gold earrings on each ear, but pushed
through a single hole. On her finger is a large turquoise ring set in silver.*

*At first I thought A.B. was Mestizo because of her looks and her Spanish-
sounding last name, as well as her fluency in Spanish. But she is adamant about
her origins. She is of African ancestry and states she is proud of her heritage.
She tells me today she is "of white and African mixture which makes me Creole." She speaks three languages, Creole, English and Spanish. A.B. has eight
grandchildren who are always nearby to assist when they are not in school and
only one daughter [their mother] who clearly resembles her, even down to their
common plumpness.[3] She also has an adopted Maya daughter who seemed
more adept at herb preparation than A.B.'s real one.*

Under Auntie Barbara's tutelage, I learned to identify, cut, and mix herbs.
Her stall at the market is a symbol of the importance of herbal medicines in
the cultural ethos of Belizeans. The ability to make a living as an herbalist or
healer was proof of Belizeans' reliance upon traditional practices either in conjunction with or as an alternative to Western medicines and treatments.

Auntie Barbara dispensed herbs with names like "Negrito," known to
cure diarrhea, "Talla walla," or "Young gal bubby."[4] "Bubby," she told me,
is a Creole word for breast. It is used to refer to a squashlike fruit with protru-
sions that resemble nipples. It grows on a shrub and is poisonous, but can be
used to cure sinus infections. Auntie Barbara told me how to perform
this cure:

*To use, you need a piece of lintel [linen cloth] cotton and coconut oil. Put every-
thing in the coconut oil and pound with a mortar stick until fine. Use the lintel
cloth to strain the mixture for juice. Make a brush [dropper] from wild cane.
Sniff in one drop at a time. Treat for about five days, one drop at a time. "Young
gal bubby" is used for sinuses and headcolds. The mixture makes you sneeze
and sometimes Auntie Barbara says, "The root of the sinus will come out black
and ugly and sinus is cured."*

As a medicine woman, Auntie Barbara was good at dispensing advice, whether it was requested or not. True to form, she advised me to take a combination of "valeriano" and "spice leaf" in a tea to settle my nerves.[5]

The stall was a wonderful place from which to observe the daily routine of women in the city. Most of Auntie Barbara's customers were women, although some men also used her services. Women customers may have been more common because they were in the market anyway. Some came on behalf of a partner or husband who was either at work or home ill. When she could prescribe on the basis of the symptoms told her, Auntie Barbara would. But sometimes she demanded that a person be brought to her stall. These were my first glimpses into the lives of Belizeans, especially Belizean women.

Auntie Barbara's own situation was intriguing. She lived in the city most of the time, but on certain afternoons and on the weekends she took off for her farm to visit "the old man," as she referred to her husband. She spoke occasionally about the white side of her ancestry, giving me some indication that a color caste system existed among Belizeans, in which lighter skin was viewed as more desirable than darker skin. Auntie Barbara had experienced the effects of this caste system when she was rejected by her white aunts because she was too dark. Her own mother's seduction (the origin of her birth) at the hands of her white employer proved that the sexual politics of slavery did not disappear with the abolition of the institution. This all suggested to me that "race" and ethnicity in Belize are more complex than they are in the United States—as is also indicated by the varied origins of Belize's people, discussed in chapter 2.

Under the strict tutelage of Auntie Barbara, I learned about the art of listening in addition to the art of healing. She saw her work as the necessary outgrowth of a gift, and she did not dispense advice lightly or for great profit. Her mission in life was to ease pain. Once she told me how she often gave medicine to women whose partners had physically and sexually abused them. She told me, "You would not believe how some men would abuse women." Though committed to helping women, Auntie Barbara had her limits.[6] Operating out of a professional ethos shaped by her spiritual beliefs, she expressed strong disapproval of women who asked her to help them eliminate unwanted pregnancies. How frequent these requests were, I don't know. My impression is that word probably spread that "you won't get that from she," so that the number of inquiries diminished over time. Auntie Barbara's mixed-age clientele included "professional" women who worked in banks and stores, identified by their color-coordinated uniforms of blazers and skirts, and women whose primary job consisted solely of homemaking. Armed with the information I had gathered from watching and listening to these women, I set off to find a research site to study women's issues and women's groups.

I found myself in the south, a place populated by "Coolies" (East Indians) and "Caribs" (Garifuna) according to one Creole acquaintance. It certainly proved to be a place where ethnic heterogeneity was highly visible. I was especially interested in the sizable East Indian population, because the voices of East Indian women, like the Maya women, were often muted. The attraction of Lemongrass as a research site had less to do with scientific criteria and a lot to do with the warm greetings I encountered during my first visit. The town's small size and its relative isolation from large town/city influences were factors that created a fairly "pristine" (if there is any such thing) research population. In Lemongrass, I could not only observe women but examine to what degree ethnicity, if at all, was a factor in the way women performed their gender roles and how it affected the strategies they deployed individually and collectively to understand and challenge gender.

Lemongrass

How you view Lemongrass on your first visit will depend largely on how you travel to the town. If you go by bus, leaving Belize City around 3:00 P.M., you will arrive near midnight (having stopped in Belmopan and every stop between there and Dangriga). By the time you reach Mango Creek, you'll be covered with red dust and aching from a ride where the bus negotiates huge pot holes at forty miles an hour while the traveler is bounced up and down at a pace that seems to be at least sixty miles an hour. Along the way, initially west on Hummingbird Highway and later south on the Southern Highway, you may glimpse the lush areas where the Maya reside or the wooden houses and shacks that occasionally double as a bus stop. If you are not shy and begin a conversation, some friendly Belizean traveler will nod toward the Maya Mountains in the far distance and point out the "sleeping giant"—a series of elevations that form a forehead, nose, and mouth and look like a huge body slumbering on its back.

After several hours, if it is the dry season, you will have learned to appreciate the wisdom of the older Maya women—brown, short of stature, with wrinkled skin and elegant red-gold earrings—who carry a towel to protect their hair from the dust that enters the windows. You may also acquire a profound appreciation for the stamina of other travelers who imbibe soft drinks but never seem to require the inhospitable outhouse at Mango Creek, where the bus pauses for an extended layover.

By the time you reach Lemongrass, it will be night and you may barely be able to discern the sea to the east and the new housing development in various stages of completion to the west. As the road curves into town, the lights of a gas station are visible directly in front of the bus and the form of a Jehovah's Witness temple stands silent to its right. This is Main Street. Most strangers exit at the first stop, a concrete hotel with rooms for as little as $12BZ a night, if you are willing to share the bathroom with other guests and large insects.[7] The next-best room goes for $20BZ night, with a private bath and two beds—it seems almost too luxurious after the trip. Across from the hotel is a bar/restaurant once frequented by British soldiers, who have now departed. The cheaper rooms face out toward the street, and on weekends your sleep is guaranteed to be disturbed. Right next door is another bar with the romantic name of "Dreamlight," frequented by locals—it too contributes to the noise level.[8]

If you are not prone to adventure and arrive by plane, you might cringe at the open field that serves as an airstrip. Your first view of Lemongrass as the plane approaches is of a hodgepodge of buildings spread out over a wide area and an unpaved dirt road that serves as the runway. When the ten-seater propeller plane finally lands, the first thing visible is the airstrip cantina, an airline office, and the Community Service building, where the town holds large events and where women's groups often meet. Adjacent to it are the mayor's and Social Services offices.[9] The buildings line a road that has no sign but can be followed right into town, where it crosses Main Street and continues on to Point Street, which faces the sea.

I have taken both bus and plane to Lemongrass and though I complain about the means of getting there, I am always happy to arrive. If you have no one to meet you, fellow travelers or curious children are more than pleased to point the way to your destination. You need only ask, "What part Miss Evelyn's house?" Most will answer, "she da there," pointing toward a path on the right that diverges from the road into town.

A Tour of the Town

With only 2,585 people, Lemongrass is relatively small.[10] Its design is like that of every other town in Belize, including Belize City—though the latter has long since abandoned the logic of design for urban expansion. There is a central plaza or park with cement benches and a few shrubs or trees. Because of the heat, the grass is always brown and patchy. When it gets too high, Maya men or others in search of work are hired to "chop bush." In Lemongrass the plaza forms an island in the shape of a V and brings two streets together. On one side are a few businesses, the local Breast Is Best office, and a multifamily dwelling. Opposite is a makeshift counter, taken down every night and set up each morning by Guatemalan vendors who have staked out this location as theirs. On Main Street, open to the sea, a variety of stores are standing, along with three hotels, one of the town's numerous churches, and one of two elementary schools. By the time children are ready for secondary school, there is no longer any choice—there is one "college," as high schools are called, in town.[11] Although there is no tuition charge for education, school fees run about $30BZ per month, not including books—a hardship in an area where unemployment is high for both men and women and among every ethnic group.[12] In such dire circumstances, youths often stop attending school in the early grades, wandering the streets if they are male and taking in laundry or doing domestic work if they are female. Males compete for the few odd jobs that occasionally pop up. Many, however, catch the fever to go to the United States, where even the most menial job offers greater opportunity than what is available in Lemongrass.

My impressions of women's lives in Lemongrass were formed by the images I caught of them as I jogged early each morning. This was an ideal time to observe women in their routines: many were up early to get water, if their houses lacked indoor plumbing, or to do laundry they had collected to generate income, a necessary job in an area where unemployment for women is 40 percent. I wrote a poem on the occasion of Mother's Day to record all these images and to celebrate the often unrecognized and undervalued work of women.

A Mother's Day Blessing

Bless the mothers of Back Street, Queen Street,
Main Street, and all the streets that crisscross the corners of "Lemongrass"
　　Town and Toledo District;
Bless the mothers soothing and cuddling their crying babies;
Bless the mothers up at 5 A.M. to wash clothes and bake bread;
the mothers who don't eat so their children can be full;
Bless the mothers who walk the hot streets and dusty roads in the midday
　　sun to sell tamales, bread, and tarts;
Bless the mothers who keep watch from dusk to dawn, without sleep, when
　　their child has fever;

To you, the Village women twisting straw into baskets for a few dollars so
　　your children's lives will be easier;

To you, the courageous women who take the last shilling and pay school
　　fees;

To you, the learned women who speak Garifuna, Mopan, Ketchi:
ancestral languages that must not be forgotten;

To you, the dancing women whose feet teach us
rhythms of joy, happiness, and forgetfulness from life's troubles;

To you, the crying women who mourn babies, youths, and husbands:
dead from malnutrition, diseases, alcohol, drugs, and bad luck;

To you, the praying women who only have God to comfort you in hard
   times;

To you, the hopeful women who dream of a better life for your daughters;

To you, women all, mothers all
in Lemongrass, in Toledo District,
in Belize, Central America;

To you, women and mothers everywhere:

We say thank you.
With every breath we take,
with every pleasure or pain that we feel,
We say thank you for giving birth to us
for guiding us throughout the years
with love and generosity.

We say Bless You.

Invisible Maya Women

One group of women who are not well represented in "A Mother's Day Bless-
ing" and whose voices are absent from the narratives that form the core of
this ethnography are the Maya. On those days that I made my circle around
town, I watched women, men, and children arrive from the remote Maya
villages by bus. It took several hours to travel from these areas because of
poor roads, made worse and sometimes impassable in the rainy season. Maya
women were more in evidence during market days. They sometimes stopped
by Evelyn's shop, where I helped out as a clerk and occasional seamstress, to
peddle baskets and embroidery. Although the baskets are generally made individually, in a few villages, some of the women have joined the Belize Rural
Women's Association. In some villages, the women would meet in groups
to weave baskets, test out new ideas or patterns, and select a representative
to attend the national meetings sponsored by the BRWA. Unfortunately, the
market for crafts in Lemongrass is limited, and there are too many women
producing the same things. Thus, though labor intensive, basketweaving is
not very lucrative, at least in Lemongrass.

I was often struck by how shy Maya women appeared. Their quiet demeanor did not seem to be just a function of their interactions among strangers but was much in evidence when I visited one of their villages. During my
visit, women sat quietly for hours. Occasionally they spoke to compare their
work, offer a suggestion, or describe a new design recommended by the
BRWA. The group shared responsibilities, and so some women cooked and

Maya woman and child,
(courtesy of Belize Information Service)

Woman cutting vegetables, Ana Gonzalez, Toledo District
(photo by author)

watched the group leader's baby while we talked and others worked on the baskets. They carried on conversations around me in their own language—despite the fact that many Maya women attend primary school, which is conducted in English. I have been told by one of the shopkeepers in Lemongrass that Maya men keep women isolated by telling outsiders that the women do not understand or speak English. Any questions must therefore be directed to women through a male interpreter. The cultural practice of discouraging women from communicating across cultural boundaries can be a major barrier to their continuing their education, working, or forming friendships. This male strategy, however, is consistent with similar patterns Mary Lindsay Elmendorf describes in her ethnography of Maya women in Yucatan, Mexico.[13] Commenting on this form of linguistic tyranny, she describes how her field research was adversely affected:

> I felt that one reason it was difficult to get to know Flora was the same reason it was difficult for me to speak alone with Luz. Both Antonio and don Trini are eager to talk, even garrulous, and any time they were in the room the women would always defer to them. I would ask them a question, and either one of the men would answer, saying something like, "She doesn't have much Spanish and doesn't understand," or one of the women would say, "Ask Don Trini" or "Ask Antonio."[14]

Only one woman in the village I visited seemed to have challenged this restrictive structure by mastering English. Able to communicate across the cultural boundaries, this individual's skills were frequently in demand by the census taker, researchers like myself, and teachers. But in general, several factors made it difficult for me to include Maya women among my consultants: the variables ranged from cultural rules that stressed a reserved demeanor, to the difficulty of getting transportation to villages during the rainy season, to my own lack of skill in any of the Maya languages. Despite this drawback, I immersed myself in the rhythms of life that made up Lemongrass, observing and participating in the cultural ethos of this community.

A Day in the Life of Lemongrass

Most women's lives in Lemongrass are ordered by routines. The day is divided into three segments, organized around meals. Breakfast is a light meal and may consist of a piece of fruit, cheese, eggs, bread or bun (a sweet bread), and hot tea, powdered milk, or coffee. Women shop early in the morning in order to begin preparation for the major meal of the day, which is at mid-day. They generally start cooking for this around eleven o'clock in the morning. This routine made it impossible for me to schedule early interviews. I was reluctant to interfere with women's duties, since for some, the consequences of not having a meal prepared on time could be severe. The major meal of the day consists mostly of beans and rice, either mixed together and cooked in coconut milk, or stew beans and rice, each cooked separately. This diet staple is accompanied by stewed or fried fish, turtle, or, when available, what the locals call "bush" meat, a term that encompasses venison, gibnut, rabbit, armadillo, tapir, antelope, and a few others. I was told that what I ate was mostly cured venison or antelope. The meal is organized around what is available, so few menus are planned in advance. Stew chicken is a favorite dish, but chicken is considered a delicacy in Belize and is often reserved for Sunday dinners or special occasions, especially at the price of $2.29BZ a pound.[15]

Schoolchildren come home for lunch at about noon and return to school at around 1:00 P.M. Those few working mothers (Creole, Garifuna East Indian, or Maya) with little time to prepare an elaborate meal may feed their children a few garnaches, a Mestizo dish consisting of a fried corn tortilla covered with a pureed bean spread and served with an onion pepper sauce, or tamales—both filling snacks. Shops also close at noon and remain so until 2:00 P.M. when they reopen, doing business until 5:00 P.M. After work, later in the evening, people have "tea," a meal consisting of hot powdered milk, tea, fruit, or fish, and often leftovers from the earlier meals. What makes up "tea" varies in each household, but as far I could tell, it is not meant to replicate in quantity or quality the noonday meal.

At the Market

On market days in Lemongrass Maya women arrive, as always, in the company of their husbands. The men either stand to the side during business transactions involving the women's crafts or circulate through town, leaving the women to shop. If the women are selling baskets, the men handle the money. Maya women also bring their children to the market, indicating that regardless of whether their motivation is business (to sell crafts) or to make purchases, they have the primary responsibility for child care. Older children do have a function. Many of them speak better English and Creole and so help the women negotiate and sell their crafts. They also assist with the care of younger siblings.

One social problem highly visible on market days is the high degree of alcohol consumption among men, most especially the Maya, who appear to have a very low tolerance and can be seen in various stages of drunkenness. A large number of Maya men begin drinking early in the morning and by evening have depleted their resources. Some beg money or find a step on which to sleep off the alcohol's effects.[16] In contrast, Maya women linger. I was often struck by the fact that they seemed to exist on the margins of the town. They stood quietly and passively at the open windows or in the doorway, watching us work or watching the business transactions that took place in Evelyn's shop. They came in groups of one or two with their children around them. The relative isolation of Maya women and their shyness made it extremely difficult to elicit information. Moreover, without the requisite language skills, any communications I had with them in English beyond small transactions and superficial questions were highly unreliable.

Adding to the diversity at the market was a small population of Spanish-speaking traders, both male and female, who came on Fridays or Tuesdays by ferry from Guatemala. Some have made Lemongrass home, staying in rented houses; a few have no permanent residence and sleep inside the storefronts they rent to sell their goods. There are also smaller traders; these are young children who sell mangoes for a shilling (twenty-five cents in Belize currency), when in season, or peddle Creole bread, Creole bun, tamales, or meat pies for their mothers. This informal vending system travels from door to door and is dependent upon the community to support it. For some women, like Rose (whom we shall meet in chapter 4), it is how they manage to make ends meet.

To a large extent women in Lemongrass are without extra resources.

Most take in laundry as a dependable source of income. Among the fortunate women are those whose husbands own shops where they and their children are the chief sources of labor. Few if any of these women are paid a salary for their contributions, however. Other women bake bread and pastries, sell frozen confections, make tamales, and rely upon possible remittances from relatives in the United States to maintain themselves. Domestic work is generally unavailable, because the income of most in town clusters around the poverty level. The exceptions are the few hotel owners, shop owners, and the miscellaneous foreigners who may occasionally hire domestic workers. The departure of the British army left a significant economic void for women in Lemongrass, who did laundry, cooked, and/or sold food to the soldiers. Without a reliable source of daily or weekly income, women make purchases daily for the meals for that day. If they have no money, they may be able to obtain credit, which is often given on the basis of a person's reputation as a reliable risk rather than need. It is in this small, semirural, and economically depressed community that I encountered Rose, Zola, and Evelyn, whose experiences as Garifuna, East Indian, and Creole women enabled me to see commonalities and differences in how women come to understand and deal with being a woman in Belizean society.

Chapter 4 *Rose's Story (Garifuna)*

4:15 P.M.   As I walk to the next informant, I hear the sound of music coming from a bamboo hut. There is the smell of incense and candles flicker in an otherwise dark place. This is Belize of the old—away from the road, on a beaten track where the bush is overgrown and wild mangoes flourish. In the quiet, the sound of an ancient Garifuna song mingles with the present.

Rose: I am the last girl of a family of seven—baby girl, baby sister. My parents were very poor. My father was an alcoholic. He died when I was seven and my mother had to work to raise us, so I grew up among brothers, so I was a very rough little girl. I climbed trees and admired their courage. When I grew up, things slowed down. I started to see what happens to women who live with an alcoholic. I tell myself, I don't want to go through that—the pain, the anguish.

   I met my husband at eighteen. But there was a problem. We were not of the same ethnic group. He was Indian [Maya] and I Garifuna.

Rose is a copper-colored Garifuna woman with long wavy hair. I have not met any Garifuna who look like her and thought initially that she was Creole.

Rose: My mother said his family would be the problem. We married. My kids came fast. Five months baby and I'm pregnant again. He was very loving, then something started happening. We were married eleven years and the last six years were filled with pain and agony. Maybe I was the one in love with him but maybe he wasn't [in love with me]. And I began to see how ethnic differences—my mother-in-law doesn't like blacks. Her daughter is married to one but he is the head, but in my case she condoned his [her son's] filthiness, and I feel that wasn't fair to me.

As her narrative starts out Rose tells us that not only is she caught in the difficulties of an interethnic relationship, revealing some of the tensions that do occur among ethnic groups in Belize, but she is also aware of the way her gender affects her treatment within that conflict. Her female status does not merit her any additional consideration and in fact exacerbates the low status ascribed to her because of her "race"/ethnicity. Because Belize espouses a public posture of racial harmony, ethnic tensions and the maintenance of group boundaries are subtly played out and integrally intertwined with issues of gender, class, and residence.

She pauses and says, "I can tell you more when you come back. I can tell you about life with my children."

> *Irma:* That is important because it sounds as if you've moved on, and so many women get stuck.

I had no other proof of Rose's husband's indiscretion beyond Rose's own story as verification of his behavior. Whether he was actually involved, however, is not as important as Rose's belief that he was and her response to what she perceived as an intolerable situation.

> *Rose:* Yes, I felt that way, and I felt I was dying, that the world was ending. I thought I was the problem. He said I was fat, so I started jogging. But it wasn't me. It was his selfish longing. He says he loves me but he also wanted to see what was out there. I call it injustice. I didn't know it. To be treated like this now is an injustice.

Rose's ability to see what is perceived by most in her culture as appropriate male behavior as an "injustice" signifies a departure from the way in which she has been enculturated. It is a sign that Rose is now able to view the problems in her marriage not as indicators of her personal failings, but as evidence of larger social issues. This ability to externalize oppression, her emerging personal self-esteem, and her growing sense of self are reflected in her words and in her obvious indignation.

After Rose was sure that the formal part of our last interview was over, she began to recall what it was like growing up in the Garifuna culture. The following is derived from what I recorded in my field notes after the actual discussion:

Rose tells me that in the Garifuna culture, the man is always served first. He has his own plate, glass, silverware, and towel and no one touches these. Also, you must get his bath and make sure the water is not too hot and not too cold. And when he enters the house, you take off his shoes and get his slippers. Rose told me, "I think I was the last person to do this. It is dead now among the youth."

Rose is appalled at how women in the United States treat men, including her sister. She describes visiting her sister and watching this sister tell her husband, "The food is in the kitchen." "And he goes to get it and warms it up," Rose exclaims. Rose then asks her sister, what happened to all their mother's teachings? Her sister told her it was dead. Rose thinks the United States and its women are "immoral."

Ironically, Rose is both a reproducer of these gendered cultural values and behavior, evidenced by her indictment of women in the United States as "immoral" because they do not perpetuate the behavior she models or adhere to the values she was taught to revere, and someone on the verge of resisting their importance in the context of her own life. Rose was taught to view the man as a king in the home, and the actions of her sister and American women challenge and reject this perspective. In addition, Rose has not made a *direct* connection between her husband's "filthy" behavior and what she was taught to accept as appropriate male behavior growing up. Yet her husband's sense of entitlement to a double standard of living and the deference Rose was taught to give Garifuna men are both interconnected with the beliefs, values, and attitudes that generally permeate the culture of gender in Belize.

At the same time Rose is herself moving away from this earlier socialization rooted in cultural beliefs that shape not only her moral judgments but also the behaviors of her husband. This shift is apparent when she denounces her husband's desire to have both a marriage and extramarital affairs. If she had accepted his wishes as part of a "man's thing," then she would be further ensconced in what is deemed to be an appropriate response by women to this kind of scenario. Instead, she does not tolerate it, rejecting the culture of gender's standards in this area of her life. Rose is now separated from her husband. She does not say whether she asked him to leave or if he decided to on his own. Ironically, by refusing to accept her husband's behavior, Rose unconsciously begins to align herself with the very women she once described as immoral, because they too reject socially prescribed behaviors. Similar contradictions and moments of epiphany are woven throughout Rose's oral narrative.

My concluding interview with Rose took place on a Sunday afternoon, almost four days after our first one. I wrote this description in my journal:

She lives in a small concrete house that is not completely finished. The verandah is crowded with old discarded furniture. From the doorway, I look in on bunk beds. A refrigerator is to the left, out of sight—I know because Rose gets me cold water. To the right is another room where the kids listen to a TV.

This second visit enables me to scrutinize Rose more closely. As I gather information, I am forced to rethink some of the assumptions I had made on the basis of initial impressions.

I had thought Rose was Creole. Her first name confuses me, for it belongs to that of a different ethnic group. In fact, she is Garifuna, but looks different from most. She has what is called "copper" skin or "clear." She is what African Americans back home would call a "light-skinned black." She has long wavy hair and is somewhat plump—I would not call her fat. Her weight is a big concern to her and as we sit down, she apologizes for smelling like Ben Gay ointment because she has been exercising.

The Constitution of Gendered Dependency

Irma: Tell me about what it means to be a young girl growing up here. You said that you were rough and played with boys and then it stopped?

Rose: Oh yes, at the age of twelve I reached a point where all my associates were boys—my brother and all his friends. I didn't have the opportunity to play with dolls. I didn't like skirts and blouses, I liked pants and shirts. I didn't behave nicely like a little girl. When I jumped sixteen, things slow down. My views change. I learned that being a girl, we have to have respect for ourselves. I learned if I conduct myself as a young lady, I'd be respected as one and so that's when the changes start.

Irma: Were there pressures from parents or friends to behave a certain way?

A car passes; Rose rushes out to check on her daughter.

Rose: My parents wanted to mold me the way they want. I wanted to be with boys; they were different, strong. I was behaving like a boy and I wanted to be a boy. I used to admire their makeup [their ways]. They would ask after me why I didn't come [play]. [They would ask] was I becoming a sissy?

I grew up among Indian people—they [speak] Spanish. They expect a little girl to behave like little ladies, to play with dolls not marbles. I didn't find it good for me. I wanted to play with what I wanted.

Throughout the interview, Rose pauses long enough to enable me to catch up as I write; she had asked me not to tape the interview.

At this juncture, Rose's narrative provides an example of how young girls are *made* into women. The category "woman" in Belize implies a certain set of behaviors to which all females must conform. Her earlier description of how the man is treated in the Garifuna culture tells us that in some ethnic communities men are highly valued. I also found similar attitudes toward men in the Creole culture, although views are changing among the young. But Rose's narrative also shows how women themselves perpetuate their own subordination. In her own telling, Rose gives examples of the ways in which cultural values and behavior get reproduced, as when she accepts the difference in her lifestyle dictated by age and the onset of menstruation.

Irma: At sixteen were your friends getting married?

Rose: I find my classmates, a few of them, got married. I noticed the behavior and they were pressured by family to get married—less burden to the family. I was the youngest so I didn't have that pressure because my father was long dead. She [the girls pressured into marriage] would be more neatly dressed [and] healthier. The husband would take care of her.

I had heard similar stories from other women about young girls who married early or formed common-law unions both to free their families from the burden of their care and to gain support for their families. (This is what happened to Elana, whose story is mentioned in chapter 2.) In these instances, the man was usually much older than the girl.

Change: Its Catalysts and Obstacles

Irma: What were your dreams in school?

As I look at this question in retrospect, I think it was my attempt to discern what young girls perceived as their windows of opportunity and to see if they felt they had any possibility of fulfilling their dreams once they were older and married or had children.

Rose: After the age of sixteen, when I was in school my dream was to be somebody like a nurse, somebody who would help. I had a lot of love for people. I wanted to help people. Though I was rough outside, inside my makeup was different. Basically, I really wanted to be a professional nurse.

Irma: What do you do about those dreams now?

Rose: At sixteen, I was active in the community—Red Cross, Girls' Guides. The roughness was still there—it would creep up on me. I found that being involved in these different organizations helped. I met the druggist at the hospital, who taught me different things about drugs and how to mix them. And I felt so good being at the hospital and learning

the different things I could learn. The time came that a little after seventeen I started working at the hospital as voluntary work. I learned
many, many different things. I found out I could learn more if I had the
opportunity. You could not fulfill your dreams because then you had to
pay to go to high school.

Here Rose refers to the fact that in the past, the only high schools were
in Belize City; there were none in the more rural districts. Going to high
school meant the expense of boarding in Belize City as well as school fees—
something few families could afford.

> *Rose:* I had friends, nuns, who teach me typing, shorthand. I started high
> school and my mother said she would help me, but I finished second
> year as what we call Standard 2 [Second Form]. But usually when they
> [people] ask I say 6 because I didn't finish what I wanted, Standard 6
> [Sixth Form].[1]
>
> I got married when I was eighteen. I met my husband at the hospi-
> tal. There was something. He knew my mother. He made friends with
> the lady I was associating with. My mother liked him very much. All
> along it was something very fast. He checked my background first, and
> that was unusual, and that behavior was good, according to my mother.
> But when she found out he wanted to marry me, my mother was scared.
>
> We were not the same ethnic group. He is Indian [Maya] and I am
> Garifuna. We chatted about the racial thing, and he said, "No [it didn't
> matter], because I have a sister who is married to a black man." But it
> did, it did later in our marriage.

This is Rose's second reference to ethnic tensions, revealing to me how much
this issue has affected her marriage.

> *Rose:* I know I love my husband very much then. My kids came so fast that
> we [could not] build our relationship. We were very young and poor,
> but happy.

Unlocking the Mythology of Motherhood

> *Irma:* What would you like your daughter's life to be like?

As I reflect now on the timing of this question, I think I posed it because I
believe that sometimes women defer their own dreams to their children. For
women, daughters often become the repositories of their ambitions, the keep-
ers of their mother's dreams. Ironically, the mother-daughter dyad is filled
with many contradictions, because while women may be envisioning a different life, a different goal for their daughters, they must prepare them for

reality; that is, they must instruct them to accept existing gender roles mapped out by the culture. Daughters may receive a contradictory message—don't let your life be like mine, but make sure you're a good wife and mother.

Rose: I wanted my daughter to grow up in a secure home. I wanted her to inculcate something she doesn't worry about later. But if she wants to be like me, rough, I will understand that. I really wanted her to grow up in a [two-parent] home where she can lean on the mother and the father. Way back there are problems in stephomes. There is a lot of abuse where the stepfather would raise the daughter not for someone else, but for himself, and he has relations with the mother and the daughter. So I worry about my daughter growing up in a stephome.

This fear is a common one among Belizeans, both men and women, as stepparenting is an anomaly here. Men fear the idea of someone else having authority over their children, and for their daughters they fear the possibility of physical and sexual abuse by other men. This latter concern is also shared by women. Most of those I encountered who could even imagine divorcing their husbands or leaving their current relationships generally talked about surviving on their own as a single head of household rather than facing the problems they anticipated with stepfathers. It is important to note that stepmothers are not immune from this assumed hostile behavior; sometimes they are viewed as harsher on children from a man's earlier relationships.

In Belize City, I once listened to a discussion on the subject of stepparenting by members of the Belize Organization for Women and Development (BOWAND). One woman told this story: "This woman I know she got two boys. One 15 is in the States, the other 8 [is here]. She marry this man now and they got two children. And she told me he say, 'One day I hope something hit that pickni [child] and take he away.' He said that!" This anecdote underscores Rose's decision to remain, if she and her husband do not reconcile, in her new status as a single woman head of household.[2]

Irma: And what do you want for yourself?

Rose: First of all, I want to have a peaceful and happy life. I know that having material riches doesn't make me happy. Now I would like to rear my kids to a certain age and then learn a trade where I can take care of myself. But right now I would like to be with my children, so they can recover from what we've been through as a family. At night, they break down and I keep hoping things will be better with their father, not for my sake, but for their sakes. If he would be sorry—really utter these words, "I'm sorry; I want to come back to my family"—but show it in his actions, because I am very terrified of all these diseases we have now. They not only affect the Belize but the world. I would have to see changes before I would get back with him.

At this point in our conversation, Rose's husband appeared for a visit with the children.

    Rose: Don't get terrified but here he is.

He rides up on a motorcycle.

    As I reflect back on that moment, I recall that at the time Rose ignored him; there was no attempt by either of them to communicate, even at the level of polite exchanges. Despite the disruption I continued interviewing Rose, trying to determine the degree to which her participation in a women's group was influential in fostering some or all of the changes of increased self-respect and independence I had heard in her story.

Institutionalizing Change

    Irma: How have women's organizations helped?

    Rose: First of all I have gained strength. I began reflecting back to when I was a little girl and I keep asking myself where is that strength. Although I was a woman, a wife, a mother, I wasn't close to women and I started learning their behavior, what they live through, and I learned it wasn't only me who went through this terrible situation. And I remember one of the women said we have to be strong, put it behind us and use it as an experience and it made me stronger. These other women support by listening, chatting about what I don't like; they had different views which I didn't like because of my religion but we could discuss. I had likes about these women but also dislikes. At first it was hard; I wasn't used to being around women.

    Interpersonal relationships between women are not often discussed, except among family and close friends, and sometimes not even then. Women have learned that silence protects their dignity, but it also shields them from criticism. Because having a husband or a partner who provides is considered a good thing, any woman who complains about the limits of her man is viewed by the community of women who have none as ungrateful. Thus, more often than not, women's friendships are filled with ambivalence. On the one hand, women are taught to rely on other women, especially their mothers and sisters, for the support that they cannot expect from men.[3] On the other hand, women are placed in competition with one another over the affections or economic support of men. Women view other women as both friends and competitors.

Irma: Do you see things changing for women?

Rose: Yes, very much. We have different people from outside. Women today have a wide field they can turn to. They have different skills methods. They just have to decide on what they want. Women today are real well advanced compared to back then. And the culture is changing. They get educated, get involved in politics. They do the both, they do the home and otherwise. The husband cannot dominate and trample them the way they want, everything is changing and that is very good.

Irma: If you have words or could send a message to women, what would it be?

Rose: We women have to be strong. Women have to be not only emotionally strong but physically. We have to be strong for our family and for ourselves. The father is important. The women is the one in the family who have all the obligations. We have to be fighters. We have to be strong. This is a battle we have to face with a smile even though it is hard. We have to face it in a positive way. I'm very proud of myself that I am stepping forward not backwards. It's not the end of the world.

The Life Course and Empowerment

Some individuals reach a turning point in their lives when they acquire the kind of inner resourcefulness that underlies Rose's words. This moment can sometimes seem to come out of nowhere, or it can be precipitated by a traumatic event. In Rose's case, she is faced with the disjuncture between the love she sees in the relationship and her husband's desire to maintain intimate relations with women other than his wife. In her mind these two things cannot exist together. Going to a women's group reaffirms this belief when she discovers that other women confront similar problems and respond as she does. In this atmosphere of camaraderie, Rose must also reexamine her interactions with women. In accepting the support of the women in her organization, she must reassess her view of women as competitors. Rose is still grappling with these new ways of understanding and perceiving reality.

Rose's self-reflection occurs at different levels. Here she muses about her love for music.

Rose: When I was a little girl I like to [play] the guitar around girls. These people today, most are musicians. [Back then,] we had sticks, boxes, and I pretend to be the guitar lady and I had a board with nails, boards and fishing string. Later I learned a guitar was very expensive.

In this part of her story, Rose connects the love for her guitar to an incident in her marriage that exemplifies the strong bond that once existed between her husband and herself and that has not been completely severed. The memory is one filled with love and makes her current situation all the more poignant. After allowing herself this momentary digression, Rose shifts back to the reality of her present situation. She talks about how she fills up her life as a single woman and a single parent.

> *Rose:* My day starts at 5:00 in the morning, read [the Bible]; we chat, prayer, we chat about our likes and dislikes. Especially my oldest son, he is the man of the house.

For a moment Rose digresses again and talks about her love for music.

> *Rose:* I need more practice. I don't know very many songs. I like romantic songs. Once I play it, it makes me feel good.

At this point Rose stops talking, the interview concludes, and I promise to send her some cassettes of music I think she would like.

Reflections

Several aspects of Rose's story conform to what we have come to expect from women's oral narratives. Overall, she is concerned with relationships and feelings. Her story concerns how she feels in retrospect about the way in which she was enculturated. The insights she reveals suggest that she may socialize her daughter differently: she may be more flexible or display more understanding of nontraditional women's behavior. Through Rose's story we learn that cultural norms for behavior are not always in the best interests of those who are expected to conform. Rose's adventurous spirit is thwarted at the onset of puberty and menses, and she unquestioningly accepts the change.

An unexpected aspect of Rose's narrative is the intensity of what I interpret as her moral indignation. When she calls her husband's extramarital relations "an injustice," this seems to me to be not just an outgrowth of her religious training as a Jehovah's Witness but a processed anger and indignation at male behavior, which she sees as transgressing the boundaries set forth by marriage and convention. I suggest that Rose is also angry at the ease with which her mother-in-law and the community tolerate and justify such behavior—her husband is not condemned by what he does; it is viewed as typical. And she is angry because she feels betrayed. Rose's moral indignation highlights real tensions between the family structure and the values advocated by her religion, her personal beliefs about how men and women should conduct themselves in a relationship, and very different (and unequal) expectations that the community sets forth for men and women. This story is one filled with conflicts and contradictions between the individual's personal ideals and community/societal norms.

Although it is only implicit, Rose has clearly developed her own standard of behavior to which she would like her husband to adhere. She comes closest to defining it openly when she makes the statement:

> If he would be sorry—really utter these words, "I'm sorry; I want to come back to my family"—

This desire for her husband's repentance is quickly suppressed or mediated by her follow-up statement:

> . . . but also show it in his actions, because I am very terrified of all these diseases we have now.

In this instance the practical overpowers what might be termed a personal desire for forgiveness—in Rose's moral understanding of the world, words and behavior are connected and must reflect each other. This conflict between the practical and the desirable is also in evidence when Rose explains why she will not consider another relationship. Cultural fears of incest between stepparents and stepchildren are powerful inhibitors to a relationship that might temporarily reduce her economic difficulties but might also create other problems.

At one point in her narrative, Rose refers to her son as the "man of the house." In making this reference she seems to diminish the changes in her life of which she is so proud. By setting up her eight-year-old son as the symbolic male authority figure, Rose unconsciously undercuts the autonomy she is struggling to create as a woman on her own and contributes to the reproduction of patriarchal values. I am forced to wonder if an older daughter would be viewed as the "woman of the house." My observations tell me that this would be unlikely. I have seen evidence of young girls who assume parenting and domestic responsibilities, but they are not given any equivalent prestige as a result. They derive no greater benefit, status, or deference, either inside the household or in the community. What they gain is a larger workload at a young age.

Despite Rose's claim that she is not like she was before, her privileging of men over women as demonstrated by the manner in which she refers to her son (even if only symbolically) reveals how much she has internalized the extant gender ideology. She is struggling to extricate herself from the system as she simultaneously reproduces aspects of it in her own home. Her story raises critical questions for me about the difficulty women have breaking out of the cycle of economic and emotional dependency and confronting the ways they have been enculturated. Theoretically, such contradictions should be expected.[4]

Another important aspect of Rose's narrative is her statement that she will accept her husband back if he repents. This willingness to take back a man who has emotionally and mentally abused her in the past, but now might profess change, is tied to the social perception of many Belizean women that there are not enough "good" men to go around. Women are willing to tolerate varying degrees of offensive behavior in exchange for tolerable emotional and financial support.

But I discern differences in Rose too. They may be barely perceptible, even to the academic eye trained to measure social transformation in individuals by the amount of ideological rhetoric they espouse or by their level of involvement in activities that are overtly political or that directly challenge the status quo. We have come to measure women's changing awareness by the degree to which they understand and follow an explicit feminist agenda. Yet most women's lives are not political agendas, but daily struggles to survive natural and man-made disasters of unemployment, poverty, drought, illness, and the like.

In Rose's life, change and consciousness are not formed by contact with external ideologies about women's equality but are strands weaving themselves out of the personal fabric of her social reality. Some of her narrative reveals her engagement in what Patricia Hill Collins, drawing upon the work of Linda Alcoff, has defined as a "process of deconstruction"—namely, exposing a concept as ideological or culturally constructed rather than as natural or a simple reflection of reality. Moreover, according to Collins, those who can engage in this demystification of social reality need not be intellectuals; they can be of the same fabric as Sojourner Truth, an African American slave who "proved herself to be a formidable intellectual . . . who never learned to read or write." [5]

Even as Rose's narrative unfolds, there are shifts and changes in her responses to situations that she identifies as different. It is a changed Rose who was in evidence toward the end of our interview when her husband drove up on his motorcycle and she ignored him.

Rose's narrative reveals a complex person who is reflective, emotional, moral, and self-evaluative. She is also changing. Her participation in women's groups forces her to view her situation not as an isolated occurrence but as part of a common set of experiences among women in her community that may cut across ethnic lines, and as part of the experience of Belizean women in general. Her story also gives some hint of the significance of women's groups in individuals' lives. As I will elaborate later, these have proved to be the arena within which women have formulated new economic strategies, gained new skills, and found the language with which to name their oppressor and oppression. Most significant, as Rose tells us, women have found refuge from the social isolation that enables men to convince women that men's oppressive behavior is a legitimate consequence of women's personal failings. Women's groups encourage and enable women to externalize their oppression, to see it as something outside of their personal selves; women's groups enable them to see their economic dependency, their acquiescence to mental and physical abuse not as individual flaws but as patterned behavior that they have been socialized to accept and that men have been socialized to mete out.

Women's groups encourage women to interact with each other in a non-antagonistic way. Bonds of friendship are fostered and often extend beyond the boundaries of group meetings. By breaking the silence, in refusing to continue to be socially isolated, women create the conditions for altering their own individual circumstances and also gain some understanding of solidarity as an attainable goal despite personal differences. As Rose tells it: "and I started learning their behavior, what they live through, and I learned it wasn't only me who went through this terrible situation. And I remember one of the women said we have to be strong, put it behind us and use it as an experience and it made me stronger." Rose sees more possibilities as a result of her experiences in a women's group and the comfort she has found in religion. Her religious faith provides a degree of support and prevents her from giving up hope. She now has aspirations that will strengthen her as an individual and as part of a collective.

Despite these transformative leaps, the change taking place in Rose's life is not complete. She is struggling to establish economic independence by making and selling tamales, and she is struggling to achieve emotional independence from the social role of wife by developing her self-esteem and stating conditions for her husband's return.[6]

My interview with Rose ended with her asking about my experiences in Belize. At the time, I recorded these field notes:

At the beginning of the interview I show her photos of my family. The interview takes place on the verandah again. At one point during the interview, Rose's ex-husband drives up on his motorcycle. She is giving a tour of the yard and ignores him for the most part. Later she tells me that she has progressed, because three months ago if he had come she would have been crying and in a panic. She is cool and calm. I believe at this point in her narrative Rose shows that she is learning to deconstruct the expectations she has held most of her life. Her house is two rooms really. One is her bedroom, the other for the children. Off of these rooms is a kitchen area. For her catering she cooks outside on "fire haat" (an open, wood-fed hearth)! . . . At the end of the interview we talk about names and she asks me about my experiences in Belize. I am very comfortable here, I tell her. People have made me feel a part of them. She tells me if I were not black she would not have been so open. Another woman and she discussed this and others agree. It is not that they are prejudiced, she says, but that certain things they will not share. I admit there are differences, but on the street women hail me as "sister." Rose says it is good that others besides whites are doing anthropology. Though Rose did not finish high school, her vocabulary is extensive. She says she reads a lot, loves to watch birds and enjoys nature, being outside.

My getting to know Rose challenged me to confront my own expectation that women's lives could be neatly divided and placed into categories. This is not true. Rose's life is filled with contradictions and ambivalence. She wants her husband back, though she stipulates he has to change, and her young son is now viewed as the "man of the house," a role that gives him symbolic power in Rose's current household configuration and to some extent reflects and reinforces her earlier enculturation regarding the superiority of male status. Rose signifies for me a woman in transition. Her sense of self is developing—she is "in process."

I returned to Belize almost two years after recording Rose's story, my transcription and analysis in hand. I felt very uncomfortable, knowing that I had to face the possibility that Rose might disapprove of how I had rendered the narrative or disagree with my interpretations and analysis. Katherine Borland refers to this as "interpretive conflict in oral narrative research."[7] She argues that a "true exchange" can only emerge through a process in which the ethnographer relinquishes some of her interpretive authority in order to hear a different perspective. This engagement she sees as a rewarding experience for both participants, because it is through this interpretive conflict and discussion that each participant learns to yield, appreciating the other's perspective without being required to adopt the foreign perspective as her own. This suggests that we must acquire a respectful appreciation of the fact that we do not all see the world through the same window and that some of us may be quite content with our angle of view.

Despite my enormous anxiety, Rose's response to my transcription was positive. She felt that I had captured the events of her life as she had told them to me; I assumed she meant if not the exact words, certainly the feelings. She told me that the narrative had helped to remind her of the tremendous pain and hurt she had endured. Her reaction to reliving this experience became clearer when she told me that her husband had returned home.

She made no apologies but said in a firm voice that this was a trial reunion only, a test he must pass. Rose's narrative, I surmised, seemed to remind her of how deep her emotional wounds were and how lengthy the process of healing would have to be. She also was very clear that the adjustments needed were to be made by him. She was no longer the little girl her husband had married, and it was incumbent upon him to adjust to her—she was not going to change. In our brief and rushed exchange, Rose thanked me for listening to her. She thought this work was important because it was not "made up" but based upon real women's experiences.

Chapter 5   *To Be a Girl:*
Gender-Role
Enculturation

Today anthropologists generally agree that in most cultures, while males and females are born, the gendered identities of "men" and "women" are made.[1] Each culture has its own rituals and rules for inscribing onto the individual ideas about what it means to be a man or woman. This enculturation, the process by which "culture is learned and acquired," begins early in the life cycle.[2] Rose's narrative compels us to ask the question: what does it mean to be a girl in Belize?

There are few descriptions of the process of gender enculturation in any of the definitive histories of, or studies about, Belize. Rich data are contained in various dissertations, but for the most part what little is known comes from literature. The Belizean writer Zee Edgell, for example, gives us glimpses of what is expected of girls in her autobiographical coming-of-age novel, *Beka Lamb*.[3] And what is most often asked of young girls is obedience and an acquiescence to domestic responsibility early in life. The following passages describe some of the tasks usually assigned to girls and illustrates the powerful expectation that parents have of young girls' full compliance:

> Beka opened her mouth, but before she could speak, her mother said quietly, "Clear the table and wash the dishes now if you are finished Beka. Your Gran and the boys ate before you came home from school. Change your uniform first."
>
> "Beka! Mama wants to know when you are going to wash the tea things."
>
> "Lay the table then, Beka, and Toycie, please bath the boys."[4]

These scenes leave little doubt that girls have clearly delineated duties, which often take precedence over their schoolwork and extracurricular activities. This pattern of early gender socialization is not unique to Belize. The roles and duties are recognizable as the same ones within which girls and young women found themselves enmeshed in the United States in the nineteenth and early twentieth centuries and which Brenda Rosenbaum links to the maturation process for young girls in her study of Chamula, Mexico: "A girl may have friends, but her life revolves around the household where she keeps busy all day."[5] As was true in the United States for young ladies in the early part of this century, as is true in Chamula, Mexico, so too is the busy world of Belizean girls structured by tasks that can be viewed as preparation for their future social roles of mother and wife.

These "home duties" generally consists of child care, cooking, and housework (laundry, dusting, dishes). The scope of such daily chores varies with age, but tends to broaden and intensify in responsibility as a girl gets older. Often this dependency on a young girl's labor is the result of economic conditions. What I observed among the Belize City and other town populations was a tendency for a preadolescent or pubescent daughter to assume the bulk of her mother's role if the latter worked outside the home or was engaged in work in the house that required a lot of attention. Girls took over child care, cooking, laundry, and discipline of their younger siblings. Moreover, they were often the individual to whom younger siblings turned to fulfill their emotional needs, especially for attention. Women in passing may speak lovingly, or sometimes resentfully, of an older sister who "raised" them.

Young girls are inculcated early into their "proper" roles, and the significance of their contributions cannot be underestimated. The importance of a girl's labor is clear if we recognize that many women are only able to participate in either the formal or the informal economic sector as workers because their daughters assist them by watching, feeding, and bathing younger siblings and by managing the rest of the house in their mother's absence. (For many of us, this description may resonate with the details of our mother's and grandmother's experiences.) While young girls' labor supports their mother's efforts to support the household, they lose out on valuable time to attend to their own personal or intellectual growth and development. I have spoken with "successful" professional women in Belize who as adults harbor a great deal of resentment and anger toward their mothers or families because as young girls they were subjected to this form of "double-duty" oppression. In most cases, they had to find a way to complete their school tasks (often viewed as the only vehicle for future mobility or job security) while serving as a pseudo-parent, the latter role leaving few opportunities or time for a social life or the rigors of being a student.

The published literature on women in Belize and my own observations of Garifuna, East Indian, Maya (both Ketchi and Mopan), Mestizo, and Creole women suggest that sex roles in this country are clearly differentiated and reinforced early in childhood.[6] In a study of the ethnic / "racial" identity formation among urban Creole children, Nancy Lundgren asserts that sex roles in Belize are rigidly demarcated: "Gender roles are clearly defined and not questioned within the context of everyday life; . . . children can be beaten for playing with the wrong kind of toy if the opportunity ever arose."[7] Although my own observations in Lemongrass confirm this early inculcation of sex roles as well as a sexual division of labor, I saw nothing that approximated the rigid enforcement of sex roles Lundgren describes. This does not mean, however, that coercive forces regarding gender-role formation do not exist, but merely that they are not always visible.

I did see instances in which children themselves instructed and were instructed about "appropriate" and "inappropriate" gender-role behavior. One example occurred on the peninsula of Placencia in the south of Belize, where I observed a group of young children at play. Two young boys and a girl, about seven or eight, were pretending to "chop bush" and open young coconuts with a machete. The boys made no apparent distinctions concerning the girl's involvement, until she was suddenly snatched away by her mother and reprimanded for playing with such a dangerous object. The boys, in contrast, were admonished to be careful, but the machete was not taken away from them. The young girl was redirected toward other, presumably safer, play activities; the boys were permitted to continue taking risks in their play with the machete. When the young girl attempted to rejoin the group, she was reminded of her "place" by the boys.

Nancy Chodorow's 1978 study on the differences in the emotional makeup of girls and boys in the United States, for all the limitations of her data set, makes some useful observations about the ways in which young girls are socialized to be less aggressive, while boys are encouraged to take risks.[8] In a more recent work that challenges the biological origins of gender, Ruth Bleier also concludes that from the moment children enter the social world as infants, they are oriented toward certain gender behavior: "It is because of the developmental plasticity of the brain and because humans learn so quickly and easily that we become adapted so thoroughly to the dichotomized cultures we are born into and we learn to accept, as *natural,* our proper place. Most of us are taught in minute detail, sometimes subtlety and sometimes with sledgehammer force, from birth what it means to be either a boy or girl."[9] The pervasiveness of gender enculturation cross-culturally is evident in Elmendorf's description of evidence of early sex segregation and a sexual division of labor among Maya children in the village of Chom Kom in Mexico. Children's play is the window through which we see how adult behavior is mimicked. This example from Elmendorf is strikingly similar to Rose's experience of having to learn to play apart from boys: "She told me that her favorite memories of childhood were . . . of playing house with her sisters. *The boys had to play apart from them* and would go off to pretend making *milpa* or other things in imitation of their fathers. We would make little tortillas with herbs and pretend to eat them and say we were making supper just like Mama." [10] Elmendorf's description and Rose's narrative both illustrate the way in which gender roles are simultaneously produced and reproduced by every age group in the society.

Because "woman" and "man" are constructed *adult* categories, gender roles tend to be more fixed regarding the specific expectations a society has of appropriate behaviors for men and women. In contrast to the rigidity of adult gender roles, my research showed that the gendered categories of "boys" and "girls" in Belize may contain variations according to age and circumstances, with the category of "boys" being more flexible in its range of duties.

Although there is a strong expectation that girls generally assist with cooking and cleaning and that boys generally do yard work or go to work on the "plantation" (farm), I found many examples of young boys who were expected to assist with food preparation, laundry, and housecleaning. This occurred in households where the oldest child was a male or where there were no female children. My suspicion that men were sometimes socialized to perform "women's work" was confirmed when in casual conversations, some older men described having cooked, cleaned, and laundered in their childhood. Regardless of these experiences, which they often remembered with a certain affection, most expressed a profound unwillingness to do any of these tasks on a regular basis as an adult man. They generally joked about forgetting these skills, although a few conceded that they cooked and assumed responsibility for child care when their spouse or partner was ill or out of town. Thus men are not at all helpless, but rather give expression to an ideological belief in the idea of separate tasks for men and women, when they refuse to assist with domestic chores. In addition, men often place greater value on the work they do outside the home, while no matter what work women do, inside or outside the home, it is devalued and generally seen as merely an extension of their home duties and therefore not important.

Women also accept and perpetuate the cultural ideology that it is an unusual or rare man who is actively involved in domestic life; yet these same women expect their sons to perform any chores they assign to them—from laundry to cooking. Their attitudes reflect the contradictory views of gender that often operate in a society. Once I overheard a group of women marvel at a man in his late thirties who went with his children to obtain costumes for a school play. The interest he showed in this aspect of his children's lives was viewed by these women as noteworthy, instead of being seen as an integral part of his parenting role. In a different vein, while I heard of no explicit stigmas attached to men who performed household chores (cooking, laundry, ironing), women who allowed men to help them or whose partners helped out were sometimes stigmatized as "lazy" for not performing these domestic tasks themselves or for needing help. The community message was clear: women who need men to help them with their work have failed.

Men who do get involved are also subjected to criticism from their male peers and may be reluctant to admit active participation. For example, one young man, recently married, whom I encountered in the market, "confessed" to preparing supper for that day. His admission was given in a conspiratorial whisper while he glanced about to be certain there were no eavesdroppers in the vicinity. His behavior supports the community belief that men who perform household work are involved in something that is abnormal. Men learn to relegate such involvement to a realm of secrecy and to participate only if the need arises. These examples indicate that while the community may not overtly restrict men from performing domestic tasks early in their life cycle, as they get older, such involvement may generate admiration for men, as shown in the above example, but provoke criticism for the woman from the same observers. Continuous performance in this area, however, may subject the man to peer ridicule, forcing men who wish to contribute their labor to the domestic arena to do so in secrecy. It is important to note that in no instance did I observe girls doing so-called boy's work. Although such role reversal is certainly not impossible, I found that if there was no boy in the family to perform a chore such as "chopping bush" around the house, a neighbor's son was generally sent for. Thus, while some of these examples point to a degree of flexibility in male gender behavior based on age, women's behavior from a young age is much more circumscribed.

I have suggested that a young girl's labor is essential to the smooth operation of a household and gets appropriated by adults early on. The need for such appropriation is a direct result of the fact that women's home duties in Belize are extremely labor intensive. Women make daily trips to the market, prepare food, have primary responsibility for child care, and do laundry several times a week. These are only a few examples of what constitutes "home duties." In addition, mothers are often the only ones available, despite this heavy load of home duties, to assist their children with schoolwork. That women are able to contribute in this area at all is remarkable, since many complete little more than a primary school education and perhaps a few years of high school.

While town women get some assistance because of electricity, in-house plumbing, and the close proximity of small shops, the lives of rural women are even more constrained and labor intensive, as the following description of a single day in the life of a Maya village woman shows. The information was compiled from a survey conducted by the Toledo Small Farmers' Development Project among Maya women in the southern district of Toledo in Belize and is further evidence of the undervaluation of women's contributions to social production:

> Most women reported that they spent from 1 to 5 hours per day on farm activities during cropping season. Their time was spent mainly assisting their spouses on tasks such as preparation and distribution of food, harvesting, and processing of produce, e.g., threshing and cleaning of rice or beans.
>
> For those with livestock 1 to 3 hours was normally allocated per day to look after the animals. Tasks include preparation of feed such as shelling corn, feeding the animals, provision of water, and cleaning of pens where necessary. The amount of time spent depended on the size of the operation, the number of animals, and whether or not help was available.
>
> Housework takes up the overwhelming majority of the time spent by women in the household. For example, most women reported that they spent between 45 and 70 hours per week doing housework.
>
> Some women reported as much as 90 hours of housework during cropping season. At this time they are usually awake before 5 a.m., prepared breakfast and/or lunch for the males in the household so that they can leave for the farms by 6 a.m. They would continue working most of the day with very little rest in between, depending on the number and ages of their children. By the time the family completed their supper it might well be long past six or seven o'clock in the evening. Children helped with certain tasks in some cases.
>
> The decision as to who should undertake which household tasks was generally made by women. That may be due to the fact that they engaged almost exclusively in the carrying out of such tasks. A full 57 percent of women indicated that they decided the allocation and sequence of household tasks by themselves. An additional 13 percent said they participated in such decisions jointly with their spouses. Thirty percent said (they let) their husbands make the decisions as to household task allocations.[11]

Few recorded descriptions exist of a day in the domestic life of Creole, Garifuna, Mestizo, or East Indian women, but much of what I observed in Lemongrass and other districts seemed to vary little from what the Toledo Small Farmers' Development Project has documented for Maya women. It can be stated unequivocally that a large percentage of women's time is given over to domestic chores. These "home duties" consume the greatest proportion of women's time, energy, and attention, and only women with daughters or women whose economic status enables them to hire a domestic worker acquire some relief from this dimension of their everyday life. As young girls mature, their labor is increasingly relied upon to lighten older women's workloads. At a more symbolic level these circumstances become a way for women

to replicate their own lifestyles and gender roles—in effect, to culturally re-
produce themselves.

Sexuality and the Reproduction of "Woman" in Belize

Rose's narrative shows that girls learn early that the sense of freedom they felt
as small children comes to an abrupt end when they enter puberty.[12] Female
sexuality in Belize and in other cultures is not only a key aspect of women's
identity but one often shrouded in silence and anxiety and marked by ambivalence. Anthropologists have asserted that negative, ambiguous, and even
contradictory attitudes and beliefs about women and women's sexual powers
most often find expression in behavior and through cultural symbols.[13] For
example, research on rural Greece indicates that social organization is structured around an ideology of female pollution.[14] This belief manifests itself
symbolically and in practices that go so far as to dictate separate physical spaces
for men's and women's activities and rituals.

Among the Maya of Mexico, Elmendorf documented cultural restrictions
regarding Maya women's knowledge of their sexuality. Some of the women
she studied believed premature or early sexual knowledge by women or understanding of the body to be sinful. Women themselves perpetuated this cultural belief and left it uncontested. Elmendorf states: "I found that sex and
related matters of womanhood are not discussed openly. The [Mayan] women
explained to me that it was considered a sin to tell a girl about menstruation
before her first period, or to explain sex to her before marriage. They had not
instructed their daughters, nor had their mothers instructed them." [15] This
silence about the female body and its processes is also prevalent in Belize. In
her study of women's sexual magic, M. Kenyon Bullard concludes that men
have a fear of how women will exercise their sexual powers; they are especially
concerned about those times when women use "magical" techniques to bind
a man to them. She describes one such ritual women are believed to use: "In
one instance, women rinse the menstrual cloth and use the water to make a
mixture known as coco-soup or sweat rice. Pubic hairs can also be added." [16]
Although Bullard acknowledges that most Belizeans find this practice repug-
nant, just the thought that a woman might actually resort to such methods
not only gives women some degree of control over men's sexual behavior but
also creates a climate of mistrust and hostility in interpersonal relationships.
In fact, a man who seems overly solicitous to a woman is thought to be under
the influence of "obeah," the Creole word for sorcery or magic: "The most
apparent effect of this kind of magic is the creation and aggravation of suspicion, mistrust, and tension between the sexes. Yet more positive effects are
probably at work. Primarily, these magical operations provide an outlet for

the resentment and hostility many women feel toward males. While females are probably not physically harming men they may get a sense of great satisfaction from the covert act of degrading them." [17]

Despite the existence of such practices or the threat of them, men also have their own strategies to gain control over women's sexuality: "Husbands restrict their wives' wardrobes to conservative clothing, and making one's self attractive and desirable is a generally suspect activity for a married woman." [18] The most common method men use is a myth of diminishing sexual attractiveness after childbearing. Some of the women I spoke with indicated that more than once they had been told by men that they had become less attractive after bearing children or while pregnant. One woman told me that her husband so disapproved of her last pregnancy that he found himself a "sweetheart." His condition for fidelity was that she get "back in shape." To the best of her knowledge, he did end his affair; she now exerts tremendous effort to maintain a slim figure. In contrast to the man who wants an attractive woman, other men view a woman's efforts to be attractive as a sign of her infidelity. Bullard explains how such suspicion results in strict control over a woman's appearance and mobility.

The degree to which such restrictions may be placed on a woman's mobility was confirmed by a Lemongrass woman. She stated: "I was mostly to myself before because my husband didn't want me to be in any social gathering. Even in school I use not to go to the entertainment. So I felt like I was penned up, couldn't talk to friends, couldn't go out or go to any dance parties. Not like you free, like confined, penned up." Examples such as these illustrate the ways in which women are confronted throughout most of their lives by contradictory messages about their sexuality. These mixed messages begin in childhood and can continue through adulthood. A significant aspect of women's personhood is a sexual identity shaped by secrecy, anxiety, distrust, and ambivalence.

As is true in most of the world today, young girls in modern Belize are almost accidentally rather than intentionally introduced to their sexuality and the responsibilities of motherhood early in adolescence. Evidence of this can be found in the UNICEF report, *Children First: A Situational Analysis of Children and Women.* The report, based on surveys conducted by the Belize Family Life Association in 1989 and the Department of Women's Affairs in 1990, states: "Belize currently has one of the highest rates of adolescent pregnancy in the [Central American] region. One out of every five births in 1985 was the result of an adolescent pregnancy. . . . Data is lacking with respect to the number of deliveries that resulted from these pregnancies. In terms of prevalence, a survey of the years 1986 to 1988 revealed that 45.6 percent of mothers had their first delivery while still a teenager." [19] These data coincide with what I saw as I interacted with families and what I observed when I participated in Belize's social night life. Young girls are sexually involved at a relatively young age, and their involvement is frequently with older men.[20] Fourteen seems to be the age around which pronounced sexual activity begins; by the time a girl is fifteen, she may have given birth. Although I observed instances of much younger girls who were actively solicited on the streets by older boys and men, the documented cases of girls under fourteen giving birth usually occur as a result of incest or rape.[21]

A visit to Belize City's nightclubs is sufficient proof of the mixed-age (young girl/older man) liaisons. Young girls, still wearing socks, are often in the company of men twice their age. I was told by some of my male consultants that certain bars in the city bring in young girls from Guatemala or hire recent refugees from neighboring Spanish-speaking countries to provide a variety of services, including sex. These child-adult sexual liaisons do not go unnoticed and serve as a common topic for community gossip. The preference by adult males for sexual relationships with pubescent girls is not unique to Belize, however. It is found in other cultures like Suriname, where among the Maroons young girls are referred to as "apron girls" and considered a prize.[22] In Suriname, among the Maroon population, these relationships are part of the culture and are condoned. In Belize such relationships are not overtly condoned, though they are tolerated. Most people ignore them and comment, "It's a private ting." For the young girls there are tremendous risks; in these situations they not only risk a loss of reputation, but generally have little hope of obtaining financial support. Most men in mixed-aged liaisons will not openly admit to paternity for both financial and legal reasons. Ellen, a counselor from the women's organization Breast Is Best in Lemongrass, comments on how early sexual experience can, not surprisingly, complicate a young girl's future.

> *Ellen:* I don't know if it is happening all over the world, but I know here in Belize it is starting very, very young right now. Girls in school are having a boyfriend and having sexual activity. I know it is very hard on the young girls. Some of them get pregnant, their parents can't even help them because their parents can't even help themselves. I know of an instance of a young girl, she just finished First Form and she is very bright.[23] She got pregnant. She's out because her dad don't have a job. Her mother is not working.
>
> *Irma:* And what about the baby's father?
>
> *Ellen:* The baby's father is denying the child because she is so young. Here in Belize if you have a young child, if a young girl gets pregnant the father can go in jail, if she is under sixteen.

Although there is some fear by men of legal reprisal, it has been my experience that women in Belize often are uninformed about their legal rights on most such matters.[24] Moreover, given that these relationships are predicated upon an emotional attachment, a young woman is unlikely to seek legal recourse to resolve her situation. Many times the man returns and a repeated pattern of pregnancy, abandonment, and return is played out. Or the young woman may become similarly involved with another man.

This pattern of what I call an "economic-sexual cycle" will be described more fully later on.[25] There are many instances where such liaisons have longevity and exist alongside a man's primary family (which may be from a marriage or from a prior consensual relationship). Finally, neither extramarital affairs nor mixed-age liaisons are confined to any particular social class, ethnic group, or occupational strata in Belize—it is common knowledge that certain prominent politicians maintain two families who may even live in the same town.

Although adolescent girls are experienced, it is clear that they are inadequately socialized to deal with their emerging sexuality. Older women, now in their mid- to late thirties, admit that in retrospect they were frustrated, ignorant, and confused about exactly what the transition from a young girl to a "woman" meant. The description of coming of age given by Ellen in the next section illustrates how socially and emotionally ill prepared girls are for the responsibilities of adulthood and the consequences of motherhood. Ellen's mother provided no guidance about the onset of menstruation and her induction into womanhood, and so her sex role was reproduced by silence. As I traveled around the country, I heard this story repeated often by older women.

Bodies and Secrets

What women say is most often not discussed are the reasons for and the methods of taking care of one's body during menses. These are rituals shrouded in as much secrecy and filled with as much anxiety as the most sacred of religious practices, where the behavior persists but the "why" is never explained, and to broach it is considered sacrilegious. Ellen describes her rite of passage into womanhood and the ritual of ignorance that accompanied it:

> *Ellen:* I can remember at the age of thirteen I started having my menstrual period. I didn't know anything. I didn't even hear about it, not even from one of my friends. I didn't hear about this thing or I didn't know about it. I didn't even see even one time. They didn't leave anything around in the bathroom or anything. When I started having it, then I

know what my sisters used to get good whipping for in the kitchen or all over the place because if they slip and they leave one thing hanging around in the bathroom somewhere, my mom would beat them up. I didn't know what she was whispering to them and whipping them for. Then when I got a dose of it, then I knew what it was.

Irma: It's a big secret?

Ellen: Ah ha, but it's a big secret.

Irma: And so your mother never explained to you before it happened?

Ellen: She didn't. None of my older sisters didn't explain to me either. I don't know how they get, I am close to my older sister. She is much older than I am, about thirteen years. Well I talked to her and she would say well, when I talk to her and tell her since I am big now, since I am a big woman right now I would tell her how I get to find out. And the reason why I talked to her about it is because she have older daughters and then I have my girls coming up. I asked her how she, if she ever tell them. I said I don't know if Ma told you but when I was growing up she never mentioned it to me and it was a very terrible thing.

Irma: And what was her response? How is she handling it?

Ellen: Well she would say, gial [girl], those days were rough days. But I tell my girls about it [menstruation], she'd say.

But I remember running to this creek; there was a little stream of water. And I had a temperature with it the first time it was coming. I remember seeing this thing and I just couldn't imagine what I am going to say to my mother. I wasn't thinking anything about sex 'cause we didn't know anything about that at the age of thirteen. I didn't even hear it. I didn't even read it. I didn't even know anything about it. So I didn't know what I did wrong now for this.

Irma: For you to be bleeding?

Ellen: For me to be bleeding. So I went to this creek and I run down there and I washed myself. And before I get back home and change again, I run there again and I change myself. And now I don't know to pin out these panties and done say why you have all these thing on the line? And my mom was strict. Every time we finish bathing, we had to wash it and pin it out. So I keep running to the stream and before I get home it is there again and I run back again. I have my work to do and then she [my mother] would yell at me and ask me if I'm not finished.

Then she noticed me running there and she said if I'm hiding something there, eating it and so. I run there every minute and come back or so. I said, no ma'am. I didn't know what to do and I start crying. She was talking to me and now I feel like it's coming down here and I run from her and went back by the creek again because it was running down now. And she said if you go by that creek one more time I am going to whip you. I will give you a good whipping if you go by that creek again, cause it's getting late, and I didn't know what to say to her.

And then I wasn't close enough to talk to my sisters. Like how my girls are growing up now, they would whisper and tell each other things. I finally told my mom that I don't know what happened and I didn't do anything. I was just sitting down and I say start feeling bad and I have a pain in my belly, then I started bleeding. Then she said, well come and I will show you what to do.

Irma: And still no explanation?

Ellen: She took some old diapers that she had from the baby, 'cause when they get old like so, we didn't have pads in those days. She said you put it on and you pull up your panty here and it will last for a few days. And she say and when you finish, everyday you wash out those cloths and don't make anybody see you. You put it in a plastic bag and you take it to the wash house, cause we had a wash house. Hang it up there. Everyday you make sure you wash out those things when nobody is around. So I do as she say. We washed them out and pin it on the line. And she say next month you will have it again and you will do the same thing. And that was it. No more explanation. Nothing more.

Irma: Nothing about having babies?

Ellen: Nothing about having, no, nothing more. Nothing. Oh what she said, she said now you can't go around boys or something to that effect. You can't go. Then every time I didn't even want to sit in the class beside a friend or so. We didn't pass close to them [boys]. And that was all we knew about it and nothing else.

Ellen's story is filled with anxiety, misinformation, and omissions. She articulates through personal experience how lack of knowledge becomes a powerful tool of enculturation designed to limit women's control over and understanding of their own bodies. They are never told what or why—young girls are kept in a darkness and silence about sexuality that is maintained by everyone in the community. Although it is important to recognize that times change, the growing phenomenon of adolescent pregnancies suggests that girls today know little more than Ellen did about the way in which their bodies work or how reproduction occurs, and that they have few guides in family planning.

Further, despite society's alarm and public outcry over the rapid increase in young, unmarried mothers, few measures have been forthcoming from either the state or the schools to educate girls about their bodies, sex, or sexuality in the form of consistent programs on sex education. The conspiracy of ignorance carried out among many mothers and fathers in Belize is similar to the one Elmendorf encountered among the Maya in Mexico—many Belizeans too believe that a little knowledge is dangerous or that knowledge means giving young girls, especially, permission to be sexually active. This situation exists largely because reproductive (or family) planning is still a controversial topic in most areas of this predominantly Catholic country. It appears that the strong link between the state and church-run schools, which dominate the educational system, has resulted in reticence on the part of the government to openly advocate birth control or the dissemination of contraceptive information. Most recently the church made explicit its official position against any form of sex education in the schools in a brochure entitled "Youth and Chastity: Essays on the Subject of Sex Education in Schools" published by the Belize Catholic Institute for Human Life. The brochure advocates chastity and sees the function of a proposal from the Belize Family Life Association to establish peer counseling training programs on sex education as one designed to "encourage our young to use contraceptives." [26]

Availability of contraceptives is not a problem for most Belizean women. The Belize Family Health Survey identifies the following as sources for obtaining contraceptives: "Ministry of Health (41 percent), pharmacies (31 percent), private clinics and hospitals (13 percent), and Belize Family Life Association, the International Planned Parenthood affiliate (11 percent)." Nor is cost of most contraceptives prohibitive. At the same time, "rural women, women of low educational attainment and indigenous Indian women (Mopan or Ketchi)" seem to be "the least familiar with contraceptive methods." [27]

If access is not the problem for most Belizean women, what is? I would suggest that the conjunction of moral codes and religious values, when combined with community ideals about family and children, produces an ambiguous and contradictory relationship with emerging adolescent sexuality that is thought to be best left alone. The following exchange between myself and a woman social service worker in one of the districts reveals just how touchy and uncomfortable the topics of contraceptives and reproductive planning are in the society:

Irma: What about birth control in Belize?

Joan: Uhm?

Irma: It's not practiced a lot or family planning?

Joan: It is. They have the Belize Family Life Association here, but I don't want to comment on birth control. It's something that I . . .

Irma: Okay, it's a controversial issue?

Joan: Yeah, but . . .

Irma: And this is a predominantly Catholic community?

Joan: Yes, and then more so I am a Catholic lay minister, so I . . .

Irma: Okay.

Any discussions of birth control, AIDS, or sexually transmitted diseases and the entire subject of women's reproductive health are indeed constrained mostly by people's religious beliefs and values. The job of informing the public about contraceptives has traditionally been in the hands of private doctors, though in the last decade this topic and the dissemination of literature and contraceptives have become the purview of the Belize Family Life Association, a nongovernmental organization.[28] This group has assumed the major responsibility for distributing information and educational materials about women's reproductive health; it is the primary disseminator of contraceptives and one of the few places where women can receive pap smears[29] and women-centered health care. Breast Is Best is another group that emphasizes women's health care and nutrition in addition to being an advocate for breast feeding by new mothers.

In most of the districts in Belize, including Toledo, where I spent a majority of my time, though community members expressed concern about adolescent pregnancies, they simultaneously disapproved of sex education classes as a standard part of the school curriculum. BFLA has organized teen groups focusing on peer sex counseling as offshoots of its organization. These groups, when invited, provide workshops in the schools on reproduction and sexuality. In general, such invitations are rare—most Belizeans view sex education as the domain of the parents. This tacit assumption in practice means that it is the woman's responsibility to educate girls and the man's job to educate boys. There is little evidence that such conversations do occur or that any traditions or structured ways of conveying knowledge about sexuality exist. Further, the Belizean adult belief that sex education in the school might be construed by the youth as permission to engage in early sexual activity is firmly entrenched. Adults do not see the contradiction of their position: that is, youth are already engaging in early sexual activity, and each year the practice seems to be trickling down to even younger age groups. Despite the objective reality, and because of a reluctance to openly discuss sex or reproduction as a result of their moral/religious beliefs and their personal upbringing of silence on the topic, adults throughout Belize are unpersuaded that sex education can either prevent pregnancies or diminish the onslaught of AIDS.

AIDS education in Belize is an area that needs to be examined more fully. Although the Belize Family Health Survey indicates that knowledge of AIDS is "almost universal," only 2 percent of those who perceive themselves as at risk of contracting AIDS actually use condoms. The study concludes that among women who perceive themselves as at risk there is a serious gap between their knowledge and their use of preventive behavior. AIDS is an invisible disease. The danger of this situation is illustrated by the *Belize Report For the Fourth World Conference on Women,* which states: Belize now has the "second highest incidence rate of HIV/AIDS in Central America. Since 1991, women have been contracting HIV at a faster rate than men."[30] This statement suggests that for women, especially, information about reproduction, sexuality, AIDS, and other sexually transmitted diseases is elusive and often shrouded in secrecy and silence.

I have discussed some of the issues that confront young girls. Once they have made the transition from childhood to adulthood, their lives become even more complex. In Belize, as in most societies, information about gender (social roles) and gender rules (the ideas that regulate behavior) are transmitted early in the child development cycle. Boys and girls, through play and the assignment of household responsibilities, are directly or indirectly given messages and symbols that instruct them on the appropriate or inappropriate behavior for their gender.

Young girls' labor is more easily appropriated by adults than boys'; as a result, women end up consciously (or not) reproducing themselves by developing in young girls domestic and nurturing skills that society considers germane to their presumed future roles as wives and mothers. As girls mature, their sexuality and knowledge of how their bodies function become a major cultural site where they are manipulated by society through the intentional omission of information.

In the past, by the time girls learned about reproduction and sex, many were already on the way to becoming mothers. Today, according to the results of the 1991 Belize Family Health Survey, "Knowledge of contraception is high in Belize, as 95 percent of women 15–44 years of age had knowledge of at least one modern method." Even with this low use of contraceptives, there is a dramatic shift from past practices under which women had limited information about their bodies and the options now available to them.

In the next story by Zola, we get clues as to how some women extricate themselves from ideas of subservience and subordination rooted in the past and work to shape new patterns that allow them to establish greater control over their bodies and their emotional health.

Chapter 6   *Zola's Story (East Indian)*

I met Zola because I had specifically asked to talk to the district's representative to the National Women's Commission. In Belize City the women I had met in similar positions were educated, well traveled, and sophisticated in their dress, mannerisms, and outlook. Many were active in one of the two political parties. Zola proved to be a dramatic departure from these other representatives. She is a thin woman with shoulder-length curly hair. At thirty-nine and with seven children (three of whom are adults), her face is ageless. For our meeting she has dressed in a fitted American-style dress made out of a satiny material. To my eyes the fabric seems too ornate for everyday use, but I have become accustomed to Belizean women wearing such dresses as they go about their daily routines.

We met in my hotel room, which held two beds and one chair. I had seen Zola in the market the week before when she stopped by Evelyn's shop. After I explained my interest in the impact of women's groups on individual women's lives, she agreed to talk to me about her work on the commission. We scheduled the interview for Wednesday, when she came into town to the market; the rest of the week, she did not have access to a vehicle. On Wednesday, Zola's husband dropped her off and went to complete their errands for the day. We talked for almost an hour and a half. Throughout the entire process, I was aware that she controlled the interview. She talked from the time she entered my room and flung herself down on one of the beds—no formalities. I asked only a few questions, mostly to clarify a point she made.

When Zola talks about her work, about her life, it is done with a great deal of ease and expressiveness—twice she knocked over the microphone while gesturing with her hands. She exudes the confidence of someone who is willing to set limits and able to accept or administer the consequences without any harm to herself. Listening to her today, I cannot imagine that there was a point in her life when she was the exact opposite, but there was. What follows is what Zola told me about her life, based on the transcripts of a taped interview and my field notes. I have edited for the sake of brevity, but have maintained the order, sequence, and richness of her oral narrative.

Zola is an East Indian woman, representing to some extent the most marginalized group of women in Belize. East Indians in the south of Belize are descended from those who arrived in the early 1900s as laborers; however, they have lost much of their cultural distinctiveness. They speak Creole, dress according to local standards, and eat whatever local foods are common to the district where they reside, with only a few identifiable traces of their heritage (yellow ginger, which may be either turmeric or cumin) in any of the dishes they cook. Many have intermarried with Creoles or Garifuna, so that it is sometimes difficult to speak of them as a separate ethnic group. In the district of Toledo there is some residential clustering of East Indians in an area called Forest Hills, though there appeared to be no strict rules that preclude them from living in other areas.

Zola's life seems emblematic of many of the stories I heard. At the age of fourteen she began living with her "gentleman," just like Elana (also East Indian, whose story we heard in chapter 1). At the time of our interview, Zola and her partner had lived together for seventeen years and had been married for eight, twenty-five years in all. Most amazing about Zola's transformation is her decision to legalize her consensual relationship. She explains why:

> *Zola:* So we are married now eight years. As I said, I always tell him, I married to you to show you the mind I had. I married to you while you were sick for nothing. I was the one who earned everything. You, a man, would have never married me on that bed. Never. I'm married to you because my kids love you and if they love you, I have to love what they love.
>
> I show him it in a way that he had to change. He had to, whether he wanted to or not. I could have said to him, when he came home, I doesn't need you. I have a house, I have a job, I have a piece of land. My kids are nearly [grown]. Two are out of school when he come back.
>
> This is what we need to educate the man about. I said I got into this thing from experience. What I went through life, I am not boasting, I doesn't treat my husband like if I have a bat over his head. He works if he coulds, and if he can'ts, that is fine with me. I doesn't show him—yeah, when you had your health I used to be dog after you and now it's my turn.

Zola challenges her community's gender system by owning her land and giving an ultimatum to her husband—he can either join her on her terms or stay by himself. She has extricated herself from one aspect of an economic-sexual cycle; her financial independence leaves the door open for freedom in other areas of her life.

The Constitution of Gendered Dependency

One role in which Zola has been most effective is as an advocate for women and their issues. Seeing lessons in her experiences as a wife and mother, she educates her community and those in a position to make policy about women's needs.

Irma: Maybe you could begin by telling me what is the National Women's Commission and what your role is as the regional representative?

Zola: The Women's Commission really is to advise the minister on the needs of our community, voluntarily, and measurement [status] of women, battered women. The abuse of women, the abuse of children, okay like for instance in a home where a woman very seldom has rights, we are not looking for as people have it on the street to see—we are looking to be above the men—we are not looking for that. We are just looking out to let we have our fair rights. This advantage that they are taking in, like for instance you are married and you haven't any rights because you are a wife. It means that you are a wife you have to be [in a] stew. Or in other words, you are tied in a home, you haven't any freedom. You are always under his roofs and we are trying to protect these things [for] women, because as we say even if you go to law, or if you go to court in Belize and you are a woman, you very seldom have a right. You has a man who is a lawyer, you has a man who is a minister [government official], you has a man who is a commissioner of police, and you has the man who is the inspector of police. And we are trying to upgrade women, that they are also human and that they also have a right. Not to put ourselves above the men, we need them, but let us go a fifty-fifty percentage.

Like for instance maybe I have a husband out there working and I am living in a rented home, and this home is getting crowded. Well, he hasn't any time to go out there and hunt for another home. I am the one who has the time. But because he is the man, he is paying the rent, whenever any fuss come in between the family, I am the one to leave. Why is it that way? Why must I leave? And when I leave I cannot have anything to leave with. All I have to leave with most of the time is my kids or our kids.

In this passage Zola describes the vulnerable situation of some women. Although women contribute to the household through shopping, cooking, cleaning, child care, and even looking for suitable places to live, when there is a conflict, it is the man who prevails because he is in control of the family's financial situation. When Zola rhetorically poses the question "Why must I leave?" she is challenging the view that women are not entitled to anything because their contributions are not monetary. The control that some men exert over the household and over their partners can also be violent.

> Zola: Or if I go in and make an alarm to the police, it's a husband and wife business and I haven't any right. You have some family where she [the woman] is tied up so bad that she even feared to come out and let the people or public or someone that can help her know what she is going through. Then instead of this [getting help], what she tried to do is just go out, make a big mistake, go out and get involved with someone else, get tied up in the same kind of home or worse home than she was already in. She feels that in that way she were helping herself. But she wasn't.
>
> But as I say we are not educated enough because we do not have enough protection for women. And that is where women go weak and go wrong. So this is what the Women's Commission is mostly all about: to help and protect women, to secure women and children.
>
> For instance we cannot make a law but we are asking for a law, where a woman can go somewhere and say I am abused by my husband.[1] I am threatened by my husband. This sort of thing. And someone come in and counsel the person and let him know where he is wrong. There is something like what you say, something like a punishment to him. Let him understand that this woman is his partner not his tools. These are what a Woman Commission is all about.
>
> Like for instance here in Belize, I can never go out and go to the social [service] officer and say, listen, my husband had beaten me last night. Most naturally we are human; we have feelings. Now he just beat me up yet he wants to have an affair with me. I cannot afford to allow him. I am very aggressive. I can't. I am hurt. Now he forced me into it and he call that consent. We the women feel like that is not fair, but there is nothing we can do about it. So I does not allow him. We fight again and he then he left me with a bruise. I go to the social officer and they take me to the police and the police say that is a private concern. These are the things we are trying to protect. They do not want to admit that a husband can rape a wife and he surely can.

Domestic violence is one of the most pressing issues for women in Belize. No ethnic group seems to be immune to the practices of wife/partner beating, verbal abuse, and emotional abuse. Further, occupation and educational levels are not barriers to domestic violence—it touches women of every ethnicity, occupation, and social status, and is generally perpetrated by their partners or spouse. According to the literature disseminated by Women Against Violence, "In every District of Belize women report being physically assaulted

by their husbands, common-law partners, boyfriends, ex-partners and relatives. Approximately 90% of violent crimes against women are committed by
someone close to the woman. Few assaults are committed by strangers."[2]
Given this, it seems reasonable to suggest that one of the underlying tenets of
Belize's culture of gender is an acceptance of domestic violence. Zola presents
a scenario that depicts how domestic violence, especially marital rape, is often
overlooked in Belize:

Zola: That is what you call rape—you has damaged that woman, you has been
so cruel to her and yet want to use her as your partner or your wife,
which as you know it is your duty. But from the way he treated you and
abused you, him lets you become his enemy. So it's just like someone
walks in and wants to abuse you and wants to have a sexual relationship
with you in the motion of a rape. It's something just like that. And yet,
in Belize they claims to say that a husband cannot rape a wife! These are
the things we are trying to protect women against. These are the things
that the mens in Belize are not educated enough to realize. . . .

But we wish that we could do it to let the people know, let mens
know that the Women Commission is not fighting to let the women has
the power over the men. It is not that. It is just that we want them to
realize that we are a part of them. We need them and they need us, but
treat us like human beings.

Like some men they have a wealth, they are wealthy. They live with
their wife until death. And there he dies and the wife is left with nothing. Sometimes the mother inherits it; sometimes the sister inherits it;
sometimes a kid in the home inherits it [knocks over microphone while
gesturing]. Things like this.

Irma: So if someone dies and there is no will you don't inherit anything? It is
divided among other relatives?

Zola: You can't have inherited anything. This all comes from the men, from
the law to show that rarely woman in Belize, very few can seek out a
right as a wife.

Another thing is as I said up in the Women's Commission at the first
time they elected me, and this is why they elected me. Not [that I am]
proud or boasting of who I am. Because some women came in and we
really relate our affairs, what we went through in the past and let us be
one as family. The women, I let them know straight out and clean that
I used to be in their shoes, where when I make my [shopping] list my
husband scratch what I doesn't need. You know? It came to a stage that
he'd give his mom money to buy me clothing and I had to tolerated it.
I was dumb to life.

In making the simple statement, "I was dumb to life," Zola both acknowledges and critiques her earlier actions and attitudes. Today she is overtly

political and aggressive, but understands her past life as one of emotional and psychological dependency. It is a life emblematic of women in the role of minors—in Zola's case this translates into a perception that she is not responsible enough or adult enough to determine when and if she should buy her own clothes. I did not encounter in Lemongrass any other examples of men creating dependency in this manner, but such personal matters are not openly discussed by men or women. What Zola's example does show is that the means by which men and society elicit women's compliance to subordination are wide and varied.

Change: Its Catalysts and Obstacles

As is often the case in an individual's changing consciousness, a single event may alter material conditions in a way that forces the person to reflect on her current circumstances. In Zola's case, the event was her partner's illness; his sudden departure to the United States for medical treatment disrupted the relative economic security that she relied upon.[3] Suddenly she found herself alone. In coming to terms with this insecure status, which left her without any financial support, Zola was forced both to confront the nature of her economic and personal relationship to her partner and to assess her own future— one in which she might find herself alone. She comments on the process.

> *Zola:* He got sick and had to get a heart surgery. We didn't had anything. Then I have to be the man. I don't know where I had that strength from and I came out and I said to myself, "No, I can't sit back. I have four kids in high school and I have one at home [knocks over the microphone], and I have him to take care of and I'll get out." I get out and then I learned that yes I didn't have to depend on you [the husband]. What was I depending on you all of these years for?
>
> He used to mean treat me, he used to beat me. Then I started to think back and see if I had done it. I had to sustain him for such a while until he could have gained his health. I got my kids out of high school. I said, well, fine, we have fifty-fifty now. If I could have done it there are many women who could have done it.
>
> I was involved in the Women's Bureau [Department of Women's Affairs] women's group. [I was] going out and leaving my home for the first time, really getting involved. He said to me, what is this all about? He had been hearing some rumors about the organization. I said, I don't know what this is all about but when I come back I will let you know what it is all about. I went out and I let myself be clear and known out there. They said, hey, if she could have done it, we can do it. It wasn't no hassle, which she tolerated—he got weak and she got strong and she realized where she was needed.

In this situation illness is the catalyst for a number of changes, especially in roles, as Zola's husband becomes economically dependent on Zola. Moreover, Zola must create strategies of survival that look beyond this particular event. In the process she discovers and creates a greater sense of self, which gets fostered by her participation in a women's group. In joining the latter she does not directly challenge the state, but she is certainly challenging state-formed relations (like marriage) that require women to be subordinate to men.

> *Zola:* This is the weird [thing], the men have to realize that you are needed or that you are worthwhile; it doesn't make sense. Some of them don't survive to know that you are needed. And then you left with that fear to go on living. [You think] well, okay I was in a rented home and he died and he didn't leave anything for me so I leave with the children. So I need somebody to take care of me. There you go and live the same life, these children [are] left [and] abandoned, because maybe this man doesn't want these kids.

Here Zola describes women's acceptance of the economic-sexual cycle that structures many women's lives.

> *Zola:* That is what I said; we are trying to become a strong Women's Commission. That we can show the women outside we are building from ourselves and we are trying to help them with some of the things we have gone through to promote themselves, to promote women in Belize, but we cannot promote them without a law enforcement.
>
> We need the police, we need the doctors, we need the ministers to do these things. Also, by ourselves, we have no law, we are not allowed to go into a home and say, hey, I heard you been beating you wife last night, you know, things like this. We need cooperation from the law and from different organizations. We need the law.

Zola points out that some change can only come about if men accept that women are equal, but she is fully aware that legislation (institutional support for change) is needed as well.

> *Irma:* So at this point there is no inheritance law that will protect women. Are there any laws that are in effect now that need to be changed, that would help women more?

At this point I followed up on Zola's emphasis on the importance of laws in the process of change. The question, however, also reflected a standard academic focus—I wanted to know about inheritance law, a question that momentarily diverted me away from Zola's story of transformation. This shift on my part is a typical example of how researchers sometimes don't listen. I was interested in learning about the structural elements that shaped Zola's life while her story was about personal things.

In response to my academic digression, Zola ignored me and remained focused on her agenda, going on to talk about the way violence is perpetuated not just in the home but also in the school. As a result of her own experience, she is well aware that abuse creates dysfunctional families and sets up cycles that can persist for generations. She uses the analogy of an unattended infection to describe how abusive behavior can be reproduced.

> *Zola:* It's something like you have a little sore and you doesn't take care of it and it really hurts. You go through it [domestic violence], the kids go through it and they see what is going on and if you have nine boys and they see what is going on you have nine men growing up that will carry on what their father was doing. So that in particular, we need a lot of law in that, as good as in the school—the teachers cannot beat the kids. It should be in the home that you cannot beat your wife. In this the family court, it is there but it is protecting the children. It is not fully enforced to protect women.

Zola's observations about the effects of abuse on women are echoed in the literature produced by Women Against Violence. In the excerpts below, the group describes the severity of domestic violence in Belize and the fear and anxiety it generates.

> Many women in our country are not safe in their own homes. Women have reported their partners for beating them with such weapons as knives, crowbars, machetes, electric wire, pint bottles, mop sticks, rocks, boards and rope. Some women are threatened with guns on a regular basis.

> Few women press charges against their husbands for fear of going to court and of further beatings. Rather than lay charges some women decide to apply for a legal separation and maintenance. Others feel they cannot leave or report the violence because they have several children to support, they do not have money or a place to live, they still love their partner and hope he will change, they want the children to have a father, they don't want their partner to go to jail or they are afraid they can't cope on their own.[4]

These statements articulate the personal, economic, and physical constraints that confront many women in Belize.

Institutionalizing Change

After this intense discussion of domestic violence, I shifted the interview focus in order to learn more about how women become agents of change.

> *Irma:* Can you just explain how you were elected to the position? Were you nominated by someone in the ministry or was it a vote in town?

Zola's answer to this question is a testament to her strong sense of the inter-relationship between her personal life and political processes. The control she exerted over her narrative throughout the interview, the commitment she exhibited in shaping her story—making herself through a narrative mode—is analogous to the control she exerted over the circumstances of her life.

> *Zola:* [I tell my daughter] if I had the education you all had I wouldn't be in that house cooking now, washing, and making baby. I gave it to you and you didn't use it. I didn't had it; I doesn't even have a primary certificate but I had more than what you have. I have something—I was born with common sense. And I use it. And [with] that I make myself who I am today.

Moreover, Zola is well aware that she has been transformed.

> *Zola:* Really, well, I am an active person and being an active person in politics, in my community and different things. Dorla [President of the National Women's Commission] asked someone here to recommend me. And there were several of us who still went up, and as I said everyone had a point of view themselves what they have been going through, see if they are strong enough to be in this Women's Commission.[5] I wasn't ashamed to say what I went through because it has made me who I am today.

Here Zola makes a clear, indisputable connection between her process of shifting from an abused woman with a minor's status to the fully responsible person she is today. More significant, it is not her knowledge of formal politics or bureaucracy that makes her a valuable representative, but the specific details of her life, which serve as pedagogical tools. She has had to circumvent the hidden bureaucracy and structures of the gender system in order to be who and where she is at this point.

> *Zola:* I doesn't have that fear anymore [where I have] to come out and say can I go to this meeting or can I go into town? I had to do that. I doesn't have to do that anymore because my husband understands. From the mere fact that I had to pick up the burden of him and five kids, that means I am responsible enough to have that right. I don't know if it is part of fear that he is sick now or whatever, but he gained understanding.

Zola says her partner has adjusted to her new-found autonomy and sense of empowerment, but she recognizes that their role reversal has spawned a fear. Such fear I found common among many Belizean men, who believe that if women become involved outside of the home, if they exhibit behaviors or attitudes that express autonomy, independence, or self-confidence, they will come back home thinking "dey the boss." Based on this male attitude toward

women and some women's acceptance of it, controlling a woman's movements—restricting her ability to see friends, go to social events, and the like—
is an important weapon in the cycle of domestic violence.

Again, the Belize Women Against Violence movement has been most successful in identifying this form of control as part of a pattern. Beyond the most
common, and thereby easily recognized, forms of physical and sexual abuse
that men use to exert "*power* and *control* over their partners," the group describes the more subtle forms that men use to force women's compliance. The
WAV brochure states:

> How do men abuse their partners? . . .
> Emotionally, by:
>> continually insulting her
>> controlling what she can do and who she can see
>> controlling all the money
>> treating her like a servant
>> making her feel bad about herself
>> having extra-marital affairs
>> keeping her from getting a job

In a study of battered women in Iowa, Julie L. Stiles and Douglas Caulkins
describe how women become "prisoners in their own homes."[6] Drawing on
Lewis Okun's theory of coerce control, they conclude: "Our interpretation
reinforces the notion that abusive isolation is a critical component of domestic
violence as practiced in Iowa or elsewhere." They also state: "Instead of implying that women necessarily invite their abuse, our interpretation shows that
abuse creates an aberrant social structure from which it is difficult to escape."[7]
Their study shows that women's participation in women's groups is of crucial
value in breaking this cycle of abuse. They argue: "One of the effective paths
for women escaping abusive relationships is . . . [through] . . . collectivist
support organizations."[8] Given this consequence of collective participation,
men's hostile response to women's groups, especially their antagonism toward
WAV, becomes understandable. Women's collective action is interpreted as a
definite threat to men's efforts to control. Men rationalize their antagonism
by asserting that women gossip and that no good can result when women get
together. Their dismissal of the worth or value of women's group, I surmise,
derives from their fear of precisely what happened to Zola—she changed and
was no longer tolerant of the limitations her partner tried to impose on her.

> *Zola:* [Now] whenever there is a meeting, unless I can't [because] I have a
> family meeting, but whenever there is somewhere I have to go, I go.
> Now I am asked to go, like campaigning for a town board election; they
> asked me to go and campaign with them. I can campaign. To go out

with them to meetings in San Ignacio [in the west of Belize], it was no problem to come out and work on the election day; it was no problem.

Social scientists are constantly grappling with the question of how to determine that change has occurred.[9] Zola gives us some useful criteria. For her, one indicator of change is the ability to control her own mobility. As we have seen, women in Belize are often kept socially isolated and their movements are severely restricted by men as a way of controlling them. In her new direction in life, not only does Zola recognize the importance of being asked to attend political functions, which indirectly affirms her power in the community arena, but she is well aware that her ability to go to these functions without having to seek permission is a visible sign that she is in control of her own life. Another indicator is the economic autonomy and sense of security she has achieved through the ownership of land.

The source of these changes Zola sees as primarily internal. Women must find their inner resourcefulness first, before they rely upon external forces in the form of organizations or the law. According to Zola's philosophy, each of us possesses the capacity to change the circumstances of our lives.

> *Zola:* Sometimes we woman has to learn and let *something grow into us that we are woman,* we are no more a kid, and we have to show that we can't depend on the law for everything.[10] We has to learn to depend on ourselves. Let ourselves grow and this is what we are trying to do. If we let ourself grow strong, a strong Women Commission, and stand up and keep what we have together, we can make a law and we can change a law. We need that strength, we need that cooperation, we need that understanding. I didn't know who was elected at Belmopan. We went for four days workshop and then I got back and had a letter from the minister pointing out I had been elected.

These words form a powerful statement that reflects Zola's current consciousness. Moreover, she is aware that the process of change is multifaceted and occurs at several levels. At the individual or personal level, she suggests that it is incumbent on women to come to some self-awareness that they are not children, not minors. Such change, she posits, must be inner directed. That is, women cannot depend upon the law to give them this inner resourcefulness or knowledge of their situation. At the same time, she also asserts that through collective action, women have the ability to transform the external circumstances of their lives; thus she attributes tremendous significance to unity and collective action, especially in the form of women's groups. Zola's "analysis" reflects a fully developed awareness of the personal, cultural, and structural basis of women's subordination. In her eyes, change on one level cannot occur without change at the other levels. In her cosmology, personal change is interrelated with social change.

This last aspect is particularly evident in Zola's narration of her involvement in women's groups, which also becomes a narration of her life. I interpret this to mean that women's groups often provide an arena for particular women's performances of empowerment. As such, women are actors within the arena of women's groups. In Zola's case, the specific circumstances of her life had already created the conditions for change, and she immediately took advantage of them. Yet, as she tells us, changing her life does not lead to community acceptance of such change and can result in alienation. Women's groups provide an alternative environment of support and nurturing, reinforcing the path of change women may be on.

What is most instructive about Zola's development is her recognition of the close relationship between personal change and collective action. She demonstrates for us that individuals do not operate in isolation; also that we are constantly in search of affirmation that the choices we make are correct, not only in terms of our individual assessment of them, but in terms of the community's assessment. Women's groups act as critical sources of affirmation. They become communal sounding boards against which women can test new ideas, interpretations, and strategies for change, all within a safe environment. This suggests that if the choices women make challenge the traditional rules and behaviors of their communities, then they must form alternative sources of support so that they may continue to function within the ever-present social constraints or boundaries. Even as women change, they are negotiating within an environment that may appear static or unassailable. As they confront the problems such a disjuncture creates, they do so with a new strength that is a combination of their own personal desires and the support of a specialized community of like-minded women.

Because of Zola's awareness and her sense of empowerment, I thought it important to determine the degree to which her reading of "the woman's problem" in Belize corresponded to other readings I had elicited from survey data and interviews. I asked her: "Are there other problems that you see that Belizean women face or women in this particular community face? [Are there] other problems that they have to deal with?" She responded:

> Zola: In our area, I mean this is something from inheritance, but as I said you women must open your eyes and see where your advantages stands and where your advantage is taken. I am not an educated person but I am an active person, outspoken person, and this is where I get around. I think that if you fight yourself out of it, you can get out of it. As I said education is a very great thing. It is something like a bank but common sense is as good and that is what I think I use.
>
> From way back especially in Lemongrass, the mens are the men. The men is the man of the home, whether you are the one who maintains

the home they stands being the men. Okay? Basically it is very rare when you hear a woman saying, "That is my piece of land; I am living on it, or those cattle out there are mine." It is something very scarce to know. These are the things I feel we must look upon. My mother had twenty-two of us, and there was one chosen son that my father left everything for. So it is something from way beyond, way, way back. Well yes, he was the chosen one. He doesn't drink, he doesn't smoke, he is a respectful brother. If we had problems we could always go to him. My mom is basically take care of by him. But how many children are there? How many boys are there that can find a wife like that?

At this point, Zola not only gives us insight into women's exclusion from acquiring property through marriage, but also suggests that wives can limit the extent to which a son will provide for his mother's needs. In her own family, Zola's sister-in-law did not have much control and so her brother took care of their mother. But because she was "loaned" out as a young child, Zola has few details about many of the dynamics of family interpersonal relations.[11] Nor did I pursue this topic as thoroughly as I might have.

Zola's concern about inheritance practices as a major issue for women illustrates the extent to which cultural traditions and life experience structure women's activism. The link between the personal and the political is analyzed more fully in chapter 9. In general, the specific problems women confront in their lives (domestic violence, inheritance) or their concern about specific issues (nutrition, breast feeding, family planning) are the motivation for their activism. These variables explain to some degree their decision to participate in particular women's groups.

Community and Autonomy

One intriguing aspect of Zola's narrative is her desire for it to be instructive for others. This is consistent with the potential for empowerment that Rina Benmayor sees in the life histories of marginalized Puerto Rican women in the United States. For these women, the significance of recounting their life histories is comparable to the role that doing so plays in Zola's life. Benmayor writes: "Hence, the life history interview has special value. . . . Clearly, both written and oral formats provide meaningful platforms from which she imparts her knowledge and example to others. Far from being self-aggrandizing, her testimony is fundamentally instructive and designed to place the community rather than the individual at the center."[12] This grounding in a community world view is evident as Zola explains why her life story is important to others.

Zola: So I try to talk to people. Sometimes my husband tells me, "You haven't any business in those people's life. They are big women and men." I tell him, I was too and I has always been a little girl until I was needed to be a woman. I had to be both a woman and a man, and I learned from my experience that other women can do the same.

Zola uses her life as a parable to instruct other women and men in the community.

Zola: [I say to women] hey you are working out there; he doesn't have to know all what you are gaining, what you are working for. Put a little aside, try to get a piece of land. Today or tomorrow you have fuss you know you will have nothing to gain because our law is for men. [If I do this] . . . you know I have something out there. I try to talk to people because rarely in . . . [Lemongrass] can you go around and it is very seldom you find a wife owning a house or a lot, or you very seldom find a wife [owning anything] because she has two or three kids and she can't go to work because nobody will take care of the kids like her.

Zola gives us another illustration of the ways in which women are dependent upon men economically. But she does not just identify issues and problems, she also offers specific strategies for women to use in order to gain financial autonomy. She suggests that when women have the opportunity to earn income, they must secretly hide part of it away for their future. Although she has traveled a long way to reach her current level of awareness, Zola has not forgotten the difficulty of her journey; she knows from personal experience that becoming autonomous and independent as a woman entails more than going out to get a job. The process involves child care and, as she explains below, also means contending with men's fear that women who work take themselves too seriously and may begin to challenge the culture of gender.

Zola: [Men feel that] the minute [women] go out and work they would try to play boss. That is the mind he has. This is why they are feeling like the Women's Commission is mostly to put women above men.

Men interpret women's efforts to gain employment as attempts to usurp male authority and power. Thus groups or other women who advocate that women work outside the home are looked upon by male members of the community with distrust and suspicion. Women's groups are frequently seen as the primary agents of change in women's status and sense of self. Because of this, the groups often operate in the midst of a hostile community, and their members risk being ostracized, as Zola suggests.

Zola: Like me, in my area [community] no one very seldom like me, but I don't care.

For the first time, Zola gives me a glimpse of the effect her activism has had on her life in this small community. She explains that her struggle for personal autonomy and her efforts to raise the consciousness of women in similar circumstances have had social consequences. She is labeled by men in the community as a troublemaker, which restricts her access to other women. Organizations that are aggressive in their advocacy like WAV, of which Zola is a member, are openly criticized by men, who see them as filled with "men-hating" or "castrating" women. Other women do not openly support the groups for fear of reprisal from their men. They then become co-conspirators in the behavior aimed at isolating or thwarting women like Zola or women's groups like WAV. Challenging the gender system can thus mean social alienation within one's own community and can involve a degree of personal risk for some women.

Yet Zola's story is not a tragedy. She has also gained a sense of belonging through participation in women's groups. Despite the negative consequences of being a transformed woman and an activist, which in a small community can be devastating, Zola persists in her efforts to convince men and women of the goals and legitimacy of her work with the National Women's Commission. She also continues to recruit members for different women's groups, emphasizing that the purpose of these groups is to educate men and not to dominate them.

> *Zola:* And I try to show them; I have my sketches of what Women's Commission is all about. It is [not] to be above men. We are trying to teach the men that, hey you need that person. You should treat that person like a partner not only like a wife, like your sister, like the way you treat your mother and your kids.

Zola's perspective is political; she possesses an awareness of broader social processes and their impact on her life and her community. She now looks back on her life as a kind of navigational chart containing territories of victimization, transformation, and autonomy, each defined by her internal evaluation of her own experiences. This perspective demonstrates that a major part of women's "empowerment" is their acquisition of self-esteem and self-confidence—their internal transformation from an identity of victim to one of agency. Her activism is grounded in an understanding of future benefits rather than immediate gratification and is based on a view of change as a process.

> *Zola:* I can't get along with [some women] but it doesn't bother me. I know what the Women Commission are and I am going to go along with it. And the women and the men will see later on. Little by little when we finally get the law changed they will know what it is all about. It's a thing really in Lemongrass that you very seldomly find a wife being somebody responsible. It is the man who has that above them that hey,

you depend on me for everything. As I say it is from your self-esteem to get out there and show them. If I am responsible enough to take care of you and the kids, and responsible enough to be your wife, and responsible enough to prepare everything for you and take care of everything for you, I am responsible enough to work with you side by side and responsible enough to let you treat me fair. That is in me.

Zola here reveals one of the major contradictions embedded in the culture of gender in her community. As a mother she is assumed to be "responsible" enough to take care of her children and maintain the house; yet women are not always valued for fulfilling these obligations or performing their work, except in the mother-child dyad during the mother's elderly years. Though not valued for their contributions, women are held absolutely accountable for fulfilling their roles as wives and mothers; they may be punished physically by men or receive community ostracism or scorn if they do not live up to the assumed, but rarely articulated, standards of behavior.

Women collaborate in this process as well. They gossip about and shape their social interactions around this widely accepted but rarely defined notion of "good mothers and good wives." As we saw in chapter 5, for example, women who do not maintain their household at a certain level of cleanliness or order are ridiculed as "lazy," and the man receives sympathy from both male and female community members. Women who are consistently harsh with their children or require them to do most of the housework also lose respect, especially among other women in the community.

Unlocking the Mythology of Motherhood

Zola's own circumstances have helped her to see that women, and more specifically mothers, are more often than not the most valuable resource in the household, and it is because their contributions are not recognized or validated that conflict arises. If men do not believe that housework or domestic matters are important, then in their eyes women sit home everyday doing nothing. The woman who wants to leave a situation in which her worth is measured only by male-oriented, community-prescribed norms is inhibited from doing so by the presence of her children. As Zola expresses it, women feel responsible for having brought their children into the world and will suffer unbearable abuse "for the sake of the children." When Zola's own children tell her to "come out and go" as a way to escape her abusive relationship, she cannot. She explains why:

> *Zola:* I let them (her children) know, no. No, no, that I am not going to leave. I am there for you; I brought you here and I am going to suffer with you here.

Motherhood in this instance is viewed as an unbreakable bond, to be respected regardless of the circumstances within which it occurs. This powerful symbolic belief is shared by most members of the community. Neither men nor women understand or respect the woman who leaves her children. According to the prevailing belief system, a woman should place her personal happiness or safety after her obligations as a mother. Any woman who is more concerned with her own personal safety and happiness than her children is an anomaly and not highly regarded.

The mythology surrounding being a good mother is a powerful controlling ethos that impedes many women from leaving an abusive or unfulfilling relationship. At some point in their life cycle, all women succumb to its power: women with no children have attacks of guilt or feelings of inadequacy; working mothers are often criticized for their absences, which are seen by the community as the direct cause of any emotional and behavior problems their children may display; and women tolerate years of emotional, verbal, and physical abuse for the sake of their children. This negative dimension to motherhood is only one component of its symbolic significance in many cultures, but it is one that appears in various forms throughout the world. The surest way to shatter a woman's confidence, self-esteem, and sense of personal power is to imply she is not a "good" mother.

But motherhood is not always about women submitting themselves to roles. Mothers can and do wield power, especially in their role as mother-in-laws. In Lemongrass, I have been privy to "bitching" sessions about domineering mother-in-laws who exert considerable control over their sons' household management and make life uncomfortable for their sons' wives. Few men seem willing to thwart the power and authority of their mothers. I observed that women are generally valued as mothers in Lemongrass, but the role of motherhood is not unproblematic. For while men respect the authority of their own mothers, as husbands they do not necessarily defer to their wives when they are in the social role of mother. Rather the authority of motherhood seems to emerge in the context of the mother-child dyad, and reaches its peak during the child's adulthood and during the mother's later years.

Virginia Kerns, in her study of Garifuna women, describes a similar older woman/mother authority configuration in her description of the extended female-headed household where stability and authority improves with the woman's age.[13] What can be a disadvantageous role at one point in a woman's life cycle and in relation to particular members of the community can acquire prestige and authority or power at a different stage and in the context of interaction with other members of the community. I would argue, as Karen Sacks has, that role subordination for women is contingent upon circumstances and therefore contextual.[14] This suggests that women's roles and status are not homogenous or universal; they can vary by individuals, circumstances, role, and age. Later in our interview, Zola returns to this theme of the mother's authority in relation to what she views as the prevailing attitudes in her community, and discusses how they shape inheritance laws.

> *Zola:* Some of the men again, in Lemongrass I'm talking about, they would rather say they have a belief that today they die, tomorrow you are married. That is what they believe. So in other words they doesn't leave it to the kids either because that is their mom, and she will still get it. So leave it for my [the man's] mom.

According to Zola, men fear that if they die, their property will be appropriated by the wife's new husband or male partner, who they assume, by the existing cultural rules of inheritance, will have full access to and authority over it. Thus, because mothers control their children and husbands control the mothers, men rarely leave property to their wives, or even to their children. Property is generally left to the man's mother, sister, or perhaps a brother.

The Life Course and Empowerment

Serendipity played a strong part in how Zola shaped her life course—a medical crisis that affected her partner altered her position in the household and shifted the balance of power in her favor. Such unforeseen events or crises are often pivotal in bringing individuals to a higher level of self-knowledge and a greater recognition of their inner resourcefulness. For Zola, this translates into becoming the power figure in her household.

> *Zola:* Not to boast but today he is living under my roof, he is living on my land, I am maintaining him.

The struggle to come to terms with the reality that her man can no longer maintain her because of his health becomes the route Zola travels to acquire self-esteem; it can also be viewed as the first stage of her politicization. Zola comes face to face with the reality that the absence of the legal bond of marriage makes her vulnerable. If her man remains ill, then she is subject to the arbitrary generosity of his kin and the same arbitrary generosity of her own kin. There is nothing in her consensual relationship that obligates either kin network to assist her. She must depend upon their sense of duty to the children from her relationship as the only reliable bond upon which she can make a claim to their economic support.

Unskilled and thus unprepared for work in the formal sector, and with limited education, Zola is forced to rely upon the so-called domestic skills she has used to maintain her household, such as cooking, cleaning, washing, and bartering. These are the undocumented skills often displayed by women who make up the invisible labor force of most developing countries and which maintain Belize's informal economic sector.[15] Activities in this area consist of involvement in small entrepreneurial ventures such as selling ice, "ideal" (a frozen confection), soda, and homemade pastries and bread. In Belize, the strong informal sector described by Lynn Bolles in reference to Jamaica and Carmen Diana Deere in reference to the Caribbean in general is not as discernible.[16] Because little research has been done on this subject with reference to Belize, it is difficult to determine the specific causes or to what degree Belize differs from other Caribbean, African, and Latin American countries in this respect. Zola explains that in the economically depressed region where she resides, she has used her "home" skills to survive:

> *Zola:* No, I didn't get a job. The first thing I went to do, I stayed right there and made pastries. I built up a little money. I had nothing, nothing when my husband was leaving me, I had nothing. It was an emergency case, he had to go out [to the States for medical treatment] and I had four kids in high school.
>
> So I had been doing pastry before he left to keep the home going because he had been sick for two years before he went out. I said to myself, if he dies tomorrow I haven't anywhere to go. Where will I go? I go to my brothers but it's only for two days with the kids. So I went to this chairman of this village that I know and I said hey, I'm a Belizean and I need a piece of land. He says, "Humph, it's a hard thing your husband have." I said listen, "I am a Belizean, I have five kids and I born in this village here that I am asking this piece of land from. There where I live I didn't born. I has a right to get a piece of land here. And he says I can't. So I didn't want everybody to know [my circumstances] that someone might come one of these days [where we were living] and take us out. So I told him what my problem is and he says okay now come here.

Zola goes on to describe how she was given a piece of uncleared land in the back of the village that the village chairman thought no one wanted. Undaunted, she took up the challenge, using her own labor and the only other labor source she controls—that of her children.

> *Zola:* The following day I took my two sons, one were twelve and one were thirteen, and we went chopping [cutting down] that place. We get it cleared up, we get the little house cleared up, we burned it and everything. And I went to my brother and I told them I needed some help and they said sure, pick a guy. And I pick someone and they paid him and we got a little hutch.
>
> My husband said no, he is not going to leave that place [the old house]. He will get well and fix that place and that is his. I said okay that is his and this is mine. I told him if you don't help me build this

little house and my brothers has to build it. I mean because it seemed
as if he wanted to go [to the States] and when he come back we had
nowhere to go, because it was his. He still doesn't know [realize] that
he were going to lose it. I said to him, if you don't help me put nothing
in that house, fix that house—its thatch is thick, it's an Indian hut—
you don't think about coming in there.

Here she explains how she built, with very few resources, the foundation for
her current economic stability and personal independence, taking advantage
of the fact that her husband was unable to stop her because of his medical
condition.

Zola invests a good amount of time in constructing a narrative self that
presents her as a savvy woman who seizes every opportunity to turn a disadvantage to her advantage, and who is usually successful. Like Anancy the
spider, a Caribbean symbol of cunning and guile, she manages to turn straw
into gold—in her case, she subverts the inheritance laws and practices. Drawing upon her devalued skills, Zola acquires property, pays for her children's
education, and establishes a secure place for herself and her family through
her own resourcefulness, skill, and cunning. But the route to autonomy is
hard work:

Zola: I got a job, I had three acres of land cut down. I paid for it while I was
working and me and the kids got up at five o'clock in the morning and
started to plant. They go to school at eight and I go to work at nine [at
the British army camp]. In the evening I come, I do my laundry, I do
their cooking, and then we get back in the field.

When he [her husband] came back I had my house, I had five acres
of land cleared, and I had my crop in and I feel like that built him up.
So I made it good. I bought a cattle, I bought a pig. I said, hey, this
man says [this] is only a house lot but he doesn't know what I'm doing
in the bush. He is seeing the bush out there and everybody afraid of this
bush. Nobody wanted this area. It was an abandoned place.

Both she and the children perform double duties, a situation that leaves
little room for a gendered division of labor. All of her children contribute
according to their age and ability. And Zola, the woman who used to have to
get permission to buy her own clothes, becomes a businesswoman who has
land and is able to maintain herself and children through a variety of means.

Political Transformation

Zola's transformation is a remarkable one, and she helped me to understand
how some women manage to alter their circumstances. Because other women
remain entrenched, it seems important to question whether the changes in

Zola's life are because of her personal qualities or her character, or whether they are the result of a series of unpredictable circumstances that crystallized in her life at a particular point. Zola's success is indicated by her having circumvented the barriers she described earlier in her narrative: she is a landowner now and financially stable and autonomous.

> *Zola:* So I just finished paying for it, just last week [April 1991]. I got my deed when I went up to see my son, I got my deed. So now it is mine. Everything is mine. I have my little bar; it's all mine. This is what I try to show: you start from nothing but you make yourself someone!

Zola's narrative serves as a testimony of transformation, but one that is explicitly political. In this life story, the process of shifting from dependency to autonomy and the self-understanding that emerges become the point of departure that enables Zola to decide to educate other women. In her new stage of making herself, Zola establishes new boundaries in her personal relationship. In doing so, consciously or not, she registers a protest against the gender system. At the individual level, she has redefined who has the right to set limits on her behavior, on her mobility, and on her ideas.

Individual, personal transformations are not instantaneous. Rather, they involve a process and can entail an arduous journey for the few who dare to change themselves in the middle of their life course. Zola, however, is not afraid to take on individuals or structures and the bureaucracies they create, as the following account of her encounter with the local political structure illustrates.

> *Irma:* How long has this taken you?
>
> *Zola:* Seven years. I saw trees all buckled up in my place. I said no, they can't go through there. So I went around and I followed the road they were pushing. When I followed the place, they were pushing through my place. All this time I had my letter informed that I should go up and get my title.
>
> So I called him. I said, "You are the chairman of this village but you aren't the chairman." He said, "Who are you talking to?" I said, "I am talking to you." "How you mean to tell me I am not the chairman?" I said, "Because if you are the chairman you should know who owns a lot, who owns a block and who is leasing a piece of land and who has title to a piece of land." He said, "What you beating on?" I said, "Because you are pushing a road through my property." He says, "What property?" I said, "Then you aren't a chairman. Being a chairman you should know who lives in the village, who owns in the village, and who does not own and who lease." He said, "But I talked to your husband."

In this exchange Zola publicly declares her independence as a woman of property. She also confronts some of that assumptions that underlie the culture of gender in her community, one of which assumes men to be in control of women's resources. In this anecdote Zola challenges such assumptions.

> *Zola:* I said, "But my husband doesn't have anything here. This is mine." He said, "I am sorry, I didn't know." I said, "Then why don't you move the government fence and put the road there? You being the chairman shouldn't use the farmers, you should use the government." So he doesn't speak to me now because he had to go and move all the fence and push the road in the government land and I fenced in my road, the road that he was pushing. So this is why no one like me in my village because my right is my right, I don't care who you are.
>
> This is why I feel like, because if you go out there and fail along with you husband you let him realize, I am no kid. From the home I can go out there and toil along with you, I am as big as you are. But I toil with my kids out there in the field. I show him that these things that are happening is because my kids are here. They are not there anymore; they are above me. And I feel like now I am a woman. So when we have a fuss he will say, I am watching you getting upstart. I say no, it's only a kid who gets upstart, not me. I am a woman. You are a man and I respect you and you must respect me.

Here Zola's resistance serves as a "diagnostic of power."[17] Through her narrative we learn that power acts to circumscribe women's mobility and represent them as minors while simultaneously utilizing their adult labor. Thus women are exploited as adults—expected to work hard and endure conditions children would not be subjected to—while being denied the recognition and status of adulthood. As a consequence of this attitude, men control women's mobility and are recognized as having the legitimate right to make decisions for them. When women make clear their resentment or attempt to challenge these constrictions, when they develop an understanding of the contradictory nature of their position relative to the power structure that governs gender representations, they are denounced as "upstart."

Language becomes a symbolic weapon that defines and reinforces the constraints women seek to challenge. In Creole vernacular "upstart" refers to children (or women) who have forgotten their proper place. It is a term intended to shame those accused and force them back into behavior that conforms. In labeling individuals as upstart, the motivation for their behavior is ignored and not viewed as legitimate. In other words, there is no reason that can justify their social transgression. By referring to women who seek to alter their position in the gender system as "upstart," their legitimacy as human agents in control of their own actions and able to determine their own future is undermined or negated. Zola has her own perspective on how women can change this situation. She advises women to establish their right to respect and legitimacy by changing their own behavior; this, she believes, will help to alter men's perceptions of women.

Zola: So I said from the point of view: if we can only use our self-esteem as a force. Hey I am going to move that bed. I can't move it, but I am going to try and move it. And finally I will move it. But if I would say I can't move that bed, I will leave it until my husband comes home because he is a man, he is the only one that can move it. There you go depending on him. So you are like a child under him in a sense and you are like a child to take the abuse in a sense. You are not responsible enough. Your self-esteem is not strong enough.

This is what I think. I said if we were being allowed, like I have somebody along with me to go out and educate the women. You are not fighting with your husband. You are not trying to be *above* him but you will try to do something that will show him, that will teach him that you are right or that you are more responsible than he thinks you are. Finally that will grow into him that yes, my wife can do it also and she is somebody.

Because they go out and they work for the money then they comes in and say hi, see the money here. And when it is done he doesn't know where to get more from and you don't know where to get more from and that causes a lot of problem in the home. But because some women doesn't show enough, that they are responsible enough to say "I can help you" or "I will try to help you" and we will let ends meet. That is like our trust. That is like I said, we want to educate the men that in a sense we are helping them and helping ourselves. I say, "Hey, why you don't want me to go out to work?" Maybe our fights is because of money, because the money is not enough to maintain the home. Then when you come and don't find things the way you feel like it should be because of the little money you brings in, there is where we go wrong. Or because I see you have this and I don't have it, I will tell you my husband about it. Hey, how that person could have such a thing. But if I could say to him, hey I could go out and look for something to do and we can make ends meet.

Let him know you can do it and show him you can do it. He will learn and finally ends will meet and he will learn to respect you because then you are bringing in and he is bringing in. But because he is the only one that are bringing in, he feels like he the boss. At the same time we are helping them. The strain and stress is not only on them. You also learn to be someone.

Zola is honest in her depiction of how far she has come in the journey toward a new self.

Zola: I came from nothing, I was a coward child. When my husband screamed at me I cried. I don't eat. When he was coming and he whistle out there

> I had gripes, I had cold sweat. I was so feared what will he come and do
> to me. When he needed me I was there and I developed that strength
> and now they can't. They can't take that away.

Although the exact sources of her personal transformation are not always
revealed or visible, she envisions that her next level of change will occur at the
group level; in her mind, the next stage of action must be collective. Zola's
narrative continues. Because her narrative structure is not chronological, certain subjects appear again and again. For the remainder of our interview she
discusses how her own abuse led her to abuse her children. In talking about
this, she exhibits a profound understanding of how a cycle of abuse is created.

> *Zola:* So I feel like not only to educate us but to educate the men. Show them,
> because some of them, I don't think, maybe it's the home they came
> from—as I said, you have nine sons imagine and they all grown up see-
> ing their father hitting their mother, cursing their mother, abusing their
> mother, they have no better to learn. Maybe one or two not the nine;
> you have seven boys growing like that to go out there and make seven
> homes and they multiply their kids into that. What you have?

She tells us that she was able to halt this cycle in her life. Zola demonstrates
that she is a woman who believes in action—and she tries to teach other
women about changing their lives by using her own life as an example of what
is possible. Again she emphasizes the importance of collective action.

> *Irma:* Do you think that having women's groups has helped you? Do you
> think women's groups are necessary?
>
> *Zola:* Well I will tell you what, like I said we had women's fears that split them.
>
> *Irma:* Now the Women's Bureau, is that the same as the Department of Wom-
> en's Affairs?
>
> *Zola:* It was similar. As we said if we have to go on and do the same thing and
> get nowhere the government would never support us, never. What are
> we doing? We do different pamphlets, let people know that we are not
> the Women's Affair or the Women's Bureau. Our responsibility is more
> greater. It's a more risk. That is why we need cooperation.

Reflections

Zola's changed awareness is not the result of external ideas or beliefs; rather,
it is the product of her own personal ideology grounded in her own experience. She now sees clearly the relationship between women making changes
in their personal lives and women possessing the power to demand changes
at the state level, the level of policymaking. In her new-found cosmology,
change is a pebble that begins at the microlevel, at the level of the individual,

and creates a ripple that keeps growing. In her opinion, women's organizations provide a much-needed platform and support for such transformations.

Sonia Alvarez has argued, in her study of women's groups in Latin America, that as women come together, they develop a new sense of self.[18] In Lemongrass, some women are now prepared to accept the consequences of joining a women's group. Many do so because they are struggling to find ways to build a degree of economic autonomy and free themselves from the fear that their man will move out and leave them destitute. Through their participation they find support and affirmation in the knowledge that their life experience is not unique. Somehow this knowledge neutralizes the emotional leverage of abuse by men that seems predicated on making women believe that they are personally responsible for what happens to them—that it is a flaw in the woman that makes the man react the way he does. It appears that when women are able to see male behavior as part of a pattern, they are better able to extricate themselves from internalizing the blame that men attempt to impose.

Although it is true that one case does not create a rule, Zola's story points toward possibilities. Zola's circumstances are not extraordinary—she begins her journey of self-discovery and transformation with few personal resources and some help from her brothers. It is, however, her sheer determination and the way in which she is able to rebound from the unanticipated stress caused by her husband's sudden illness, coupled with a desire to provide greater security for herself and her children, that drive her. In this respect, she is exactly like many women in Belize who are anxious to fulfill their traditional roles of mothers and wives/partners as best they can. They too are now looking beyond their desire for individual men to live up to their obligations to demand that the state and the political party that supports it intervene and provide women with greater access to strategic resources.[19] Although on the surface Zola and other women in Belize who find themselves faced with the question of everyday survival do not reject their traditional gender roles, they are challenging the availability of the resources they need to be a good wife/partner and mother. In so doing, they chip away at the institutional structures that support the status quo of the culture of gender. Their actions are sometimes conscious, as Zola illustrates, but not always.

Chapter 7 *Women's Subordination in Modern Belize*

The voices of the following Belizean women, like the narratives of Rose and Zola, reveal the scope and contradictory nature of gender in Belize:

> Some women will think husband the boss so they have to live by that rule/ regulation from him; they don't think they have the right to think for themselves. Things are changing because women work. Most husbands don't like their wives to work.
>
> *Thirty-three-year-old East Indian woman (married)*

> I think women are emotionally abused and financially abused as well as physical abuse. The first two happens so much.
>
> *Twenty-nine-year-old East Indian woman*
> *(married, but would prefer to be separated)*

> What I personally face [is] the way men think because of culture. [It is] difficult for one to pursue and do the things they want to do in life. You are suppressed. In my case [my] children are bigger. I can't have any more so I feel confident. For those women who have a lot of children, it's difficult but once they get a certain age, I think they too will break it. Women are with their behind out the door. They are left alone; they don't get educated because the men don't want them to. That's what we try to teach in BFLA [Belize Family Life Association]. If they can control just even their reproductive system, then their life will be better.
>
> *Thirty-four-year-old mixed[1] woman (married)*

> I think the men don't respect the women much. Men like to molest you and ask you to go to bed even if married. Women have too many children with too many gentlemen and get no support. And the government doesn't give support. Women leave children to go anywhere.
>
> *Forty-five-year-old Chinese woman (married)*

[There is the] problem of mothers without fathers, mother coping with bringing up fatherless children. [They] have to do everything—man and woman's job. *Thirty-year-old Garifuna woman (married)*

These words confirm that women's problems straddle multiple cultural domains—social, political, economic, and personal. At the same time, although many women's lives consist of economic uncertainty, variation in personal relations and family structure, and physical and mental abuse, other women assert that these issues are irrelevant to their own personal experience:

No problem as a woman. *Thirty-two-year-old East Indian woman (married)*

I don't have any problems. [Other women have] too much beatings. *Twenty-two-year-old Maya woman (married)*

Still, even these women generally concede that economic inequality, primary responsibility for children, and domestic violence are salient features in the lives of the women around them. Women's personal experiences are one proof of the power of gender. But women's lives are not lived in isolation. They are affected by institutional, political, and economic structures that help to develop and maintain Belize's gender system.

The Economics of Women's Unequal Status

Many women in Belize today believe they occupy a fairly marginal and devalued position in society. Their observations are not just personal musings, however, but social facts confirmed by the government. In a comprehensive assessment of the position of women known as the "Policy Statement on Women in Belize" and first articulated in 1988, the government commented: "While women are now participating at all levels in national development, they are hampered in utilizing their full potential as agents of development and they do not benefit equally from the development process."[2] This unequal position of women is not unique to Belize. The existing literature on women in the Caribbean and Latin America confirms this as a regionwide phenomenon. The policy document further states that "despite the testimony of history, tradition, culture and statistics to the crucial role women play in Belizean society women's activities in the family and the workplace remain undervalued and under supported."[3] Past and present research on specific ethnic groups discloses relatively few structural variations in economic status among women in Belize despite different languages and value systems. Virginia Kerns, for example, has written about Garifuna women's access to economic opportunities: "Women, like men, find work primarily in the manual labor and service sector. But in nearly every other respect, the work experience of men and women differs profoundly. The labor market is occupationally segregated, and men work in a wider range of industries and fill a greater number of occupations."[4] And Olga Stavrakis and Marion Louise Marshall in their study of Maya women provide parallel proof of this economic vulnerability: "The decline of the milpa, the obsolescence of the kitchen garden and the shift towards purchased foods have had a negative impact upon the activities of the women. As a result, women have lost much of the control over their productive resources and have become economically dependent upon the males."[5] Such findings all point to the fact that across ethnic boundaries, Belizean women hold a uniformly tenuous economic position, one characterized by the absence of financial autonomy, economic dependency upon men, underemployment, low wages, limited access to training, and insufficient resources to create economic alternatives.

Assessing the economic status of women is somewhat difficult, since as the *Belize Report for the Fourth World Conference on Women* notes, "reliable gender-disaggregated data are historically limited."[6] Despite this problem, this report concludes that women are severely limited in their access to the labor force, that they are concentrated in lower-paid jobs, and that rural women suffer the most.[7] The report points out that while "the female labour force doubled between 1960 and 1988 . . . the actual numbers of men in the labour force still exceed the numbers of women by a ration of 3.4 : 1."[8] Although women's participation in the labor force is growing, they are still severely underrepresented in comparison with men. Further, women have virtually no presence in the strongest areas of the national economy (agriculture, fishing, and forestry). In fact, "such sectors employ 33.8% of adult males but only 1.2% of adult females."[9] Finally, whereas "40% of all adult males earn less than $4320 per annum," twice as many women (84 percent) fall into this category. Such statistics confirm the conclusion reached in *A Poverty Profile for Belize* that "the poor in Belize appear to [be] somewhat older, more likely to be headed by females, and come from families of larger size with a greater number of members under 14 years of age."[10]

The opportunity to achieve a modicum of social mobility through employment is virtually impossible for women, who are often denied the opportunity to complete their secondary education after giving birth to a child. Such practices relegate women to domestic and factory jobs. Beyond secondary education, 1.6 percent of Belizean men go on to graduate from postsecondary (college) programs, whereas only 0.9 percent of women do so. The *Belize Report for the Fourth World Conference on Women* also documents women's underrepresentation in "administrative/managerial positions." Women hold 36.5 percent of these positions as compared with men, who make up 63.5 percent. These figures include those who work for the government.

Most women appear to accept their unequal status, but a few recognize the urgent need for employment that will enable them to subsist at an adequate level. One such group of women mobilized themselves forcefully and brought the problem of economic inequity to the public's attention. In April 1991, the first labor union solely for women was organized and set into motion events that would ultimately lead to the establishment in 1992 of the first minimum wage in the country.[11]

"Stop Tek Chance of Our Workers"

The formation of the Women's Workers Union (WWU) was an unprecedented effort by women to organize on the basis of gender issues. Their struggle highlighted the dilemma of working for companies in export-processing zones which deny women adequate wages, benefits, and environmentally safe working conditions and brought to a public forum their government's complicity in the creation of a growing underclass of female laborers.[12] What women protested was the inadequate wage of $56BZ for forty-five hours. When women measured their salaries against the expenses of bus fare, lunch, and child care, they found them wanting. In response, approximately 120 women workers charged the Civic Textile Company (a Taiwanese garment factory) with failure to meet minimum standards of health, sanitation, wages, and proper working conditions. The working conditions were described in a pamphlet produced by the Society for the Promotion of Education and Research (SPEAR),[13] a nongovernmental organization, in order to educate the public:

Working Conditions

Wash basins—The 120 women workers employed at Civic Textiles found it impossible to share four washbasins within a time limit of 1/2 hour during lunch break. Some proceeded to work without washing their hands, soiling the garments and were accused of producing low quality work.

Toilets—Six toilets are available for these 120 women. The breaks of 10 minutes two times daily is inadequate for everyone to use the facilities. This leads to waiting in lines or not using the toilet at all.

Seating—Stools were used as seats at the facility. Chairs with backrests were recommended to alleviate the risk of back injury or backache on the job. These stools are uncomfortable for working a nine hour day schedule.

Cafeteria—Civic Textiles has recently built a shed with long tables and benches to serve as an eating area for the workers. Mobile vendors sold food outside the gates of the factory.

Security measures—At 7:30 a.m. on working days the gates of the factory were padlocked. Only the company's management personnel have access to keys opening the gates. In case of emergency, no alternative exit exists, increasing the risk of panic and disaster on the compound. The women feel that working under such highly scrutinized measures gives the impression of working in a prison. In addition, women's purses were taken away from them at the beginning of the working day and placed in a cage so that access to personal belongings was limited.

Work schedule—Women reported to work from 7:30 a.m. to midday and from 12:30 p.m. to 5:00 p.m. with two 10 minute breaks daily. The women worked alternative Saturdays and skipped alternative Fridays, totaling 90 hours every two weeks. Wages were calculated on this 90 hour period rather than weekly.

Wages—The flat rate for sewing machine operators is $0.63U.S. per hour, the cost of a tin of condensed milk in Belize. Piece rates were $0.12 for hemming a dozen pockets and $0.30 per dozen for sewing down the labels. Although these wages are below the basic cost of living in Belize, the Company did not break the law by paying low wages because Belize has no general minimum-wage legislation to protect workers.[14]

The company responded to the complaints women made about the working conditions by firing the union's leaders and its most vocal members. Striking women were barred from the factory by a padlocked gate; in a final gesture to prevent the formation of a union, several newspapers reported that Civic Textile had threatened to withdraw from Belize. This tactic, if true, is a typical example of the union-busting and economic coercion that often accompanies foreign companies' investments in underdeveloped countries like Belize, Mexico, Colombia, and many others.[15] What really angered these Belizean women, however, was their government's collusion and its inadequate response to their needs. They felt the Labour Office was not sufficiently concerned with wages and work conditions. In a small country like Belize where people are involved in patron-client relations, they are accustomed to having the ear of the political parties they support with votes. For the women the battle lines were clearly drawn along two divides: gender needs versus political needs and local people's interests versus foreign investments. The force of their anger was evident not only in their deeds but also in their words, as the signs they carried during the strike revealed:

We run things. Things no run we.

What does PUP have against women?

UDP supports women now.[16]

Belizean women demand a just wage.

These slogans captured the women's sentiment that their rights as workers were not adequately protected by the government solely because they were *women.* Other signs the women carried directly questioned the government's relationship to foreign companies:

> If this issue were political this company would have been shut down, but when women try to save themselves, they [the government] say they can't shut it down.

> The problem in Belize is Belizeans have no voice. The Taiwanese have more rights.

The WWU strike persisted for almost three months and culminated in a prolonged hearing.

On July 20, 1991, a Statutory Instrument (No. 84 of 1991) was passed, exempting the Civic Textile Company Limited from some of the provisions of the "Labour Act, Chapter 234 of the Laws of Belize, 1980," but with certain conditions that were somewhat more favorable to women—no longer could women workers be required to work more than six days a week, the work day was decreased to nine hours total per day, and the total hours over a two-week period could not exceed ninety hours. Yet the wage issue and the subordination inherent in factories operating in export-processing zones were never addressed.

Less than a year after it had woven women's issues into the public's ethical consciousness, the WWU ceased to exist. Internal leadership conflicts and economic impediments led to the union's demise. One contributing factor was the failure of male-dominated unions to support the fledgling group. This conflict between "male-dominated unions and working women," Safa contends, is merely a reflection of the gender asymmetries present in the workplace.[17] Yet in its brief existence, the WWU provided the motivation that forced the Ministry of Labour to review the country's minimum wage policy. And certainly the WWU should be seen as the source of inspiration for the minimum wage campaign mounted by the Belize Organization for Women and Development (BOWAND), begun in July 1992. Initially the government announced an increase in minimum wage to $2.25BZ for agriculture and export industries, both of which are areas of the labor market dominated by men. A nongovernmental organization, BOWAND lobbied by attending hearings on the topic and by distributing flyers and brochures written in Creole and intended to educate women about the issue. As a result of these activities, they were instrumental in getting the Ministry of Labour to raise the wage scale for those jobs dominated by women. Women who were "shop assistants working in establishments where liquor is sold, for domestic workers in hotels, rooming houses, hospitals and other institutions" would receive $2.25BZ an hour, and "other shop assistants and domestics working in private homes" would receive $1.75BZ.[18]

Revealing the Work Women Do

One of the key questions that arises regarding the WWU's activism is what would cause ordinary garment workers to stand their ground and take risks. The examples from women around the world are discouraging, since efforts to organize unions are often met with severe repressive measures dispensed by either the government or the factories themselves. One reason the Belizean women stood up for themselves may be their limited options beyond domestic work and factory jobs to develop alternative sources of income. The formation of the union can be read as a desperate act, when no other options were available to draw upon. While Jamaica, Haiti, and many African countries have in place a strong informal sector of female hawkers, traders, and entrepreneurs, Belize has no such counterpart of any note. In the market, both women and men sell vegetables, and street vendors are as likely to be men as women. Although a small group of women in Belize City and throughout the country seem to have carved out a small niche selling pastries and meat pies, most women supplement their income by taking in laundry and performing domestic work. For rural women, the options are even fewer because the population is not large enough to require domestic services. Thus "women in rural areas are more likely to suffer inequitably." [19]

In general, most working women in the country rely upon factory jobs in Belize City and domestic work in the larger towns to generate income. [20] I met women in Lemongrass who leave their small children with relatives while they go to work in the factories in Belize City, a seven- or eight-hour bus trip. They live in the city and return home once or twice a month. Here is one woman's story of the difficulties she and other women experience in trying to sustain themselves and their families:

> The major problem here is that we find the economy, or the financial economy, is very low. You find that the woman have to work very hard, very hard to cope with the financial problems, especially in the home. You find most women (the Garifuna race) they would bake bread and the children would go home and go out to sell. Well some of the Creole, well they, some of them make pastries.
>
> I noticed the East Indians, they make food to sell at the market. So that is the problem of women here in [Lemongrass] especially. They have to work extremely hard to cope, to balance that home you know, to balance that home and to provide for the home.
>
> It happened in Belize City too because I taught there for some years. The poor women, the Creole women in Belize, they would take in washing. They would do some little housework you know for these people who have big businesses and so. They would take in washing. I was renting a house. I was upstairs and this woman was downstairs and she took in three different wash-

ings this lady downstairs, just to keep her child going to high school—three different washings, big bundles of clothes. I said, "My God, poor woman." The other one, she used to go out and clean out these offices. So the women in Belize work very hard to keep up [with] this financial problem.

Although such circumstances make these women easy targets in the politics of multinational corporations and foreign factories in the export-processing zones, they can also harness their vulnerability and make it the motivation for resisting such conditions, as the WWU did.

All over Belize, the hard work that women do is very much distorted by the fact that it is masked. The consistent jobs that women perform in the small informal sector take place behind closed doors or are done concurrently with routine domestic duties and so are difficult to separate from their ordinary routines. For example, in Lemongrass I observed that women sold bread, buns, cakes, tamales, ice, ideal and milky ways (frozen confections), and soft drinks and took in sewing, all within the privacy of their homes, where with the exception of an occasional cardboard sign, their arduous labor was virtually invisible.

No one has yet documented the actual size or complete impact of Belize's small informal sector. This makes it impossible to determine how much of the work women engage in—which is often quite labor intensive with minimal economic return—directly contributes to their livelihood or to the country's economic growth and development. What can be culled from available data is the fact that in a country where unemployment among women is over 20 percent and 21.8 percent of all households are headed by females, women are forced to rely upon marginal subsistence strategies in order to fulfill their obligations as mothers and/or heads of households.[21] With so few options, it is not surprising that some women might view a strike as less risky than their current predicament of insufficient housing and food. A successful solution to a strike would be a vast improvement over their current situation.

According to the 1980 and 1991 censuses, Belizean women are rarely involved in agricultural production, despite the availability of land. Agricultural production is primarily the purview of three ethnic groups: Maya, Mestizos, and Mennonites. Women in these groups rarely own or participate in large-scale farming. A few work on small home gardens or assist on family farms, but generally are not in control of production. Few Garifuna or Creoles are actively involved in agricultural production either for profit or for personal use.[22] While in other Caribbean and Latin American societies women may have access to small plots that they can use to attain a certain degree of economic stability and autonomy, nothing comparable exists in Belize.[23] The 1991 census indicated that there are three major industries in the country: agricultural

Market Vendor, Irene Swazo, Belize City, new market
(photo by author)

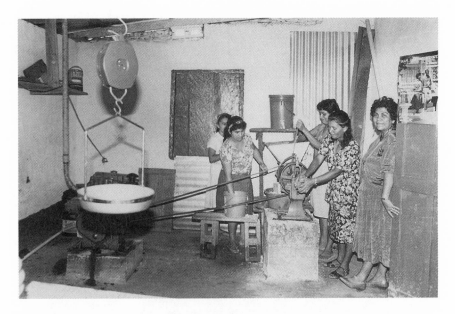

Women working in a corn tortilla factory
(courtesy of Belize Information Service)

production, hunting, and forestry. Of the 16,973 workers in these industries, 97 percent (16,422) are men and only 3 percent (551) are women.[24]

Women, for the most part, are concentrated (or marginalized) in different industries: manufacturing (3.9 percent of women workers), wholesale and retail (4.9 percent), hotel and restaurant (3.3 percent), education (4.0 percent), and health and social work (1.8 percent). In addition to these, a large number are employed in private households as domestics (4.5 percent).[25] One reason women tend to be relegated to service jobs is their lack of previous employment. The majority of them (68.8 percent, or 35,274) have never worked previously, compared with only 14.4 percent of men. This suggests that because most women spend the greater part of their life performing home duties, when they do seek outside work, they tend to turn to familiar employment, building upon existing skills. The forces of a labor market that favors men neither encourages women to move beyond jobs linked to their domestic roles nor fairly compensates them for the work they do. Women are segregated in the garment and domestic service industries.[26] The government as an employer also participates in subordinating women. Although the Belize Civil Service is the fourth largest employer of men (7.7 percent), it employs only 2.2 percent of those women eligible to work. While there has been no study to prove that intentional discrimination is at work, de facto discrimination occurs because women more often lack the higher educational skills needed

Basket weaver, Trefosia Coye, Belize City
(photo by author)

to perform many of the jobs. Moreover, since appointment to some jobs is a political gesture, women lack the political capital to draw upon for assistance, a matter I will return to later. It is these historical practices of de facto gender discrimination that have created the reality of occupational and economic inequities and disparities that underlie the protests of the Women's Workers Union.

Despite their disadvantaged position, women find ways to manage their survival. One strategy they rely upon is a system of informal exchanges and obligations developed with family, friends, and neighbors. The system is based upon a provisioning of services such as child care, laundry services, and food in exchange for material goods. Yet despite this system of reciprocity, numerous barriers still impede many women's ability to help themselves.

All of the conditions I have described explain why women depend so heavily upon husbands or male partners as their most viable resource for economic survival.[27] Unfortunately, this reliance, rather than alleviating women's economic problems, often ensnares them in an immutable cycle of strong economic dependency on men. Further, inherent in the cycle is an emotional, psychological, and sometimes physical powerlessness that weaves a pattern of dependency in women's lives, structuring their most intimate relationships and creating a set of dynamics in family or household interactions that support women's subordination.

The Economic-Sexual Dynamics of Personal Relationships

Multiple consensual relationships (also called common law or visiting) are the most frequent type in Belize. The reasons for such relationships, in opposition to monogamous legally sanctioned marriages, have attracted the interest of anthropologists and other social scientists from the time of Melville Herskovits in the 1930s up to the present day.[28] Contemporary research on women in the Caribbean has taken as its major subject the impact of the absent male in the construction of gender roles and women's economic status. The origins of consensual relationships in Belize, as well as in the rest of the Caribbean, are often attributed to slavery and the retention of African traditions of polygamy. The strong predisposition of most ethnic groups toward consensual relations has been commented upon by researchers studying kinship in the country. Anne Sutherland and Laurie Kroshus confirm this preeminence in their study of kinship in Caye Caulker specifically and Belize in general. They state: "Mating patterns on Caye Caulker are very similar to the patterns found in the Caribbean area in general. The three kinds of unions, found in Barbados and in Belize in general . . . are Christian marriage, consensual unions and . . . [visiting] relationships."[29]

When formal marriage occurs, it is most often among the elite or professionals, though even this is not guaranteed. Legally sanctioned monogamous marriages represent the ideal in Belizean society. Yet there is little or no social stigma attached to men and women who live together in consensual relations, though men are freer in their movements than women. "Marriage is valued; but consensual unions are the norm."[30] Data from the 1991 census indicate that only 38.7 percent of Belize's population are married and 56 percent have never been legally married.[31]

There are striking differences among ethnic groups in this aspect of Belizean culture. Of those married, Mestizos have the highest rate ("46.8 percent of current married females and 48.3 percent of the currently married males are Mestizos"). This trend contrasts sharply with marriage rates among Creoles. In this ethnic group, only 22 percent of males and females legally marry. Given this low marital rate, it is surprising that Creoles have the highest divorce rate of any ethnic group in the country: 49.6 percent for females and 46.5 percent of males compared with 21.7 percent and 30.3 percent, respectively, for Mestizos.[32] Among most of the ethnic groups, the Roman Catholic Church exerts the strongest influence, but there are no data that show a correlation among ethnicity, religion, and marriage practices. Creoles exhibit very different marital patterns than those of Mestizos, their fellow Catholics.

The majority of consensual interpersonal relationships often have an economic basis. The woman involved tends to place great value on having a man who will provide for her and her family, just as married women seek security for themselves and their future offspring. Bullard found in a study of such relationships that both men and women see marriage as "a highly economic proposition."

> A woman looks for a man who will hold a steady job and contribute most of his income toward housing, food, clothing, and maintenance of the children rather than spending it on liquor, gambling, marijuana, and other women. Romantic love is definitely secondary to the desire for a good provider. Men prefer mates who will be faithful, save money by doing all domestic tasks themselves rather than hiring assistants, cook tasty dishes, keep their clothing in good condition, and, by staying home, not interfere with non-domestic aspects of male behavior.[33]

Beyond these expressed domestic responsibilities, one other "duty" is expected of women—their sexual compliance.

Mary, a professional woman working with one of the nongovernmental organizations that focuses on women and health, talks about some of the beliefs and behaviors that influence personal relationships in Belize. Her observations are based upon her interactions with women during the course of her

Women working in a furniture factory
(courtesy of Belize Information Service)

job. She sees a number of women from a broad age range. Below she describes a scenario typical of many first-time relationships. Although Mary does not speak to the emotional component of relationships, her comments are telling: many young women begin their primary relationship inspired by romantic love, however, pregnancy changes both partners' expectations regarding the issue of obligation and the degree of responsibility each expects of the other. Both from gossip and in my observations, I learned that once pregnant, women seemed constrained in their lives by an economic-sexual cycle. Mary describes the way in which this cycle is responsible for the proliferation of female-headed households:

> We have in Belize again the situation where a lot of these young people when you sit with them and you talk with them if they have three children, many times the three children have three different fathers. So it's that cycle of—I have this young man, he walked out on me, I got pregnant and he walked out. Some other young man starts looking at you soon after when you look as if you're ready for a relationship. But sometimes they target women I think because they know that they are in need of economic assistance.

Her description points to a tendency by men to use women's economic vulnerability as a way to extract sexual favors or as a way to develop a temporary consensual relationships.

Market Vendor, Luz del Carmen Cortés, Belize City, old market
(photo by author)

That's the premise on which sometimes these relationships start. That you
will look after me and my little one and more often than not that doesn't work
out so you have second one and he goes and the third one comes along. Well,
after you reach four or five [children], you're lucky if anybody looks at you
because they're not about to take on the responsibility of these four or five
children.

These relationships often exacerbate a woman's subordinate situation, because in exchange for temporary economic stability she is expected to produce
a child for the union. This act of reproduction, which men interpret as proof
of a woman's commitment, becomes part of a system of economic exchange
whereby women's reproductive capacity is commodified. Sexual reproduction
becomes the one commodity that they have to bargain with, but in the process, they lose control over the ability to decide when reproduction should
occur. Ironically, in adding another child to her family, a woman may be sow-
ing the seeds of the relationship's end. If the cycle continues and a woman is
required to produce a child for each consensual relationship in order to obtain
needed security, she may find herself with a larger family than she intended and
which she is unable to support. "The Total Fertility Rate (TFR) has traditionally been high in Belize," reports the government, "from around 7.0 children
per woman in the 1960s, to about 6.0 in 1980. The TFR averaged 5.3 be-

tween 1980 and 1987, was 5.5 in 1990 (Vital Register) and had dropped to 4.7 in 1991."[34] With such a large family, a woman has little likelihood of marriage or a long-term relationship, since many men are reluctant to assume the support of someone else's offspring. Mary confirms this viewpoint:

> Some women have been lucky and they have found men who have [taken on the responsibility of four or five children] but most of them don't. And I remember when I was growing up in Belize, if you had a child and you weren't married, well your life was perceived as pretty much finished. You know in terms of the social system, you were lucky if you got married again. You were considered lucky, and if you had four or five [children] and you found a man, I mean you were extremely lucky.

Bourque and Warren document similar patterns of relationships in their discussion of the *madre soltera* or single mother in Peru.[35] In Belize the circumstances that surround the cycle of economic dependency that develops in conjunction with sexual unions also have moral and social implications, which in the past put women at a distinct disadvantage. The social stigma of being an unwed mother is eloquently conveyed by Zee Edgell in *Beka Lamb*. One of the characters, Toycie, discusses the moral and practical conundrum many girls face: "'He said he doesn't believe the baby can be his, if I am pregnant, because his body didn't go into me and anyhow he could never marry anybody who played around with him like I did, because if I can do it before marriage, after marriage I would do it with somebody else and his mamacita would collapse if he married somebody that wasn't a virgin because she's so religious and she raised him to be a modest Catholic boy.'"[36] Although today single motherhood is viewed with somewhat greater tolerance, some social stigma still obtains. In *Beka Lamb* the nun upholds her decision to dismiss the pregnant Toycie from school on the grounds that appropriate conduct is the girl's responsibility: "[I]t is entirely up to the modesty of the girl to prevent these happenings. Our girls are warned of this likelihood, and the possible consequences. . . . 'We women must learn to control our emotions, Mr. Lamb. There are times we must stand up and say "enough" whatever our feelings. The rate of illegitimacy is quite high and has been for a long time. The women will have to decide for a change in their lives, otherwise they will remain vulnerable.'"[37] This moral stance may seem outdated and Victorian, but its underlying premise that girls are ultimately responsible for their "fall" still prevails in modern Belizean society. Most schools have no formal policy to prohibit pregnant girls from completing their education, but the informal practice is that they are not allowed to continue. When all is said and done, young girls assume both the moral and the economic responsibility for any children born outside the sanctity of marriage. The result is a tangled web of

economic dependency predicated on unwritten, but firmly entrenched, social standards that define appropriate and inappropriate behavior for men and
women and ultimately create a double standard. Mary elaborates: "More often than not when a woman, a young teenage [*sic*] gets pregnant she drops
out of school. She's dependent on her family. The male may stay in school, so
the impact, economic impact hits the female more because she is the one left
with the children, and she is the one not getting the training and the additional skills in order to improve her situation so she finds herself doing mainly
domestic tasks in homes and now . . . [they become] factory workers." In
Mary's mind, there is a strong link between girls getting pregnant at an early
age and the myriad issues that affect women's lives in Belize today.

The social circumstances of women, like their sexual development, are
filled with contradictory messages. Pregnancy signals a young girl's achievement of full adult status, yet many confront motherhood without any opportunity to understand the full significance of their new role or to set personal
goals. Very few have planned to have a family and are emotionally prepared
for the responsibilities.[38] Further, if they are rejected by the baby's father (as
Toycie's ordeal in *Beka Lamb* shows), their self-esteem, which is at a crucial
stage of development, atrophies. Given such inexperience, young girls on the
verge of womanhood are easy targets for males who perpetuate the economic-
sexual cycle. At the core of the cycle is a belief system that assumes women to
be minors, sex objects, and exploitable, discardable property.

The Discourses of Domestic Power Relations in Belize

The discourses of domestic power relations in Belize are varied and played out
in a number of ways. They are supported by cultural perceptions of women as
"less than" or as "different" from men. Such ideas appear to be rooted in the
prevailing cultural belief that women's anatomy, to a large degree, dictates
their place in society. It is an ideology most men subscribe to, although they
do not necessarily articulate it openly or on a daily basis. One male consultant
made this comment when asked what he thought about the problems women
face in his community: "I don't think woman is equal to man. I will never
look at women as equal . . . because men and women's bodies are different;
they are not equal." In this man's mind, sameness means equality. Another
male interviewee expressed the same idea but from a sociocultural perspective
when he stated that women are not equal to men because "women haven't
begun to do men's job as yet." These two examples suggest that "biology as
destiny" and other cultural beliefs about men's work and women's work are
integral aspects of Belize's culture of gender.

Another tenet upon which this culture is founded is the belief that women's primary obligation is in the home. The importance that Belizean society places on women's responsibilities in the home may help to explain why in the 1991 census, as noted earlier, a majority of women (64.9 percent) identify "home duties" as their primary work or "economic activity." According to the census report, men defined these home duties as "expect[ing] to have a homecooked meal and have . . . [a woman] take care of the kids after she's worked all day."

The census separates out home duties (that is, housework and food preparation) as a separate category. This division makes it hard to interpret unemployment figures for the formal labor sector; should home duties be viewed as unemployment or as a distinctive category of unpaid labor?[39] This question is significant, because of the 51,238 women in Belize aged fifteen years and over who are eligible to work, only 23.2 percent are actually employed in the *formal* labor sector, while 64.9 percent are "involved in 'home duties'" (of the remaining 12 percent, 8 percent are students and 4 percent are described as primarily looking for work or disabled; there is a small number whose status was unknown). These numbers contrast sharply when compared with those for men in the same age group. Seventy-six percent of men are engaged in some type of employment, meaning that they collect a consistent wage. However, only 4.4 percent of these working-age men are involved in home duties, making it clear that the society as a whole sees this area as "women's work." The number of men who are students is slightly lower than women (7.4 percent). Retirement is extremely low. Many cannot afford to retire; in addition, Belize has an extremely young population. Seventy-eight percent of the people are thirty-four years old and younger, with the largest concentration (47.9 percent) between the ages of fifteen and twenty-four. People over the age of sixty-five represent only 4.2 percent of the total population. Many elderly migrate to the United States to work or reside with family. Still, within the small group of elderly, the possibility for retirement is greater for men (3.1 percent) than for women (0.9 percent) and this gap is widening—ten years ago the figures stood at 2.5 percent for men and 1.3 percent for women.

The majority of women in Belize, regardless of their ethnicity, thus have extremely limited social and economic options to improve their status. They are further constrained by a social belief that their primary responsibility is the fulfillment of home duties. Their identities remain linked to the roles of mother and wife/partner from the onset of adolescence until they die.

Among Belize women, these beliefs and practices have spawned the kind of economic dependency already described. It is this context of economic vulnerability and social ideology that has also produced women who are emotionally and psychologically dependent on men. Coupled with this dependency are individual feelings of low self-esteem and worth, as Rose and Zola so eloquently tell us. And it is within the boundaries of the institutional and ideological dimensions of gender that the dynamics of power and subordination among Belizean men and women are very often set up and executed through physical and mental abuse.

Although men exercise real economic power over women, they still exert their authority and control through physical battering as well. Up until 1992, when the Domestic Violence Bill was implemented, this behavior was viewed by the police and much of Belizean society as a "private ting." Domestic disputes were regarded as something to be worked out between the individuals, regardless of how severe the battering, in the privacy of their home. Violent acts thus go unacknowledged by the community, unreported to the police, and remain rarely discussed among friends and families. Domestic violence is so acutely invisible that it did not warrant any mention in one of the most important official documents produced by the police, the "Report of the Belize Crimes Commission."[40] Yet the local papers run stories several times a year of women mutilated, burned, and murdered by their husbands or partners in domestic disputes.

Both Rose and Zola provide evidence of the way domestic violence manifests itself in individual women's lives. As their stories indicate, patterns of physical and mental abuse appear early in a woman's life cycle. These are often established when teenage girls become involved with an older boyfriend or older man—the latter representing a de facto father authority figure. One way men exercise their gender power is by controlling women's movements. A retired schoolteacher describes what this pattern looked like in her life: "That is it! I was a prisoner! That is the word. I was a prisoner. He was afraid that other men would talk to me. So I was a prisoner. So you see they afraid. To me, most of the time he would talk, I would sort out that he felt like inferior. Inferior. That's the way some men feel, you know." From a man's perspective, women who freely travel about the town and city alone are rebellious and need to be controlled and contained. When a couple begins to live together, males expect that a woman's mobility will be limited by the requirement that she attend to her home duties. In this traditional way of life, a woman's path is generally confined to the market, school, church, and home. Dances, bars, and other activities that place a woman in a public space and in the scrutiny of other men are discouraged and in effect deemed taboo.

Another way men exercise their gender power is through social isolation. Some women are denied the privilege of having friends and visits in their home, a restriction most commonly explained by saying that women gossip when they get together and men condemn this behavior.[41] A woman's friendships then are limited to those relationships established prior to her marriage with school friends, women kin, or those neighbors who travel the same circumscribed route from kitchen to market and back again. Some women told me that although they had lived in their communities for years, they had little more than a "good morning" relationship with most of their female neighbors.

One of the most powerful holds that men have over women is the threat of abandonment. To avoid abandonment, women in Belize practice endurance. Since the intent of the threat is to gain compliance, women's failure to do anything that provokes such a threat can be read as acquiescing to male needs and authority. Bullard describes women's behavior under these circumstances: "A Belizean woman will accept much abuse and tolerate a great deal of offensive behavior from her mate in return for the economic security of his wages, so great is her dread of being left alone. This is a fairly common fate, and almost one-third of the women classified as 'mothers' in the 1960 census had never been, or were not currently, living with a mate." [42] Erica Jong, an American writer, once commented that the worst slave was the one who beat herself—making the point that women participate in their own subordination. They seldom challenge male behaviors or expectations for fear of being cast in a negative role.

This threat of abandonment shapes not only how women interact with men, but also how they relate to one another. Women feel competitive with one another in the face of a limited male population. The irony is that numerically the Belizean population is almost equally divided by sex. Further, there are equal numbers of men and women in the same age groups despite the popular perception, regarded as "truth" by both women and men, that there are only a few "good" men available. [43] Since in reality there is an adequate number of men, the question becomes what exactly is meant by a "good man."

Popular culture often provides the clues we need to interpret cultural meanings. [44] Music, and songs in particular, frequently convey people's understanding or interpretations of normative social expectations in both values and behavior. One song in Belize, popular during my stay, attempted to answer the question "What is a good man?" The song asks, "Where have all the good men gone?" and responds, "I don't know." The song incorporates a dialogue about the issue.

Dem Bow[45]
[Woman:] Where have all the good men gone?
I don't know.
. . . I have got to find a man
who will stick to one woman
A man who'll never lie to me
who will love me faithfully . . .

> [Man:] . . . Gial [girl], if you want a man with no problem
>   Get the ugly one no gial no want him
>   Handsome man have woman all bout
>   Gial love pretty face and sweet mouth . . .
> [Woman:] . . . Where have all the good men gone?
>   I don't know.

According to the song, there are very specific qualities and characteristics by which a woman can identify a "good" man. What is valued in a man is honesty and emotional involvement (that is, someone who is kind, sexy, and understanding). A "good" man is also monogamous (meaning faithful), an almost unrealistic expectation for most Belizean women, given that male infidelity seems to be a virtual norm. The song warns listeners against "handsome" men, who are depicted as capricious and unreliable. Yet despite the advice, the song contradicts itself, subverting the message it is intended to convey. With the line "gial love pretty face and sweet mouth," we are told that in fact women prefer the very type of man they should avoid. The line indicts women for making decisions based on superficial qualities; in so doing, it turns the intended critique of male behavior into a critique of female judgment, making women the problem. In many ways, this reversal is no different from the way in which the culture of gender operates on the assumption that women cause their own victimization.

Both Rose and Zola describe feeling at fault for their own subordination. Blaming the victim is one of the most critical issues that women's groups confront, just as it has been one of the central themes around which Western feminists have organized. Because men point to women's personal qualities (weight, personality, attitude, anatomy) as reasons why they view them or treat them as inferiors, women are made to feel individually and collectively responsible for the circumstances that make their lives difficult.

Connected to these feelings of guilt and inadequacy, which can be fostered by early sexual encounters in which the girl feels she has no choice but to comply or lose her man, along with insufficient education, inadequate job skills, and unemployment, is child abuse. As I suggested in my interpretation of Zola's narrative, women may sometimes turn on their children as a way to gain a measure of control or as a way to release the frustration and helplessness they feel. Mary describes the way in which abusive parental behavior is produced by circumstances and lack of options:

> [Women] take up jobs in the factories and they're paid very, very low wages and they can hardly survive and it ties in also with the issue of child abuse. Many times they come home, they're tired, they're frustrated, they beat the children severely because they may have left them with parents or friends [and] the

children are walking all over the place. They're getting into mischievous, typical children things. But it's because of a lack of guidance and support systems
for them [the mothers]. [They lack] daycare centers or people they can leave
their children with and feel secure that while they are working their children
are being taken care of and [they] are [not] able to pay adequately for that
kind of support as well. So it's all, it's all interrelated and then I think in terms
of other issues for women. There are so many who have the availability for
opportunity and training, and further improvement, [but] adult education
opportunities are just not there.[46]

UNICEF, in an analysis of the situation of women and children in Belize, also
identifies child abuse as a potentially serious problem, though not an excessive
one at this time, despite the high birth rate and youthfulness of Belize's population: "Indeed the figures for child abuse are low relative to the population
of children in Belize, but they are remarkable given the fact that there are no
child abuse reporting laws, [and] no systematic data collection on child abuse
cases."[47]

Further, UNICEF gives a positive assessment of Belize's efforts in the
area of child-care facilities: "Seven Early Childhood Development Centres,
serving as prototypes, have been organized in Orange Walk, Corozal and
Stann Creek districts, attended by approximately 209 children."[48] My own
observation, however, was that such centers are often constrained by community politics, personality conflicts, and frustration brought on by a lack of
funds and facilities. Indeed child-care centers seem to better serve the agendas
of the external consultants paid to assess them than actually meet the needs of
the women and children who use them. This view is confirmed by the *Belize
Report for the Fourth World Conference on Women*, which states that "the continued absence or unaffordability of child care centres, including work-based
centres, remains a serious barrier to women more fully achieving a more eq-
uitable LFP [labor force participation] rate."[49] On the whole, Belize lacks
social institutions such as subsidized daycare or other social services to assist
women who struggle with problems of unemployment, child abuse, underemployment, domestic violence, and low self-esteem.[50]

Chapter 8 *Evelyn's Story (Creole)*

Evelyn's narrative, like Zola's, goes beyond the simple narration of events and resembles a life story in form and content. My relationship with Evelyn was, and still is, more intimate and intertwined than with the other two women. I worked in her shop, helped her cook meals, and often took tea with her family in the evenings. We shared stories about our children and discussed the significance of my research as we walked the dusty streets of Lemongrass or shared a beer at one of the local restaurants. For these reasons, I cannot say with any degree of certainty if Evelyn's narrative is completely spontaneous or if it is the accretion of the months we spent working together and becoming friends. What I can say is that I learned about her life over a period of time, although the actual interview did not take place until a few days before I was to depart.

I delayed interviewing Evelyn until the end of my stay for several reasons. Above all, I found I had tremendous anxiety about the task. These feelings were the closest I came to experiencing a moral dilemma as I asked myself whether to include her—she was like a high school friend whom I had just rediscovered. My concerns reflected the debates I had with myself over the ethics of fieldwork. In the course of collecting data, researchers interact with a variety of people on a daily basis. I wondered: How much of what we learn is legitimate "data"? Do we include in our published writing the private sharing of feelings, frustrations, and dreams that occurs between two individuals?[1] At times the thought of recording Evelyn's life story seemed almost a violation of the intimacy we had developed in our relationship. Textualizing her revelations was further complicated by my fears that there might be repercussions for her. What if Evelyn's husband did not approve of my description of him or resented my making public details of their life together? Because I had no interaction with Rose's or Zola's spouse, I feared no such threats or repercus-

sions—a classic case of out of sight, out of mind. With Evelyn, I also anticipated that her husband might act to curtail our friendship. These are the kinds
of risks with which I believe every ethnographer grapples. In the end, the
decision is a judgment call. Sometimes the result is favorable, sometimes not,
but often the consequences are not felt until after the researcher is gone. We
remain safe and distant, while our consultants continue to live their once private lives as public parts of our research. There is a certain imbalance against
which I continue to struggle.

Evelyn is an attractive thirty-nine-year-old Creole woman with large ex-
pressive eyes. Brown-skinned with large hips, about which she usually com-
plains, her shoulder-length hair is parted down the middle with French braids
on either side to frame her face. She exemplifies the mixtures that are reflected
in the ranges of skin color and hair texture found among the Creoles. She tells
me that her grandfather was a very light man of Jamaican origin; her paternal
grandmother, Belizean born, was very dark. Evelyn's youngest daughter suggests other mixtures beyond West Indian—she is a very thin girl with smooth,
dark skin, and long, wavy hair. To me she looks East Indian or mixed. Evelyn
says some of her own appearance and elements of her daughter's derive from
her maternal grandmother, who traced her origins back to the country of
Sierra Leone in Africa.

Evelyn married at the age of eighteen and is the mother of eight children,
the eldest of whom she had, out of wedlock, at the age of sixteen. In response
to one of my more direct questions, Evelyn says that she stays with her husband out of habit. A thriving entrepreneur, she has a successful business, but
is always on the lookout for something new to strengthen her financial security. She has not relied on her husband's income for years, if ever, since it is
highly erratic. When it is there, it is there; and when it's not, it is not missed.
Like many Belizeans, Evelyn has a plot of land in one of the nearby villages.
Such areas away from an individual's home are called "plantations." The husband or son will often take off on the weekend to work the land in hopes of
producing enough to supplement the family's food supply or to sell in the
local market. Evelyn has banana trees, pineapple plants, citrus trees, and pigs.
The investment has proved to be a wise one, for it keeps her youngest son
occupied whenever he decides he is not interested in attending school. She is
open-ended about her future; she alludes to the idea that once her youngest
child completes high school, her obligation to maintain a family structure will
be fulfilled. Once that obligation is complete she poses the question: what is
to keep her in the marriage?

The threads connecting Evelyn to the ways of her past are rapidly diminishing. She married the man her grandmother thought was the right person

and remains in the marriage more because she is supposed to than out of a desire to be there (her love, she says, dissipated years ago as a result of the abuse, humiliation, and economic difficulty she suffered). Today she is deeply involved in community issues related to domestic violence and would like to see a woman's center established in the town.

Each time I visit Lemongrass Evelyn seems to have acquired another position of leadership. The respect and prestige she has earned is recognized by the community. At the same time, this status is barely acknowledged by her husband. He finds fault with her work, her appearance, her business ventures. I see this as his attempt to maintain a control he thinks is eroding. Although Evelyn appears to ignore him, her decision not to leave him attests to the strength of his hold over her. His comments seem to fester and create pockets of self-doubt in her life as well as emotional pain. As a result, Evelyn is not always confident about her abilities, despite countless examples of success that prove her talents.

My interview with Evelyn took place two days before I was to leave Lemongrass. There had been one false start a month earlier in my stay, which I had terminated. It happened during one of the quiet moments in the shop. Evelyn began to talk about her life, especially her separation from her mother and the death of an infant brother. She was overcome by emotion, however, and could not continue. After this I again delayed interviewing her until time forced me to.

One night after supper, at the kitchen table, I asked Evelyn to talk. She shooed all the children outside in her usual brisk and threatening tone while I set up the tape recorder. The interview lasted for four and a half hours and covered three ninety-minute tapes. Initially I was concerned about privacy: children floated in the front door and drifted through the kitchen out the back; also, one of Evelyn's sons sat listening to local music not three feet from where we sat. If we could hear him, I had no doubt he could hear us. I worried too that Evelyn might not be comfortable talking to me because of her husband's presence. He lingered about the small house and could hear much of what we said. There would be no secrets. But none of these distractions seemed to matter to Evelyn. Her attitude reminded me that in the past she had openly discussed with me, and with anyone else who would listen, the problems she faced and was attempting to overcome in her marriage. In a sense, telling her story to me, revealing her life in such an open way, fixing it in the record of my research, destroyed the potential power that secrecy might have bestowed upon her spouse.

Everyone in the community—friends, neighbors, her children—was well versed in the chronology and details of Alan's infidelities. I interpreted this public knowledge as Evelyn's personal method of achieving empowerment—expose the secrets. She invoked her own personal commandment for confronting abuse: thou shall not cover up for the perpetrator. The effect this produced on Evelyn's family was an interesting one. Alan contributed very little or nothing financially to the maintenance of the household or the upkeep of the children. Of the eight children, six were living at home in 1991, aged twelve to nineteen, and two were working in the United States. Because Alan contributed nothing financially, he had no visible role in his family. Unlike other men I had met or heard about in Belize, he lacked any power to legitimately invoke the authority they seem to believe they hold by virtue of birth. In reality, the ability to exert such power is learned, and Alan seemed unskillful in this aspect of his gender role. He roamed the house more like a phantom than a king, and was often ignored.

I observed Alan's interaction with his children over a period of time. His reprimands were generally shrugged off, and the children rarely invited his opinion on any issue. Mostly he voiced his criticisms to the open air, empty of an audience. Threats he made were dismissed. In contrast, Evelyn's yells and threats were heeded, sometimes with humor, other times more seriously. Whatever Evelyn wanted done was ultimately completed.

What struck me most about Alan's tenuous position in the house was the isolation he faced from his children. His response to this was to direct his frustration and anger toward Evelyn. Any chance he got, he attacked her. Most of the time his tone was humorous, but nonetheless, she could do nothing right. He ridiculed the work she did, despite the fact that her efforts alone enabled the family to maintain a reasonable standard of living. Evelyn's physical appearance was constantly the brunt of Alan's jokes or commentary. Her solution was to not bother at all about how she looked. She wore her hair in braids or pulled back most of the time, rarely wore any makeup, and for a woman who could whip up a dress out of the creative corners of her mind in an hour or two without a pattern, Evelyn paid very little attention to her own clothes.

Although Evelyn did not divorce her husband or put him out of the house, she somehow managed to uproot his place as an authority figure and unmask his undesirable behavior in a way that gained her respect in the community. In her household there were two adults, but only one parent—there was "mom" and there was "Alan." Most of the choices Evelyn made in her life were not accidental but a combination of enculturation and a struggle to resist the same. She presented herself as a mixture of the traditional and the modern Belize. Just as O. Nigel Bolland describes Belize as a new nation in the making, so too is Evelyn a new woman in the making.[2]

The Constitution of Gendered Dependency

Evelyn: So where do we start?

Irma: We'll start with your life and what it is like growing up in Belize as a young woman. Give me your background. You are Creole? Where were you born and all that?

Evelyn: Maybe I should start when I was two years old. (Go play, pickni [kids].) At the age of two I was brought to live with my [maternal] grandmother. I could recall, I always recall the very dress I wore. It was a polka dot dress. I started school at the age of six because I couldn't learn English, because . . .

Irma: What did you speak?

Evelyn: Spanish.

Irma: From the time you were born? So where were you born?

Evelyn: In San Pedro Colombia [a village in the Toledo District]. My mother only spoke Spanish. I was back-ordered [in] my language because I didn't socialize with none of the kids around. So my only friend was my grandmother. I think that kept my learning English backward. I started school at six. As since I started to school I picked up a lot. I learned Creole fast. In our days, they didn't have kindergarten. You go straight into Infant 1 [first grade]. I pick up the language fast enough to come in 80s in my first year. And from since then I remain an "A" student.

Irma: Now where is San Pedro Colombia?

Evelyn: It is twenty-one miles away from here [Lemongrass].

Irma: And it's a Spanish village?

Evelyn: The village was Ketchi, but Spanish people lived on the other side of the river.

Irma: Now how did your mother get there?

Evelyn: My mother's mother died when she was eight years old and she was given to a family—a distant uncle. This family she lived with they did chicle work [extracting the base for chewing gum] way back in the early, I don't know what year it was, but they did chickle and mahogany work. They used to camp. I don't know which one but there were different camps and when they left from there they settled in [San Pedro] Colombia and that's how my mother became a resident there.

My [paternal] grandfather, he's from Jamaica originally and loved farming. When he came to settle in this country, he lived in Guatemala previously to living here and he was the foreman for the United Fruit Company at that time. When he migrated here he wanted to do farming, [so he] went straight to Colombia and that's how my father met my mother, in Colombia. They had six children: three lived and three died. When my youngest brother was a baby, that's when they separated and when they were separated, that's when I was given up.

Irma: Do people do that often, send kids to stay with relatives?

Evelyn: No. My grandmother wanted the company.

Though Evelyn states that "giving up" or lending out children is not a common practice, Kerns has documented it among the Garifuna in Belize and Zola in chapter 6 indicates that she was "loaned out" (adopted) as a young girl.[3] No systematic study of Creole or Mestizo kinship—with the exception of the brief study on Mestizo kinship by Sutherland and Kroshus mentioned earlier—or family structures in Belize has been conducted, so the frequency of this behavior among these groups is not known. The pattern, however, is documented among people of African ancestry in the Caribbean and the United States.[4]

Irma: Were you the only girl?

Evelyn: Uh-hmm.

At this point in the interview Evelyn begins to cry, and I ask, "Are you sure you want to do this?" Like Rose and Zola, Evelyn did not grow up with her nuclear family. She was part of an extended family household that emerges out of economic necessity (the mother is working a distance away from home or has immigrated to another country) or the desire to provide companionship for an elderly relative. Children (and the practice seems to be biased toward girls) often grow up with two sets of parents and authority figures in their lives. This can result in conflicting value systems; children find themselves having to conform to the more rigid standards of behavior set by grandparents or elderly relatives in contrast to what many Belizeans view as the laxity of such standards among modern parents.

I have frequently heard such conflict discussed in relation to children whose parents work in the United States. The parents are viewed as initiating the problem, because they often leave adolescent children in the care of grandparents who are physically unable to contend with the strain of raising a teenager in today's world. Moreover, absent parents often send their remittances directly to their children, who spend them freely, or lavish gifts upon them to the extent that others see such children as having little understanding of the value of material goods. Many Belizeans attribute some of the rise in adolescent crime and street children to this practice.

Yet one reason parents either leave their children with this established kin network or send them back during summers and other vacations to elderly kin is because they hope that their own parents will be able to instill in them better "manners" and proper behavior.

For Evelyn, being sent away to live with her grandmother at a young age is still an emotionally charged issue almost thirty-seven years after the occurrence. She continues, ignoring my question about stopping the interview.

Evelyn: I used to visit my mother during the holiday, but it was like once during the summer vacation I would visit them. I never got real close to my mom since when I used to visit her I spoke Creole and all the other kids spoke Spanish. So we weren't close.

Irma: So the Spanish you know now is what you learned from high school?

Evelyn: Yes. After I learned Creole I just forget everything. When I'd go and spend holidays, I would spend a month. I'd come back speaking a few sentences. We didn't communicate because all my mother spoke was Spanish. All the commands and things. Very few Creole I would hear when I would be with them. And I think that is why we didn't get close. Anyway [long pause] I was the only one with my grandmother for several years until my aunt came home to live. I think she couldn't make life over in Guatemala, and that's when she came home with [her husband] along with five children.

    Sarah [my cousin] she is two years older than me, but she came and they didn't know how to talk Creole.

Irma: So she spoke only Spanish too?

Evelyn: It was like a mixture, in between, because since this man [my aunt] was living with was Spanish, the children tend to speak Spanish more. Well, the year she was living with us, [my cousin Sarah and I] didn't see eye to eye. The very day she entered our home, she liked to fight. Since then I got even closer to my grandmother because when [Sarah] came she was two years my senior and she could beat me up. She used to pinch me up. So as to get protection I didn't play a lot in my childhood either. I would always be with my grandmother since she was old, she was always sleeping and would be in her room, or eating or doing something. I always tried to be in her eyesight because whenever Sarah get a break she would come behind, sometimes for nothing, come at me and pinch me. When I cry she would say, well I didn't do anything. I'd never fight back. I would never, always, when it get too much, then I would go and tell my grandmother. My grandmother would lash her. But that didn't stop the issue. She kept on, all during my teenage. At one point my grandmother had gotten enough of this [my aunt's husband] because all he did was drink. He didn't like to work, didn't contribute to the house and he would get drunk, come home and be rebellious. Once my grandmother put my aunt and him out of the house. Then I was alone again for almost two years.

The scenario described by Evelyn of living in an extended household is revealing. It gives me insight into the fact that her childhood evolved in an environment that was emotionally volatile and unpredictable. Evelyn's description of her aunt's life choices may also explain Evelyn's own acquiescence, an attitude that I think derives from a fatalistic view of life, a belief that this is the way things are. The latter also seems grounded in the view (validated by the community) that her aunt's behavior or pattern of life was generally acceptable as a survival strategy.

Evelyn: After they left she tried living with him but things didn't work out when she was on her own. So after that she came back home. She had given up on him. When my aunt came back home, he still used to come around our place but only when he was drunk. The last time he came was, I was about twelve years, he came out to the neighbor's house one day and he sat there all day sharpening a knife. He said he was going to kill my grandmother. He sat there cursing under that tree all day. My grandmother, well, she didn't go report him or anything because she said, well, he is not on her property. In the evening about five twilight, he went around to the back of our yard and jump right through the window with this sharpened knife. He jump on my grandmother but my grandmother was a big woman. Although she was old, she was about two hundred and fifty pounds, still big. My grandmother took an iron pot cover and she wopped him in his head and he couldn't even use his knife.

When the police came it was him who had all the damage. My grandmother was unhurt. That is when he went to jail and that was the end of their life together. After he left, my aunt got on with her life. But when she left she had a young baby and my grandmother took care of the baby and she went to work. And so now me and Sarah was like the two little ladies of the house. We did everything, we shared the work. At that time we started to see eye to eye. We quit fighting and she didn't beat me. We shared the chores. If she washed, I cooked, because this time my grandmother was getting down. She had hypertension and she would always be in bed. There was this baby to take care of. So he got attached to me. Most of the time he slept with me. This continued for five years.

Sarah and Evelyn are integrated into their grandmother's household as both companions and helpers. True to the process of gender enculturation, they become socialized into domestic routines very early in their life.

Evelyn: Within that five years my aunt, when she was working at a new settlement in Mango Creek, she fell in love with a Mexican guy. She went to Mexico to live. She left for two years. When she went she wrote occasionally, once in a while. In that time my grandmother took care of the kids all by herself.

My grandmother also had an income from a sawmill that she bought from the compensation when her son died in the Second World War.

We didn't have it all that bad, we had a weekly income. She cared for all of my aunt's children. When my aunt came back she brought a little girl. She had a little girl for this Mexican guy. She came back and she had to go back to the same way of life. She left the baby again and went off. My grandmother took care. Again me and Sarah were taking care of these children. So then it was only me and Sarah who were the two oldest and then four small kids. We went to school. We went to high school. Sarah came out of second form and she got pregnant and had Annie. She was still at home at the time. So again I took care of Annie most of the time because she went to work.

Irma: Almost the same kind of cycle?

Evelyn: The pattern, uh-huh. So it was the same thing. Annie was attached to me because most of the time. Sarah [her mother] was out. She worked all day.

Irma: What kind of work did they do?

Evelyn: She worked at a store. When she got pregnant with her second child that is when she went to live with this guy, Annie's father. They didn't marry right away until after the last child. She had three boys. She left home after she got pregnant after the second child, and my grandmother said no, this is it. [My grandmother] spoke to the boy; he was willing to take her home but didn't want to marry right away. They went to live.

As I listened to Evelyn, her story was replete with vivid illustrations of the patterns of behavior that form the economic-sexual cycle. Sarah, Evelyn's cousin, models herself after her mother and seems to expect that her grandmother will support her in the same way. She then mimics her mother's course in life: working, relying upon kin to take care of her children, continuing to be sexually active, and becoming pregnant again. Because her kin network provides her with basic support, there is little to motivate the father of her children to assume any financial responsibility for his offspring. Sarah's life, in this respect, acquires the neatness of a self-fulfilling, cyclical prophecy: adaptive strategies reproduced by both mother and daughter. As for Evelyn, without her own mother to set an example, her life too becomes guided, to a large degree, by the actions of her aunt and cousin.

Evelyn: Now it was only me and my grandmother and these children, four children. I continued school and in third form I fell [got pregnant] also. That is when Alan also started coming around. In the beginning, when I first met Alan, everything looked bright and beautiful. After I got to know him I didn't like him. Then my grandmother liked him. So she encouraged him. He wrote a letter. She asked him to write a letter as a permission to visit the home. He did. Of course this was against his mother because his mother didn't like me. I was black.

Irma: And he is?

Evelyn: White.

Irma: Clear? [5]

Evelyn: Uh-hmm, yeah. It started in the beginning with just letter writing. We would write to each other. And then after he started to visit my home, I said no, this isn't my choice. He was too jealous because we had about eleven girls in my class who were always together, we did everything together.

That is because when we were going to school we separate ourselves from the Carib (Garifuna) people. It was eleven Creole girls. Our fights in school would be that because if we were taught by a Carib teacher, she would pick on us all the time. Then if we were taught by a Creole teacher, she would try to separate us, so as to socialize with everybody. She wouldn't favor us. She would say it is not right that you separate yourself. We would always have fights in class concerning this because then if one of our girls, one Creole girl, would quarrel with a Carib girl then everybody would just . . . , but they always outnumbered us so we were no match for them. It just continued all through the years.

Irma: Why the separation? What difference do you see?

Evelyn: There is no difference, but it's from our parents because in our home my grandmother would—it's from way back. It's from generations and generations. When my grandmother talk about Garifuna, she would say they are cannibals. She would talk of them like they are inferior and then we grew up with that. We were born in it. So we always felt that we were better. I know it was wrong but it happened. That was the life we lived and even in high school we continued the same thing.

Irma: So you wouldn't interact, you wouldn't consider marrying a Garifuna?

Evelyn: No I couldn't, even then. No. We were taught that because we are all human we were to bid them the hour of the day and be nice to them to a certain extent but there is a boundary. We grew up with that. I don't know if it is worldwide, but if one of her grandchildren would fall in love with somebody, they would come and say grandmother this is my future. This is my fiancée, meet him and then she would ask what is his background? Who is his [family]? That is the first thing she would [ask]. Sometimes we would ask her, what's the difference?

She would say there is! And then she would rant and rave. She would say look in the fowl yard: we have ducks, we have chickens, we have turkeys. Do you see the ducks breeding for the turkey? I said no. She said and those are birds. We are people we are different. So we grow up with that.

I consider myself from childhood as a person. I like another person despite the fact of all of that. I had my friends. I had my Garifuna friends that I get along with. But of course they weren't allowed home to get too close. When I started high school, two different occasions two Garifuna boys tried to be friendly with me and write me letters and so. I didn't respond because first of all, you know, it's like who are you to try to come and get close to me? I shun them. That didn't last.

At present I grow out of it. Or try to grow out of it, [laughing] to a certain extent. That is what makes sense. Even after I got married I still had that slight resentment. After I started studying my Bible then it started to fade away because I consider in the eyes of God we are all one. That resentment started to weaken.

Evelyn's discussion illustrates how stereotypes are produced not only through cultural beliefs but may be reinforced, or challenged, by what Louise Lamphere calls "mediating institutions" such as schools.[6] And although these issues of color, "race," and ethnicity are important to Evelyn, it is her stormy courtship and subsequent marriage to her husband that provide the continuity of her narrative. Yet even that aspect of her life is shaped by the complexities of color, "race," and ethnicity.

Evelyn: I left off when we were talking about falling in love with Alan and being close to my friends, the girls I used to associate with. When I started to respond to his letters, he started to make more demands, like I don't want to see you with those girls; they are too rowdy.

When he hit that, that is when I said no. I won't allow that. These are my friends. How can you want to separate me from my friends? But then at this time even though I started to put my foot down and say, well, I don't like you, I don't want you to come to my house, I don't want you to visit me, he had already gotten close to my grandmother and my grandmother liked him.

Irma: Why do you think she liked him?

Evelyn: Because she didn't like black people. She was black. My grandmother was jet black, but didn't like [it]. . . . [S]he'd always say, you—you find somebody blacker than you, uglier you, then you would produce a monkey. That is what she would tell us. So then I think that is why she encouraged Alan. But still on the other hand she welcomed Alan, but she didn't welcome this American guy. Two different times, two white American who fell in love with me and went to my home. She said no way! She said a white man has no love for a nigger! That was her response, so then that was off. Done. No.

Ethnic relations in Belize are marked by certain boundaries that affect friendships as well as mate selection. Thus while people of different ethnic groups may interact casually on a daily basis, their actions do not go beyond the realm of common courtesy into friendship or love. These lines seem less of an issue for the younger generation, whose members mingle more freely. Evelyn's recognition of the contradictory messages communicated to her as a child is particularly striking, for it demonstrates that such biases are not innate but socially constructed over a long period of time. Her grandmother inculcates a sense of difference between Creoles and Garifuna that suggests that any intermingling between the two groups is a transgression of nature. Evelyn is thus confronted early in her life with the perspectives of a grandmother who posits that Garifuna are as different from Creole as ducks are from turkeys and the views of a Creole teacher who encourages her to socialize with everyone equally. Not only is Evelyn enculturated into the social role of a woman, but she learns her ethnicity as well, absorbing without question the biases and boundaries that tell her what it means to be a Creole woman.

These attitudes determine and dictate who is an acceptable man for Evelyn to marry. Her "freedom" to make a life choice is based upon the values she has internalized and her desire to please her grandmother, the only parental figure she has ever known. Her grandmother's own self-hatred reflects the colonial (British) heritage as well as the contradictory image of Belize has constructed of itself as on the one hand an extremely heterogeneous and tolerant country and on the other hand a country with ethnic boundaries and social rules that accompany them. That everyone seems to know and respect the rules reduces tensions on an everyday level, but they do exist and they do affect the decisions that individuals make in all aspects of their lives.

Evelyn is not the only one being enculturated and learning to act out social roles. Alan also has learned how to present himself as an acceptable male. In his case, this means showing one face to Evelyn and a different face to her grandmother.

> *Evelyn:* Between this time when I was going to school. Alan used to come to my house every day. As long as he was in town he would be at my home. Then I started to hate him more and more because he was spying on me. He was jealous. I couldn't say anything about him because I would tell my grandmother, well, you don't know Alan. Oh no, she would say. No way. He is not like that. Alan is a nice boy. He is well mannered. Everything good. So this kept on for over a year.

Evelyn learns early in her relationship that Alan is possessive and wants to control her mobility, yet her narrative suggests that she believed herself unable to challenge the relationship. As long as her grandmother approved of him, she felt she had little choice in the matter. Alan thus consciously manipulates the power of Evelyn's grandmother to influence her. There are many more interesting anecdotes that Evelyn relates about her courtship with Alan, including her attempts to encourage an American suitor in hopes of dissuading Alan from pursuing her. She is unsuccessful. In addition, she is dismissed from

school for a prank and goes to work for her friend Elana. Although they are
the same age, Evelyn is more skilled than her friend. As she describes it:

Evelyn: I went to work until school opened again. So I went to work [with
Elana] for almost eight months the first time. That is when Elana had
her first baby.

Irma: And she was how old?

Evelyn: Fourteen years. I am months older than her but because we were raised
up the hard way, I know how to cook and wash, I know everything. Her
husband, he hired me. When the baby up, I help her with the baby. I
wash early in the morning and in the afternoon I help him in the shop.
I was getting kind of comfortable with that kind of life. I was making
ten dollars a week. That was a lot of money in my days. I used to give
my grandmother five dollars, and I keep five. With five I saved and buy
my clothes. You know I have money to spend. I was getting really comfortable and I didn't want to go back to school.

Finally I made up my mind. I said I am going back. That is how I
went back to school. The changes started when the next year, I went to
school. It was in December. We had this school party. The first teacher
that I said had fell in love with me, he had left. This was another one
who came. He would say you have such great eyes and stuff like that. I
didn't think it was anything, just flattery. In that same Christmas season, he stopped by one day and he brought me a Christmas card and it
was not one you would give to a friend. I think that was the beginning
of that one again.

Well it didn't take Alan long to pick up on that [the fact that the
teacher was interested in Evelyn]. He didn't last too long because the
next day [Alan] went and told my grandmother. So before it could ever
start, my grandmother was right there with all sorts of threats. If I ever
hear you are walking with this person or talking to this person what I
think I will do is send you to your mom. When I heard that, at this point
I did want to continue school. I was very smart in school at that time.
In months I was the top student in my class. When she said that well,
I'm going to take care of the school, this is the second time this is happening, I will just send you off to your mother, that wasn't my choice
so I said no it won't happen again. I won't speak to him. Then Alan was
happy again because I'm free. After that, well, then I had almost given
up on that part. Of course everyday my grandmother would say something nice about Alan. Oh just a nice boy. He is so lonely. He would
make such a nice husband.

So now here I am kind of rejecting Alan. My grandmother on one
side pressuring me. [My cousin] started having an affair with Alan. I
think it is between jealousy or not jealousy. I don't know what term to
use for it.

Irma: Like get back at her?

Evelyn: Uh-huh. Well I could win this time and that's when I went all the way and got pregnant.

Evelyn's life unfolds almost like a soap opera drama. She gives in to Alan's persistent attention out of adolescent feelings of jealousy, possession, and, I think, frustration that nothing could ever change. In this part of our interview she went on to talk about traveling to Mango Creek, where she worked for an American family. The job introduced her to the life of a domestic servant who is overworked and underpaid, though for a young girl any amount of money seemed enough. She did not realize she was pregnant when she left home but when she did find out, she feared telling her grandmother.

Evelyn: I took over two people's job because there was this woman who was washing and one cooking. When I went there [Mango Creek] it was just me alone. [My uncle] went to this woman and suggested that she pay me more. The woman said, Evelyn is young, what will she do with all that money? I was kind of satisfied, twelve dollars meant a lot to me. In that time you could do a lot with twelve dollars. A yard of cloth, good material, it cost like $1.50, print was $.45, so it went a long way. I stayed there for almost two months working during the summer vacation but it was then that I found out I was pregnant.

So I had two choices, whether to stay on and just continue working for the summer since I wasn't going back to school, or come home. My grandmother wrote and said she missed me, I must come home. Of course I didn't tell her anything, I wrote Alan. Alan went and told her. When I came they both knew what was my destiny.

As Evelyn describes it, her destiny is not hers to make. Everyone knows what it is except her. She is too young to marry, and Alan is under age. She therefore falls into the same pattern as her cousin and her aunt, residing with her grandmother until circumstances change. During this period her grandmother takes charge of the baby and Evelyn goes to work again.

Evelyn: Even after we got married I stayed with her for company's sake. She needed someone to be near. After [the baby] was born, she took this baby over for herself. Like I wasn't involved in this child rearing at all. She did everything, except I would wash. That is about it: she feeds the baby, she takes all day, even to sleep—she wants to be asleep with her. My aunt would go there and say you are old, you aren't supposed to have this baby sleeping with you. This child will weaken you. She will suck your strength or something to that effect. My grandmother was insistent. She said I don't, well she wouldn't curse, she had a version the same as I don't give a blast. This is my grandchild and I am going to raise her how I want.

> [My baby] got attached to her too. In this same time Elana had her
> third baby now and [her husband] asked me if I could come and help
> Elana in the home and at the same time around his store.

Like many women in Belize who find themselves wanting to or needing
to work, Evelyn relies upon the skills she has learned as a young girl under her
grandmother's tutelage and refined while working as a domestic in Mango
Creek. Yet because these skills are so directly linked to household tasks, they
limit the employment options open to women like Evelyn.

The ambiguous life usually associated with being a domestic worker is
mediated to a large extent in Evelyn's case by the fact that her employer is her
best friend Elana or, more precisely, Elana's husband. In the context of this
employment situation, Evelyn is expected to do housework, which Elana
seems unprepared for—probably as a result of having left her own family at
such an early age—but Evelyn also provides companionship for her friend.
This latter dimension changes the dynamics of their interaction and seems to
have eliminated the tensions often found in the social relations between domestic workers and employers.[7]

Change: Its Catalysts and Obstacles

Evelyn: I worked there for a year. From since [Elana's son] was born, eleven
months. I quit when I got married. Because when I got married and
Alan moved in with us, it was too demanding. I got pregnant with [my
second child, a son] so then I quit and stayed home. The first year we
got married and Alan got a job at the post office. He worked for almost
two years. Then right there within that time he started this alcohol problem. He didn't stay. He just kept going from one job to another because
it was then that every time he get settled in a job, he goes on a binge,
just forgets about work. And by the time he gets up he lost his job.

Evelyn's unplanned pregnancy is the first major change in her life that in
her words establishes her "destiny." It is to be the first of many. Events happen in her life one right after another, and her response for the most part is
the passive acceptance she demonstrated earlier in her childhood, when her
cousin used to harass her.

This coping pattern of passive acceptance enables Evelyn to endure and
keep functioning under the most difficult of circumstances: these include an
alcoholic and erratically employed husband; working while raising two small
children; her husband's marital infidelity; family tensions among her relatives
when her grandmother attempts to bribe her out of a dysfunctional marriage
with the promise of an inheritance; and her grandmother's favoring of Evelyn's first child, who is light-skinned, over the second one, who is darker, on

the basis of a deeply rooted color bias. These are just a few examples of the events in Evelyn's life cycle, discussed in detail in the next few sections, that seem to prevent her from taking any action on her own behalf.

Evelyn: [My daughter] was still her favorite, her baby. I could see how she treats both of them. Of course in this time when [Alan] started drinking that is when my grandmother started to turn the other cheek. She didn't like him anymore. Everyday she would nag about leaving him or what are you doing with this guy. She made me different promises. She would say, well, if you leave him at this point, I will give you the house. I will sign the [business] over in your name.

Because I knew Alan was insistent too I didn't bother because I knew even if I had, well, my grandmother was getting sick at this time. She was really going down. I would say this stemmed from this pressure—Alan was drinking. So then I said, well, if I move out it would be less on her because she wouldn't see or hear when he comes home drunk. So I decided to move right beside Alan's mother's house. We moved in. The problem was still there. He didn't change. He continued.

I didn't have a mother to turn to. My mom had enough of her own. My father isn't the type. He wasn't a father because growing up I could recall and at Christmastime and my shoes would be out or I needed new clothes and my grandmother would say [to my father], I want someone to buy new clothes for this child. He would plain say no, or I don't have money or something, you know. He never maintain me nor contribute to my growing except he was a farmer and he would come down here, he would bring some plantain, some ground food, stuff like that. That's about it.

So then, throughout my, when Alan was drinking, I was alone. I didn't go to nobody. I put up with it for ten years. And ten going into eleven, I said no, this is it. One of my cousin came down from the States, Sarah's sister. She said she heard about Alan's problem. She thinks the solution is I should leave. So I said I'll leave Alan, but then I need some help. But who would take care of the kids? So she said, well, the first thing for you to do is you need to take out your passport.

It was a hard decision for me to make. I said I'll see what's the effect. I'll tell Alan about it when he gets out. He was in the hospital at the time. So when he came out I said this will be enough of this scenario. I had enough. He said, well, like the only thing about him was you come across men that drink and you know rowdy, curse and quarrel and want to fight? He wasn't like that. He was the kind of alcoholic who would go out, get drunk, come in here and I'd be cursing and he would not say a word. I think when he comes home that's because he is really exhausted. All he wants is sleep, and he would sleep. Maybe at four in the morning he would sneak out. That is how he would do it. We didn't have any quarrel in the time he was drinking. No fights, no quarrels, he just well when he would come he would say, well, give me some soup.

So this last time I recall when I had decided I said, well, you know this is it. He was in the hospital and I think I had decided to tell him then. When I saw him I told him, I said Alan you better get strong. As soon as you come home, I forgot who I told him who was going to take care of the kids, but I'm leaving. He said where? I said I am going to the States. He said no, you can't do this. I said yes I can. Anyway this was the last time he was going to drink anyway because he quit for a long time.

Evelyn's threat to leave Alan is a turning point for both of them. For her, it marks the first time she has openly confronted him about his problem. For Alan, Evelyn's decision is the first time that she has given him some indication of what type of behavior she will not tolerate. Evelyn delays her plans to leave. Their truce lasts almost a year and then Alan has a relapse. He joins Alcoholics Anonymous and remains sober another year. During this time, he leaves his stable job as a civil servant and opens a business—a restaurant/bar. Within a few months, however, Alan is drinking again. This time Alan believes he is near death and confesses to having an affair with one of Evelyn's good friends.

Evelyn: In that same time he was running his business he ended up in the hospital. This time I don't know if this was what really change him.

I think this [other] guy must be eighteen and twenty, he couldn't be older than twenty. Some says he was taking Valium and drank liquor with it and he died that same morning. Alan was sitting there waiting for the doctor to arrive for his bed because now he is throwing up. This guy died in front of him. To top it off he had to go lie on that same bed.

While he was in the hospital the priest usually runs ward and would take confession from patients. I recall when he came back the day he said Evelyn do you know why I came home? I need to tell you something. I asked why? What do you have to tell me? He said, well, before I say, promise me that you will forgive me. I said yes I will forgive you, whatever it is. Now during all of our life together I have never had any problem with any affair. If anybody come and say I saw Alan with a girl, I wouldn't believe because he was not that type. He said promise me; well, I was confessing this morning, the priest took my confession. After he took my confession he said I will absolve you from your sins but [Alan] this will remain on your conscious unless you confess to your wife. So he said, well, I had an affair with your best friend.

Like many partners of alcoholics or victims of abuse, Evelyn is eager to believe in Alan's recovery. Any change he makes is sufficient to deter her from her plans to leave. Although we did not discuss this issue, her own feelings of having been abandoned as a child combined with her strong Catholic upbringing were most likely major factors in her willingness to ignore his behavior as long as he and she were able to maintain the semblance of a family. Further, because the community does not ostracize men like Alan, and indeed may sanction some of their behaviors, Evelyn is left with little institutional validation for her side of the situation, except among her women friends—and even here, she is betrayed by the friend who has an affair with Alan.

Throughout the interview I was struck by the candor with which Evelyn spoke about this part of her life. We had known each other for only a few months, yet she showed no inhibitions in discussing her situation. For me this seemed to fit in with the idea that women are more open about what men would consider to be "personal" matters. This contrasts with the unspoken folk rule in parts of the Western world that says people should keep their skeletons in the closet or their dirty linen hidden.

In American culture, it is this "rule" that has contributed to the silence about matters of sexual abuse (such as incest) and domestic violence. Victims are afraid to speak out for fear of public reprisal or reprimand while perpetrators feel safe that no one will learn about the indiscretions—because people don't want to know or discuss what are "private" or "family" matters, regardless of their severity. In Belize, however, some of the women I interviewed and encountered in the course of my research seemed uninhibited about discussing such matters among themselves. Generally the listeners were female relatives or close female friends.

Evelyn: After he told me this I still couldn't believe. [T]wo of his sisters came and told me the same story. Well, after that, the rumors started to come out and people started saying that this girl is pregnant for Alan. When the baby was born I was there. I went to her house. This time Alan came home and told me that she sent to him for money because her man that she was living with refused to give her any money because he said the child wasn't his. I said, why would she send to you for money? He is trying to be honest. He said, well, do you think maybe the child is mine? I said I would go see. So I did go. I went there and said I came to see this baby. Whether the child is his, he did say that she said the child is yours but she put it in the man's name she was living with. So up to now that still remains a mystery. That was the last time I spoke to her. We weren't friends anymore. She left and went to the States.

This was the beginning of a new era—Alan womanizing. Every new girl in town, he was to be the king of. He has to conquer that girl first before everybody. That is what he lived for at that point. Every new girl that comes, you know, rumors would go around: "I saw Alan at the dance with this girl or he was at this restaurant."

Alan's infidelities became more open. For herself, Evelyn maintains that during this period she was "too busy with my life, trying to make something of myself." Her ability to accomplish this was built upon skills she had developed on her own when she was confined to the house as a young mother. Years later she would convert these same domestic skills into wage labor in the United States,

The Life Course and Empowerment

> *Evelyn:* I started my sewing career when [the second child] was a baby; just before [my third] was born, that is when I really started. Since I had [the first baby], I used to sew just old pieces of fabric, pull the clothes out and rip them apart. Now I was really into sewing. I think I was too busy with myself to even care what he was doing and try and to something for myself and my kids. There were times that I would stay up. I would sew like, I would just go right through. I have hired a maid and I sewed from morning until sometimes two in the morning, I'm still sewing. I recall like thinking back I would sew like ten dresses a day.

Evelyn reflects upon what her life was like in the early phase of her marriage and upon the series of events and circumstances that led her to separate from Alan, rejoin him, and eventually begin what would be a series of journeys between Belize and the United States, initially accompanying Alan and later alone.

> *Evelyn:* I didn't work [then]. I guess that is the reason why I picked up sewing because it was something that I could have done right in the house. I didn't have any skills when I just got married. I used to take washing. I washed for his parents, for his mother, since [his family] had maids for everything. At that time all of their maids ran off with boys and left them without maids.
>
> At this time his mother got an operation and her business was going down. So she couldn't afford to pay a decent salary for any maid to come in. So since I was living right beside her I started washing for her. Washing and ironing. In those days it's not just wash and press, it's washing [and] what we used to call pressing just the clothes off the line. That is, like you press tee shirts, [but] blouses, shirts, pillow slips, those you have to put in starch. So then I used to do that for his mother for five dollars a week. I did it for almost two years and then she died. So after she died I still continued doing it a little. But then Alan didn't like the idea either.
>
> In my spare time apart from doing [laundry] I used to sew, learning on old pieces of scraps. That's how I got started. Not going to anybody either, because in my early marriage, Alan was very jealous. I couldn't

go out. A lot of things I couldn't do, a lot of restrictions. I came a long way and through a lot of changes. I couldn't wear pants, I had to wear my dress long.

[Alan] didn't want to work for nobody at this point. When one business would fail he would do another business—all bars. Why did I leave him? It was because of a girl who had come from Belize [City]. He was getting to the point now that he did what he wanted to do and he didn't care who saw. He was just, his life was run by what he wanted. He would come home and eat, sometimes he didn't come home. He had his bar. He would come home almost every night past one o'clock. He wasn't there for the children, not at all.

During this time we had been quarreling a lot. Because I guess he comes home, I'm tired, he has a life of his own. We are in two different lives. So we didn't communicate a lot. We didn't see eye to eye. He had given previous to this, he had given me a thousand dollars to start a business.[8]

I started a grocery business by the drugstore. My business grew. With his actions I decided this isn't for me. I'll just leave him. So I packed my stuff. When I left him he was quite upset. He was his father's eyeball. So his father would come and talk to me and say why I'm leaving Alan? Try to cover up for him. I had made my mind. I said I will stick to my business and do what I have to do. I won't be bothered with him.

Anyway this was the same time this old guy said Evelyn the house is for sale. If you think you can raise the money then I will give you first preference because you are living [upstairs] and you have a business downstairs. So I said well give me two weeks. Alan kept coming back and forth and then I suggested to him, well, you know this house is for sale. Well, that's when we got together again. He sold the one we were living in. I put the balance down to buy the house. We bought that one and moved my business since I didn't have to rent. I didn't have a great expenditure. So everything I got I just put it into assets. It kept growing and growing.

This time [Alan] didn't have any kind of business. He chose to be free. One week he's in Belize [City]. He was just having fun with the kind of life he was living from one girl to the other. I was too busy again with my life, taking care of my business and my business was growing.

Women sometimes become involved in interpersonal relationships that are more economically based than romantic, as I discussed in chapter 7. Although Evelyn's relationship with her husband does not exactly fit the model I described, it is a variation on a theme. Alan has access to resources (land, credit and some prestige by virtue of his family's name and status in the community), and Evelyn is willing to remain in their relationship if he can provide her with the needed resources (even if sporadic) she needs to maintain herself and her family. In exchange, she ignores his infidelities and erratic work behavior. Though the situation is not ideal, Evelyn maintains the semblance of a family, while Alan may be able to use his family obligations as an excuse to extricate himself from sticky relationships. On the surface the marriage is functional.

When Alan receives an invitation from his sister to emigrate to the States, Evelyn is eager for him to go. She expects no financial support from him, but his absence will alleviate the stress she feels from his lifestyle. She is even willing to help pay for his ticket.

Evelyn: Because of what he was doing I said okay this is a chance [for him to go to the States] and I guess he could go and find a job. At least I have carried on with my life and I do what I want to do. I helped him with his ticket. I bought the ticket. He left. What he had, he needs spending money because it is a strange place. He left. And as sure as God made Moses, twelve days after, Alan was home.

It was a Saturday night. I had locked up late that night because it was usually a busy day. I was just closing the door when a truck stopped. I heard his voice and I couldn't believe it. When I looked out there, Alan jumped out. I said what are you doing here? He said I missed you first of all. I missed the kids. America is good but we need to go together. He said so much girls and he told me about all the tourists and skyscrapers. All the highlights about America.

I still didn't want to believe it because he was suggesting now, it was like a year ago he had bought this place [he was suggesting] that we sell the place and leave. I said no, because Alan's like that, he keeps changing. Nothing suits him for too long. Everytime he wants something different. He has a business this week, next week that business is over with. He just never stay long enough in something to see if it works. I said no. I am not giving up the business and I don't want to go to the States. Everyday he would keep bugging me about it.

When he see that I wasn't interested he decided to get violent. [He says to me] all this house is mine. I'll sell it and I will give you your share and I will take my share. I will leave and you will never see me again. At first I said no. I won't sell it because it was in both of our names. When he started nagging for real I said no this house isn't worth my happiness. Now at this point I was down to a hundred and ten pounds.

I said, well, do what you want with the house. He sold it and we went. I left four thousand dollars in the credit union. We took about four thousand and with the stock we left money for the kids and [someone] took care of the kids for us.

Two weeks after we were settled. I went on an interview for a job. He said this isn't my life Evelyn I think I want to go back to Belize. Now this time I am saying you are going back? I'm not going—we just sold our house; we sold the business. Going back to what? He said we would survive. Remember I have a truck back home. I said yes that is a truck, we can't live in a truck. He said we will make money off the truck and then we will rent a house. I said no you go. I'm not going. He left. He left [and] he came back [to Belize].

Irma: And you stayed? So this was your first trip to the States?

Evelyn pauses in the interview to buy sweet buns from a little boy who sells them. It is late evening and she yells to one of her children to "get one basket with a cloth" and continues as if no interruption had occurred.

Evelyn: Yes. I was lucky because two weeks after I settled, my cousin's sister was working with these people and someone had a test-tube baby. So five of us went on this interview. I said this is my first trip to the States, I have no experience. I was very pessimistic about this job. After the interview the woman told me well, Evelyn, I can't give you an answer right away, I will call you tomorrow. When she called the next day she said I want you to start on Monday. Now Alan didn't left as yet. He said you stay and work, but I am not staying here. I don't like this place. Now [Alan] hated everything about the States. All along he loved the States and now he doesn't like it. I said, well, go and I will stay. I stayed on and lived with them. I did a live-in job.

Irma: The first time you stayed for how long?

Evelyn: Eleven months.

Irma: And how did you feel about leaving your kids?

Evelyn: It was very hard. It's my first time leaving them. I think that most of all why America didn't, I didn't have that fever [to go the States]. With all the hardship, with all the misfortune, with all that I went through [in my marriage], I still couldn't make up that mind to leave them. When I had left, I had left with this intention: I said if things work out, because now I had reached a point to where I said that my marriage isn't working. I need to do something, you know, drastic. I need some changes in my life. So I said probably if I leave. I spoke to my family and they said what they could do is help me get the kids over one by one and I could resettle in New York. So I saw it as, that was my . . .

Irma: Goal?

Evelyn: Uh-huh. In eleven months that I was there Alan made three or four different trips. He would stay two weeks in the States and be back and forth.

Irma: Where did he get all the money? Was he working?

Evelyn: No. He had a truck that was running. [Also] the woman that I work with, she gave me money. She would say, "I know you are married and there are times that you feel lonely," because of course I would sit down and tell her all my life story. Sometimes Alan would call and she would hear us talking back and forth and she suspected that he wanted me to go back. So then she did everything to make him happy. So what she would do, she would give me money to send him for a ticket. She would say Evelyn here is five hundred extra. Send this to Alan so he can come and visit you. I was illegal [at this time].

Alan knows that I really loved the children. That would be the one thing to bring me back. This time [my youngest] had gotten sick and he called and said that [she] is running a fever regularly and they don't know what it is. So then I got [the lady who watched them and she says] yes she is running a fever, that is when I decided to come back. Now when [my employer] came home I told her about it. I said I am going home. She said why. I said because my baby is sick. She said well, Evelyn, I can give you money so that they can take the baby to Belize City. Let her see the best doctor.

Before I had made my mind to leave. We called and she was feeling a little better but by this time I had made up my mind that I had missed them and wanted to come home. She offered me three thousand dollars [She said] if you stay I will give you a bonus. This isn't your pay. Just stay for one month more, I will give you a bonus of three thousand. I said no. My mind was made up, I wanted to come home. So that is the first time I came back.

[Alan] started his same nonsense all over again. Like I came back to the same old story. I told him this time I am going on too. He sold something and gave me a thousand dollars again. He said do something for yourself. I chose to go to Belize [City] because with my past businesses I usually end up having a lot of credits, people are owing me. I blame it on everybody knowing me, and I am sympathetic and things.

Irma: Soft touch?

Evelyn: Uh-huh. It is hard to say no to especially friends and somebody poor. Somebody comes to you and says please could you give some flour [for] my kids, so it is hard to say no, so that is how a lot of people got away with it. I'm going to the City. I'll move to Belize. I'll open a business there and see how it goes. It was working.

Irma: What kind of business?

Evelyn: I opened a saloon and a restaurant together. I stayed there for six months and everything was working. I did make it to a certain extent, [but] [t]here were a lot of thieves. Then Alan wanted me to come back to [Lemongrass]. Now this time he was running his bar again. I didn't want to come but he kept insisting you better come home.

This time my mother was taking care of the children for the first time. I had three of hers. My sister Alice, her brother, and a nephew. So now I had eleven children.

At this point in her story, I am struck by how much Evelyn's life begins to mirror that of her grandmother, who also supported an extended household on her own. Evelyn moves back home and sets up a business. The year is 1984. Her good fortune, however, is short-lived. In a fire that destroys her home, she loses all her clothes and other material items and has to start over again.

Evelyn: Fire was already in the ceiling. We saved nothing, nothing, nothing. This was a time that I had a lot of things because all the time I was in the States I bought a lot of sheets and towels and curtains and household stuff—our house was well put together. We were completely burned out. Nothing was saved. One thing that saved was a dish pan. That's because we ran to the well and got some water. The fire lasted about forty-five minutes.

We left from there and went to stay at my brother's. But he was miserable. He's a miserable guy, always fighting with his woman, so I didn't stay too long. To top that off they made some contribution around town. But people always think that, I don't know if it's Alan's lifestyle, [but] every person asked to give say Alan has money, he's rich. On the contribution list from this whole town, all they collected was a hundred and seventy-nine dollars. That is all they got.

The house wasn't insured so we were left almost penniless. He had his little business and then I had my little business. But right then my business started to deteriorate because I had to buy [school] books, I had to buy clothes. It start going down until it almost went to nothing. When I saw that, well, it was going down for real, I asked a guy to take it over for me. He said he didn't have the money. I said, well, I am going to the States. With this stock I have here, you could start. With the money you have you could invest it and then you have a business of your own.

Within a two-year period, Evelyn's life is filled with tremendous change. Her way of coping both personally and financially is to become one of the many Belizean émigrés to the United States, living with relatives first in New York and later in Chicago.[9] Many Belizeans travel either legally or illegally to the United States to work for short periods (two to three months) in order to earn quick money. They rely upon a network of relatives and friends to find them jobs and also maintain contact with past employers who have been satisfied with their services and will rehire them or refer them to friends. Some of these international workers go with appropriate visas, but many end up staying past their visa deadlines or entering the country illegally. Once in the United States, they join workers from all over the Caribbean and Mexico who make up the ranks of a huge unskilled or semiskilled labor force. Many of them are women like Evelyn who find jobs as domestic workers (nannies, cooks, maids) in which they sometimes suffer from not only low wages but humiliating living or work conditions. Many do not speak out for fear of reprisal.[10] Because they are often illegal workers, they are at the mercy of their employers. And although they eke out what most Americans would consider only a meager wage, it is enough to allow them to sustain themselves in deplorable conditions in the United States and still send home remittances to sustain their extended household. For most, there is something waiting for them upon their return home. This was not the case for Evelyn; in her absence, Alan goes on a selling venture once again.

Evelyn: I didn't get one blessed thing out of the business. Nothing. He sold everything or almost everything. I went to the States for six months. When I came back he handed me one pigtail bucket of goods. He said this is what is left from the business. Anyway I took it because there was something that I could use like thread and stuff in there. I started over again.

Now this time that I went to the States I was in Texas.[11] I went about September in 1985. That time I stayed six months. After six months I came back. I started sewing again. I don't think I stayed a year, because I went back again. I went back in 1986. I stayed six months again.

Irma: And was this just to get away or was it a way to make money?

Evelyn: Both. There was time now both to get away and also to make money, because at this time no business, mostly sewing I depended on. I didn't stay long that time either. I went down to Texas and I worked with a psychiatrist. The woman was nice, the man was crazy. I stayed about two months with them and then I went back. Well, like every job, the people didn't suit me.

When I went back to New York, the minute I went back I got a job that same week, but this was with a woman who was very prejudiced and segregated. She was the one who told me that I am not allowed to eat at their table and stuff like that. I stayed with her two weeks. In that two weeks I picked up my passage money and I was ready to head back home. I guess because of the job experience I didn't stay the expected time. So I came back and I, what I did? I sew, stayed home and sew.

Irma: And when did you start thinking about bringing your sewing outside the home?

Evelyn: October of last year [1990]. So I stayed on again. I stay again [in Belize] and I sewed a little and watch how things were going. Just living from day to day.

During this period of traveling back and forth to the States, Evelyn worked on the seamstress skills for which she was noted by the time I met her. By then she had a small shop, with two young women (one Garifuna and the other Maya) working for her. Evelyn did all the cutting. She could look at a style or listen to a description of what someone wanted and was able to cut a pattern with virtually no guides. Within a week after my arrival in Lemongrass, Evelyn moved into a shop on Main Street, near the sea. There she increased her stock, beginning to carry ready-made clothes for which most Belizeans express a preference. In addition, she began to make ready-made clothes under her own label.

She also expanded her inventory to carry T-shirts, for the few tourists who peruse the stores in town but rarely buy anything, and a vast assortment of other dry goods. It seems that in Lemongrass, stores survive best if they have a little bit of everything, because people rarely shop with one item in mind. If a store carries shoes, underwear, deodorant, clothing, and make-up, the shopper only has to make one stop and is likely to return there again. Some of the other stores that carry clothes also carry groceries as well.[12]

> *Evelyn:* Now before I had come back from this last trip, then I went again. I went in 1986. Four different times I gone. I worked in New Jersey the last time.
>
> *Irma:* So your last trip was in 1988?
>
> *Evelyn:* Uh-huh.

Evelyn gives me a detailed description of her travels between 1984 and 1988. Her narrative provides the essential context that I was lacking when we first met. I recall on our first visit that I left with the impression that for all her being a small-town person, Evelyn was very well traveled. In our initial conversations, Evelyn told me about her trips and the jobs at which she had worked. Although it wasn't clear when she first told me, I now understood that the trips represented both an escape from the domestic turmoil in which she lived and the opportunity to earn money quickly.

On her last trip, which began in 1988, Evelyn stayed for almost two and a half years. She began to follow her earlier plan of bringing her children over one by one. Her two oldest daughters were already living in the States, having followed her pattern of working as live-in domestics as well as going to school. Evelyn sent for her oldest son, who went to work for an uncle in New York. She moved into an apartment and began the process of trying to get her papers legalized. At one point, her employer was transferred to Boston. The family made her a generous offer to move with them. Eventually she talked to her children, who all came for a visit, and decided to move to Boston from New York. This settling down, however, had an adverse effect on her husband.

> *Evelyn:* This time Alan is back and forth. He wants me to come home. This time I was insistent. I had made up my mind, I am not coming back. It is over, because now this time when he came and visit I said no, I put up with your shit over the years, this is what I want. I settled in. Well,

he saw it for himself and then he must have said, well, I'm on the losing side this time.

Everything he did; he tried all different fronts. He even moved in with a girl. Maybe he must have said, well, if I did this she will hurry and come back when she hears this. Nothing didn't move me then. Anyway this girl that he moved in with got pregnant. He came and he told me about it. I said that is good. Go and live your life. I'll be happy for you if things work out. He said Evelyn, I can't believe I am actually hearing these words. You have changed. I said, well, it is a part of life. I change over the years. I am changed because now, this is the first time I don't care what you do. At first he would give me an ultimatum, he said if you don't come by the end of next month I will put somebody in the house with the kids, and then he knew I would jump. But this time I didn't. Well, when he saw that he was on the losing side, he decided to report me to Immigration, which he did.

Having been identified to Immigration as an illegal alien by her husband, Evelyn continued her legal battle to stay in the United States, fortunately with the support of her employers. Despite her efforts, the law required that she leave the country until her case was reviewed. Just before her return, Alan made one last trip to the States to convince Evelyn to come back to him. During this final visit he was finally confronted by his children about his behavior.

Evelyn: Well we had a big fight. It started he was very nervous. The same time now he started tell me [my oldest daughter] intervened and she told him throw out our years. She think it's time to quit. She started telling him what she had in mind. What she had wanted to tell him a long time ago. When she started he couldn't take it. He got up and started hitting her. When he started that [my son] came and they jump on him.

He got real angry and violent. We came out of our apartment and went upstairs to our friends. He came up and burst the window with a piece of iron. He made a wreck of the whole front. The woman had called the police and they cuffed him. The apartment was full of police and the ambulance outside. I guess they came with the intention of finding this violent [man]; [instead,] they found [him] sipping beer, taking his high blood pressure. They said is this the guy who did all of this? We said yes. [They said] how could you change so quick? Here you are taking your high blood pressure.

They look at me and asked me what do you want? I said just let him pick up his stuff. I want him to leave and ask him not to come back here no more. He said do you hear that? He said yes I will do that. [The police told him] if we ever hear you come as close as the corner of this block we will throw you in jail. They said what about the damage, do you want us to sue for damages? I said no. I'll pay. So he left.

After he left, he didn't go straight to his sister's. They took him a couple blocks away. I guess they put him on a subway. He called a taxi and went to the nearest phone booth and called and called. He said he was cold and freezing. From there he called and first it was regrets. Then he called and wanted forgiveness. Anyway he didn't stay. He stayed on about two weeks after that and he came back home [to Belize].

Of course I had this case pending [on my immigration status]. I didn't get that letter until after he left that trip. I'm in Boston now, the case is pending. I went to court. The same attorney, he defended me. The judge said is three months enough for you to get yourself together before we give you a voluntary departure? I said yes. Well then I had made up my mind to come home because I saw now I would have to leave.

Irma: So you would have to leave the country anyway?

Evelyn: Yes. I would either be a fugitive; you know a lot of people get caught and get these letters and just run. I said no, I will do it legally because my papers are on file. I spoke to the other attorney I had in New Jersey and he said I advise you to leave. Once you leave voluntary you have hopes of coming back because the paper is progressing. I left three months after that, the ending of July.

Evelyn had just been back in Belize for six months when we met. At that time she was just about to expand her sewing business into a full shop. She had also just been elected president of the local chapter of Women Against Violence. Like Rose and Zola, Evelyn also seemed to find solace in her participation in a women's group. Safa confirms this dimension of women's groups and draws from the examples of women's collective action in Latin America. She comments: "Participation in these movements has apparently led to greater self-esteem and recognition by women of their rights."[13] This aspect of women's groups is discussed more thoroughly in chapter 9.

Institutionalizing Change

Irma: When did you become involved in Women Against Violence?

Evelyn: In 1990.

Irma: So you just got back?

Evelyn: Recently.

Irma: And why?

Evelyn: Because I saw the need for it. The experience I had in the past. First of all the protection. Why I stayed on in America was after the same old women that I told you I worked for that had the bed and breakfast, we talked a lot. She would tell me about all the rights and she gave me different phone numbers. She gave me pamphlets and things. She told me about the protection women have in America. That's why I decided to get involved. Because I live it.

Because if it was here that such home violence took place, you know the cops would never—there were times when I went to the police station with blood running from my mouth, and they would say Mrs. ———, that's wife and husband affair and we don't want to get involved. That's what you would hear. That's domestic violence.

Irma: What are women's options? Is divorce an option, or separation?

Evelyn: Divorce is something almost unheard of in this country until the past two years when a law came out that both parties doesn't have to agree on the issue. Two different laws concerning [that] came out. That's when things started to change a little but in the past divorce wasn't an issue then.

That was just a word, not an option. As for domestic violence most people live with it.

In contrast to her experience in United States, where the police assisted her when Alan became violent, in Belize Evelyn, like Zola, can cite striking examples from her own life in which the male-dominated bureaucracy has created a safe environment for perpetrators of domestic violence, in effect ignoring the rights and safety of the victim completely.[14] Further, Evelyn's knowledge of those laws that help women is a direct result of her participation in Woman Against Violence. Most of the Lemongrass women I questioned, however, knew little about the laws or how they might directly affect them. In response to the question "It is true that there are laws in Belize today that help you as a woman," of the 57 women surveyed, 18 (or 37 percent) had no knowledge of any such laws. Although the majority of women surveyed felt there were laws in the country that helped women, they could not identify any specific one. Among this latter group, most had a general knowledge that there were laws on divorce, rape, and employment, but they were often unaware of how they might use this information on their own behalf. The most pressing issue for women at the time of my study in 1991 was domestic violence. There was then no specific legislation that prohibited it as a distinct form of assault.

Irma: So you think [domestic violence is] common?

Evelyn: It's very common. And to some point it has become a way of life, you know. Women accept it. There are some women who, well, most women, you would see them with their swollen face or black and blue eyes. And they would actually cover up. [A friend] would say, well, you got hurt, how did this happen? They would cover up and say I fell down or some lie. They hide the man.

Like Zola, Evelyn also has intimate knowledge of the secrecy and fear that surround domestic violence and become part of the cycle.

Irma: Is it that they fear more violence is going to happen and there is no safe place for them to go?

Evelyn: That's the greatest issue. At least that was in my case. Because you go to [your husband] with lines like I'm going to the cops. [His] answer would be I don't care if you go to the cops or not, or also it will just get worse and stuff like that. Men know that they can do these things and get away with it, so it just happens.

Irma: What other kinds of abuse do you think women face besides physical? Mental, emotional?

Evelyn: Mental, emotional.

Irma: What forms do they take?

Evelyn: Most Belizean men think life should revolve around them. It's what they want you to do. Like a woman doesn't have say. Like for instance last night I wanted to go that dance. Alan didn't want to go. If I had said, well, I'm going, then that would be a big fuss. A woman doesn't have a rights to a certain extent. You only have so much rights.

Irma: Do you think you were brought up to accept that?

Evelyn: Yes. The man is the head of the house, yeah. Even though, well, I didn't face no man because my grandmother didn't have any man around, except my aunt had that guy for a short period of time. My mother had different children for different men. I think she never stayed long enough in any relationship or didn't take anything from any men. I guess as she found one man, got pregnant [and left], it wasn't what she [wanted] then.

Now where the violence lie, was where I saw it was with my father. My father is a cruel man. Everytime we visit him, or we'd be there for vacation, we would actually see [him beat] this woman, you know. When I say beat, it's not like a lash or giving a slap or so. He would actually—at that time she had long hair [down] her back—he would wrap that hair around his hand and pull her like the pigs. These scenes that you would see in cavemen, when they are dragging their woman behind them by the hair? These are things that I actually saw. Sometimes he would use a machete to lash her. He would use a machete scabbard that is a thick leather. He was a *cruel* man.

Sometimes in the midst of, you know she would be preparing our supper or making lunch, in the middle of that he would beat her. Then she was forced to, after getting this beating, I could see she was in pain, sometimes her nose would be bleeding, but she would be forced to finish our supper. With all the pain she's in, she was forced to do what he said, she's supposed to do it. And she had to do it.

There were times when he would come down to town, he would drink a little. He goes home very violent. He gets home, pulls out his gun, and just start firing. The kids have to take [cover]; once we had to sleep in the forest. He was a very *cruel* man.

Evelyn too learns early, from her intermittent contact with her father, that women have few choices and must acquiesce to men's violence and abuse. She learns that passivity is one strategy that women may deploy in their defense and for their survival. This model obviously affects the decisions Evelyn makes in response to the tensions, violence, and frustrations that emerge within her own marriage later in life. Without any other models to learn from, she has a hard time envisioning alternative responses or solutions.

Despite this lack of role models, Evelyn has developed a clear and insightful critique of the way powerfully entrenched gender roles and rules bind men and women to behavior norms that assume passive women and aggressive, authoritarian men, who are also the providers. In her analysis, she sees men as expending their energies trying to uphold the standards and feels that women are left with little choice in the matter. For her, so far, this is the way things are.

Irma: Do you think things are changing? Like your daughters? Do you think from what you see in Lemongrass, I mean you've lived in Lemongrass all your life, do you see change?

In asking this question, one I had also posed to Rose, I wanted to understand how much Evelyn was conscious of her own passive behavior and whether she reproduced her own circumstances by passing on this gender message to her daughters. I also wanted to see whether she believed that changing her personal circumstances was enough, or did she think that institutional changes were needed. Such a way of seeing the world is a major step toward social, rather than personal, transformation.

Her response indicates that she had given these matters a great deal of consideration and that her involvement in Women Against Violence was a conscious decision to address change at the societal and institutional level. Choosing to respond in this way was not without great personal risk, since the men in Lemongrass (including her spouse) and in the rest of Belize were openly hostile to an organization they viewed as intrusive. WAV uses public exposure as a threat in the face of a culture that believes that male authority as exemplified in domestic violence should remain secret. Breaking the web of silence is the organization's most powerful weapon. For women who carry this strategy over to their personal lives, it produces fear on the part of men and creates new levels of freedom and relief on the part of women.

Evelyn: Yeah, it is changing and it's changing a lot to an extent, I would say with the different groups and social departments and police on a whole. It is a different story from experiences that friends give me. It's not like before. You would go there and you do get justice.

Irma: So now there is more in terms of law and enforcement?

Evelyn: Yes.

Irma: Do you think the women's organizations have helped?

Evelyn: I would say it helped. It help a lot because for instance look at Elana. I think if this was like in the past, because [her husband] had divorced his previous wife to marry Elana, and you know he didn't have any problem at the time. But now whenever they would have any fuss that he would always mention oh you're in that group, WAV, so I'll do things the legal way. He would always bring up something to that effect.

Irma: What would you like to see changed in Belize? What changes would you like to see? With all these listening ears [laughing] over here? [Evelyn's children have all drifted inside the house by this time.]

Evelyn: For women? First I would say more protection, like a shelter. Where if things get out of control, a woman has somewhere to go to. That would be some consolation.

Irma: How would you manage something like that in Lemongrass? I mean, it is so tiny.

Evelyn: Well maybe the law would have to be involved. The man's like, well, okay, once the law gets involved, saying in this issue, well, you can't touch her and if you do they send you to jail. Making different demands on, I don't know. I think it will work, it depends on the law. You know you can't fight the law. Once it becomes law you know people just learn to live with it. At this point, despite the fact we have WAV, violence still exist and abuse, but you know there is just so much, you get educated by it. Maybe if men would get more involved in the organization, then they would see, well, this is what I am doing wrong or this is what we are doing wrong. But at this point men are more offended by the organization . . .

Irma: And they dislike it; they really do dislike it?

Evelyn: They do because they feel like it's interfering in their lives.

Irma: What about your sons; how do you teach your sons different?

Evelyn: Well I always use their father as an example and I say you are not supposed to act like him. That's not the way.

Irma: What's going to happen with WAV here in Lemongrass?

Evelyn: Well, if I happen to leave it should go on and maybe [the former president] would be willing to coordinate it once more. As soon as this hectic week is over, I will call a meeting and do suggestions like meeting a certain day every month. I hope that will work.

When I first broached the idea of studying women's grass-roots organizations in Belize, I started from a Western point of reference. My models of organizations assumed a consistent membership, a hierarchical structure within which a leader directed the group, and clear organizational aims and objectives. I found in Belize that while my model might have been suitable in the West, it could not always be found in the exact same form in Belize.

Irma: It seems like it is real hard to have an organization where people are trying to live their lives; I mean, it takes time.

Evelyn: It does; it does if it is worth it.

Irma: What do you get from the organization? How does it make you feel?

Evelyn: First of all it is a big challenge for me because at least at this point in my life, because in days past the way Alan used to act I would never dream of even maybe going to one of those meetings. Because he would say, well, it is either you go and stay there or stay [here]. Life is changing. He has made a big change in our life.

Irma: It sounds like you've made more of a big change.

Evelyn: Maybe on both sides. But I think it all came about when I decided, because I think all along, during our marriage he thinks of himself as this great catch. Like I couldn't live without him. So when I had showed him that I could do it and of course I keep saying, well, if things don't work out I can leave. We don't have to be with each other. At first like I wouldn't be rebellious. If he talks to me too hard I'd cry. I was really a softy when it comes to him. I would never think about answering him. No, I used to fear him in one way. He really felt supreme until I made my stand and said, well, this is what I am going to do. He has talked to different friends and they would tell me you know something Evelyn, Alan said that you don't care about him anymore or you don't love him or stuff like that. This is what he would tell his close friends. I'm glad that he feels that way, because at least now he doesn't feel that he has me covered.

At that point Evelyn laughingly whispered, "He's coming," as Alan returned to the house. I stopped the tape for a brief moment and the interview went in a different direction. We talked about some of the tensions between the national office of WAV and the local chapter in Lemongrass, which feels it does not receive many of the benefits that other districts have.

Irma: So there is a difference between the local and the national office?

Evelyn: Yes. They feel like everything going to Belize [City] and the last meeting [someone] came down [from the national and] she said Corozal got this TV and video. At this time I had become a member but I haven't went to many of their meetings. Usually the timing wasn't right. A lot of people I heard was interested in the beginning. But you know news flies fast. They said that [someone] had offered them the little room by the church. They didn't use it because it didn't have a chair. And then they sent and asked [the national office] and they said that they could get some chairs. When they went for it, she gave it to some [other] group because they didn't come in time. And I think that is what discouraged the first set of people. At this point it has been hard to recruit them back again. Maybe this week I will see how much people in town and try to meet this week, one day.

Here I turned off the recorder because Alan had joined us at the table. Alan said in a joking way that he wanted to talk about "abused men." We talked briefly about his point of view. Later Evelyn and I continued our discussion. One topic that seemed to flow in and out of her narrative was the role religion played in her life.

Much of Evelyn's determination to go forward with her life and assist her children in building their dreams has been fostered by her religious beliefs. In some ways, she balances the difficulties in her life through her spiritual involvement. This emphasis on spiritual reward and fulfillment and an acceptance of secular trials and tribulations is a strategy often used by those who face harsh conditions in life. Religion as an adaptive and coping mechanism has been discussed by many anthropologists. Yet this perspective is not without its own set of limitations.

Evelyn: My mother would say is it religion or my belief? Apart from my belief, it has helped me over the years, because there came a certain time in my life that I believed deep down that if I didn't have the Bible to lean on I would go stark crazy. I needed it not only as a support but also using different [strategies], like forgiveness. If I didn't have that I wouldn't be here with Alan.

In the beginning Alan did oppose. He fully opposed me studying [the Jehovah's Witnesses]. I couldn't attend meetings and I guess that's why I haven't committed myself. If he would go there and finds these people home studying with me, he would rebel and start throwing down things and cursing and then they would leave.[15]

It took me years of studying before I attended a meeting. He just wouldn't hear of it. The strange thing about it, when he did me all these evil things I would say to get him to overcome the hate he had for these people I would tell him it's only because I study the Bible that I can live with your wrongs. Then he started turning around. I started attending meetings.

Even in practicing religion, however, Evelyn faces constraints. Although she renounced Catholicism because of its restrictive nature, her interest in the beliefs espoused by the Jehovah's Witnesses carries some limitations as well. One, which has prevented her from actually joining the church she attends, is their prohibition against political involvement. Evelyn is well aware that should she become a Jehovah's Witness, she would have to relinquish her participation in women's groups and community affairs. She is not quite ready to do this and so instead faithfully attends her study group, just one step shy of absolute commitment.

Political Transformation

As was evident in both Zola's and Rose's narratives, change is a process, and its impact is different for each person. In Evelyn's case, she has altered her views of how she would act in certain circumstances, if given a second opportunity, but more important, she has conveyed this message to her children, especially her daughters. The two eldest have finished high school and continue to pursue advanced training. Of the younger six, at the time of the interview, only one son had graduated; the remaining sons were in various phases of leaving school either voluntarily or by request, as a result of poor attendance or lack of performance. The two younger girls continued to express greater interest in completing school than their brothers.

Like Zola, Evelyn also sees women's salvation as primarily internal. She believes in skill development and developing greater autonomy before entering into marriage as a long-term relationship.

Irma: If you could change something in your life as a woman, what would that be?

Evelyn: I wouldn't marry early first of all. I always advise my daughters, and this is because of my experience, make yourself into what you want to be. Then if you really want to marry, regardless of how long it takes, accomplish your goal, then settle down.

Irma: So do what they want to do first?

Evelyn: Yes.

Irma: Are there some dreams that you had that you weren't able to accomplish because you were a wife and mother?

Evelyn: Growing up as a kid I always had this yearning to be a teacher. I did had a couple months' experience in teaching, but then first of all I didn't graduate and I did this at an early age. I was only fifteen when I really had this experience. So I had gotten disappointed in the expectation of, I was young and easy also maybe because the kids took advantage of my soft heart, they were hard to control. So that kind of abolished that yearning. Apart from that, deep down I always reading different stories, persons like Florence Nightingale and Joan of Arc. I used to always and I still maintain it. I want my name to go on someway or the other. I want to be famous in some . . .

Irma: So that is what you are working on?

Evelyn: Yes. I still have dreams.

Given her vision, Evelyn's participation in WAV and her ongoing community involvement have already gained her a degree of status in the community where she lives. Her opinion is sought after, and she is actively involved in people's lives, especially in issues of domestic violence and sexual abuse.

Irma: What would you like to see changed for your daughters? Do you think that they are growing up in the same way that you did or do you think things are better or worse?

Evelyn: It's better in a sense that, well, I provide, I try my best to provide for them. And I didn't have that. Although my grandmother tried to help us there was still something lacking. All I want for them is to accomplish their dreams. Whatsoever they want to be, I support them fully. No holding back.

Community and Autonomy

At the conclusion of our interview Evelyn described some of the barriers that have stopped some women from participating in women's groups. Part of her explanation was supported by comments women had made to me in the context of the survey I conducted. However, she also pinpointed a different obstacle not usually discussed. This is the barrier of existing divisions within the community that polarize one group of individuals against another. In the case of Lemongrass, and Belize in general, organized political party politics represents such a divisive element. As mentioned earlier, Belize operates under a patron-client system. In effect, votes are used to elicit favors from politicians, and often resources are distributed along party lines. When a party is out of favor, one may find oneself jobless or without access to certain resources until the next election.

Another divisive element is alliances based on kinship or friendships. Where these exist, people are likely to take stances on an issue not on the basis of its merits but on the basis of how that particular issue affects their relationship with friends or kin. Ethnicity in some towns may also be a key variable that divides people. This was not the case in Lemongrass, where there is a high degree of ethnic intermixing, especially among the youth. Finally, differences in the membership's view of what the goal or vision of the organization should be can have far-reaching effects on the group's ability to recruit or may create the conditions for members to withdraw. As Evelyn describes, all of these elements determine the effectiveness of a group to create and maintain activities that are valuable to its members or to the community. Some of these aspects of women's group dynamics are discussed below in the context of Lemongrass; others will be explored more fully in the next chapter.

Irma: How hard is it to organize women? I mean to have a women's group?

Evelyn: It's kind of hard.

Irma: What do you think are some of the problems?

Evelyn: In a small town like this, things just like would happen, and then word spread fast. When I started that group we had about twelve people total. This is the [sewing] group that came over from Women Affairs that closed down. . . . I have all the names down in the book.

I had been directed to Evelyn's sewing group before I arrived in Lemongrass. The group was perceived by some staff members in the Department of Women's Affairs as being fairly organized. The resignation of the town's women's development officer (over what she says were political party politics) had left the women involved with her skills development program faltering. They had appealed to Evelyn, who had been hired by the DWA to give sewing lessons, to continue. Out of this specific activity had evolved a small group of women who eventually joined Evelyn when she became a member of Women Against Violence. They continued to take sewing lessons from her at the shop for about $5.00BZ a week, but much of the time was spent socializing.

Evelyn: Little things spark off conflict. . . . Miss Eleanor used to come. She has a close friend who is her *comadre* [comrade or friend]. When Mrs. Melendez [the wife of a high official in the PUP, the People's United Party] started to come to the place, I was passing one day and she told me she heard about this group. Her husband just got into the government and she needed company. She's bored and she asked me . . . is it political? I said no. She said okay, well, if it's not attached . . . [to any political party]. So she started coming. When she started coming that is when everything started drifting. First of all Mrs. Melendez is PUP and Miss Eleanor is UDP [United Democratic Party]. That break up people. That is one of the biggest separation here in this town—politics.

Irma: That really works here.

Evelyn: Even in death! You know you will actually hear people say, I'm not going to funeral, he's PUP. When Miss Eleanor saw that Mrs. Melendez started there, she quit. Now Mrs. Melendez is a heavy PUP [and] they know that I am UDP, but I don't practice. We raised up as at that time as UDP. So deep down you tend to [go along]; [but] I quit voting. You have it in your system.

[Mrs. Melendez] she know because like when little arguments, some political issue would come up, I pass small view. They know that I am UDP. So when Mrs. Melendez started, Miss Eleanor made it her duty and went to Mrs. Melendez's house and [asked] her if she is joining the group? She said yes. She said you know something, I would not advise you because I am quitting. All they talk at that place is politics. Well, since she said that, Mrs. Melendez came back and told me because we are friends from way back.

So when she told me, one day I did mention it [to the group]. I just said it openly. I said one thing class, I want this group to remain non-political. We aren't going to discuss religion, politics, not your personal lives in here. We will keep it mainly on what we are doing. Then [Miss Eleanor] must have [realized] and said, well [Mrs. Melendez] told me. She didn't come back. Since she didn't come, her *comadre* quit coming.

Evelyn goes on to report that conflict over how to use the money the group made from a collective project further divides the group. Some members favor taking their individual share; others want to use the money on a project that will benefit poor youth in the community. More women leave the group when they are unable to agree. Evelyn sees such conflicts as endemic to a community the size of Lemongrass.

Evelyn: In a small town it is hard to keep people organized because little things just make them break up, and word spread like wildfire. They just want a little thing to break up.

Another thing too people don't like for others to see someone getting ahead and making success. . . .

Evelyn here describes what Peter J. Wilson refers to as "crab antics."[16] Her words depict the dynamics of social relations within which certain individuals who lack the necessary resources for socioeconomic mobility either resent those who have it or covet whatever it is that brings it about. At the same time, those who have achieved socioeconomic status, but even more those who aspire to it, feel that they are being held back or resented by others who have not reached their level of success. This behavior pattern seems to characterize some of Belize's political interaction, and may be behind the highly personalized attacks on political party officials that are flung back and forth from one newspaper to another under the guise of keeping the public informed.

At the level of individual membership, the tenacity of party affiliations has been known to divide families and split up relationships. Thus Evelyn's friendship with Mrs. Melendez, which extends across oppositional party lines, is viewed by many in the community with suspicion. That the latter's husband has been a ruling party official with benefits generates envy as well. To some, this relationship is comprehensible only if they believe that Evelyn derives personal gain from the political privileges that Mrs. Melendez has had access to. Ironically, this is not the case. Although Evelyn is a seamstress, Mrs. Melendez only occasionally utilizes her services, and Evelyn, well aware of public opinion, refrains from asking any favors.

Reflections

Much of what Evelyn recounted to me about her life was so clear and concise that to offer commentary seems redundant. Many of the themes that appear in her story also emerged in the narratives of Rose and Zola. Evelyn describes quite vividly the limitations of women's roles, the use of domestic violence as a means to control women, the conflict between women's personal aspirations and community and societal expectations, and finally the double standard of behavior that exists for men and women.

What stands out about Evelyn's narrative is her tolerance for the numerous crises that have marked her life course—she has endured more in the first forty years of her life than many individuals encounter during their entire lifetime. Her coping strategies, moreover, are largely self-taught. From youth to adulthood, she has had few reliable models to learn from. Her coping patterns include passive acceptance (resignation) and withdrawal (trips to the United States), yet she maintains a high level of energy and commitment to work in the face of great odds. She is not daunted by failure, and is able to recoup quickly and move forward. What the narratives by Evelyn, Rose, and Zola reveal is the enormous capacity some individuals have for dealing creatively with the constraints that govern their lives.

When I first interviewed Evelyn in 1991, she seemed hopeful about her marriage on the basis of observable changes in Alan's behavior.

> *Evelyn:* He changed a lot over the years, you know, no drinking. He used to be a smoker. With the doctor's advice he threw away the cigarettes. His biggest problem was womanizing. I won't say [he] give it up because I don't know, but he seemed to kind of give up womanizing. Of course this is after sitting and listening to [his] confessions. . . . Deep down Alan feel himself very eligible and prince charming, that he cannot be resisted. When I put him down that was a great hurt to him. He just couldn't understand. He would sit there and accuse me of having an affair. You don't want me because you have another man. That is why you don't want me. I said no, it is not that. It is just that I don't want you because I had enough. I could live without that. It took him a long time to really get his act together.
>
> When I had come back from the States I was still angry at him. He kept dogging me at my mother's house. Because my mother was sick, I didn't want him to go down and make scenes. So that is one of the

reasons I came back. Just one month he would say. Just one month I
need Evelyn. If you don't see any changes then you can do what you
want with me. I said okay I will give you one month. Since then he's
trying.

The tenuousness of Alan's ability to fulfill his promise subsequently became
evident. Some months after I left Lemongrass and Belize, Evelyn wrote to say
Alan had begun his extramarital affairs once more. Her response was to file
for a legal separation. The action had an effect—Alan begged her before the
magistrate to give him another chance. Evelyn conceded, in part for her own
personal reasons that are tied to her upbringing and her beliefs about the
sanctity of marriage vows, in part owing to the social reality that Belizean
courts make it extremely difficult to get a separation or a divorce. Their goal
is to preserve the marriage, and so women especially are encouraged to be
tolerant and forgiving. If an individual plaintiff does not want to humiliate the
person she is separating from, she can easily be persuaded by the court to try
again.

When I returned to Lemongrass a year later in 1992, Evelyn and Alan
seemed to have declared a temporary truce. On the surface, their lives continued to operate in the same manner as they had before; Evelyn was still busy
with her shop and making plans to move to a different location. I asked her
why she had decided to remain in the marriage. "Habit," was her only response. But she followed this up immediately by saying that she was not afraid
to leave after their youngest child completed high school. This gives her four
or five more years. In the meantime, she continues to prepare herself for whatever comes along—she now has a multiple-year visa that enables her to travel
back and forth between Belize and the United States, and she anxiously awaits
being awarded a green card, which would allow her to work legally. This,
coupled with her earnings from the shop, provides the means to get away
whenever the situation warrants it. Her trips to the States are not only an
escape but can also be read in a different way. Leaving Belize whenever the
circumstances exceed her patience may be construed as her own personal form
of resistance, although she might hesitate to define her actions in this manner.

In Evelyn's narrative, I noted a progression in her demeanor, in her perception of her situation, and in her responses to specific events. At the beginning of her story, she presented herself as a passive participant; by the end of
the narrative, she was an active agent. I see this shift as directly linked to Evelyn's broader social exposure to alternative models of behavior in the United
States. The refinement of this shift into a political perspective, however, can
be traced to her involvement in women's groups in Belize.

Chapter 9

The Quest for Female Autonomy: Women's Groups in Belize

> Power concedes nothing without a demand. It never did and it never will.   —Frederick Douglass, *Life and Writings*

They come, young and old, with a host of children straggling behind them. They are married, common-law, divorced, widowed, and single. They arrive from places with names like Guinea Grass, Chan Pine Ridge, Barranco, Mango Creek, Crooked Tree, San Antonio, or Big Falls. Some of the women must rise before 5:00 A.M. to catch the bus that passes through their village or town at that unseemly hour. Others have been up early to cook rice or bake fresh tortillas for husbands who will not tolerate leftovers. They wash, cook, and clean house at the approach of dawn so that there can be no excuse to detain them.

They come, wrapping a few tortillas or pieces of Creole bread in a towel to snack on along the way, knowing that a free lunch will be served. Some have never heard of a "workshop" before. Most are shy; they stick together and speak in Mopan, Ketchi, Creole, or Spanish. A few come because they want to share their knowledge and experiences. They are women who have earned the right to speak (like Zola and Evelyn), who can now say they have *trained* their husbands to eat leftover rice; trained their men to accept the fact that once every three months they will attend this meeting for women. They ignore the male comments implying that when a bunch of women get together no good can come of it; they refute the male belief that women only come together to gossip; and they tolerate the male fear that women coming together means that soon the woman will try to wear the pants—"She de get upstart now." [1]

These women, Creole, Mestizo, Maya, Garifuna, East Indian, and mixed, play games designed by the facilitator to put them at ease and get them to learn something about one another. When lunch comes they organize themselves to serve food so that everyone gets a plate and some can take home leftovers. They listen eagerly to the workshop presenter, who is a younger, single woman, educated in the States. After listening for a while, they think maybe she is not so different. She tells them how she too was trained to cook and wash clothes by hand, even if she had a washing machine. She encourages them to participate with this simple statement: "Every idea is a good idea." She lets them know that she truly believes women have valuable contributions to make.

In every district, they meet in schools, at rooms over bars, in community centers, wherever space is made available. They travel far because they believe in this entity called a women's group. They are members of organizations like the Belize Rural Women's Association, Belize Women Against Violence, Belize Family Life Association, Breast Is Best—national organizations, with local chapters, that have sprung up over the last twenty years, partly in response to specific community needs and partly as a result of the momentum generated by the United Nations Decade for Women. And for years they have formed their own community or village groups with names like the Lufuliria Women's Group, Sandy Beach Women's Cooperative Society, Ltd., Maura Lopez Designer Group, Columbia Women's Group, Caledonia Women's Group, Orange Walk Rotary Ann, and Xunantunich Cultural Committee. [2]

The catalyst that brought each group into existence is often obscure. It may have been the vision of an individual woman, who has long since left the group but whose spirit remains; it may have been the persistence of domestic violence in the community and the bravery of a few women who dared to speak out against it; or it may have been a desire to change local women's economic status. I am told, however, that many came in the beginning because they felt the need to come together with other women, just to talk, to learn—there seems to be security in numbers.

While the reasons for the formation of these women's groups in Belize are varied and their origins often obscured, what is evident is that throughout the country women are engaging in collective action. They come together not just to share stories but also to act together on behalf of specific social goals such as increasing women's representation in the labor force, obtaining maintenance from fathers for children born outside of marriage, gaining better housing, and setting up job training to prepare women for employment.

Under the auspices of women's forums, where they meet to discuss issues ranging from domestic violence to child care to teenage pregnancy, women's groups create the structures and emotional support that will foster each member's journey toward her own autonomy.

The common thread in the narratives of Rose, Zola, and Evelyn is their involvement in such women's groups. In a community of kindred spirits, they have found a source that motivates each of them to some level of personal action as well as community concern. Women's groups in Belize, as elsewhere in the world, are often the catalyst that some women need in order to become active agents in their own lives.

Understanding Women's Groups in Belize

As the narratives of Rose, Zola, and Evelyn, illustrate, women's groups play an important role in women's lives. They provide the means by which some women, for the first time, may gain insight into the reasons for their circumstances. For those who have already acquired this knowledge, women's groups form a base from which to mount specific strategies to address problems as they see them.

In my study of women's groups I often found that women were more likely to organize around issues that were specific to their community or that affected their social roles as wives and mothers and might also help them in the activities they performed in the domestic sphere.[3] This merger of domestic concerns and social action is consistent with Johanna Brenner and Barbara Laslett's assertion that it was "through voluntary association that grew out of their responsibilities for social reproduction (for managing homes and raising children . . . [that] women developed the political resources necessary for collective action."[4] I found women in Belize similarly occupied with issues related to social reproduction and the management of their roles as wives, partners, and mothers. Their lives, and thus the organizations they formed, were concerned with school activities, job skills training, cultural preservation, domestic violence, religious training and recruitment, political party politics, family health, nutrition, and personal relationships.

Yet these groups do not exist in a vacuum; they are subject to community and individual scrutiny. Because some of the issues they deal with are controversial (and sometimes contested), the groups are not always free to openly advocate their interest in certain subjects. They fear reprisal by men and isolation by their communities. As a result, they rely upon subversive strategies, capitalizing upon the fact that it is far easier for women to gain permission or approval to come together to practice or improve their crocheting skills or cooking techniques than to gather to discuss domestic violence or sexual abuse. To forestall confrontations or disapproval of their activities, women's groups rally together around traditional domestic topics, relegating the discussion of controversial subjects to the privacy of their meetings.

In this respect, the groups embody dual messages—one public and acceptable, the other private and subversive. In Belize, even breast feeding becomes a negotiated arena and can entail a "trickster's" approach to social action. In Breast Is Best, young girls are (publicly) educated by older women about breast-feeding techniques, while the subversive agenda emphasizes personal health care, self-esteem, assertiveness, and leadership skills. Moreover, the organization encourages mothers, especially young, unmarried ones, to return to school or acquire job training as a means of challenging the low social expectations for their future set by society. Despite the social relevance, and sometimes the ramifications, of such agendas, few of the women's groups I encountered describe themselves or their goals as "political," in the sense of having an expressed political agenda or ideology. Yet much of what goes on in these groups precisely fits Brenner and Laslett's definition of "political self-organization" as "any collective action in which women as activists and leaders define goals and construct strategies, [and] not only self-consciously feminist organizing."[5] From this point of view, those activities that call into question cultural practices or beliefs which tend to place women at a disadvantage and organizations that self-consciously develop strategies to change this situation must be viewed as political.

Women who participate in such groups sometimes incur great personal risks as they deviate from the traditional, nonparticipatory stance women are expected to assume in their communities—as Zola so poignantly explains in her narrative. I often heard men threaten those in women's groups, especially if they worked on the issues of domestic violence or family planning. One man went so far as to proclaim that if his wife persisted in her involvement in Women Against Violence, she would find herself in the midst of a new group, Women Without Husbands.

For those individuals who choose this unpredictable path to empowerment, their willingness to join these groups raises several critical questions: How do women develop the awareness that their lives are constrained by political, economic, and cultural structures or institutions in their communities or their country when historically they have been granted limited access to explicit knowledge about the inner workings of these structures? How do women decide to commit themselves as activists to political self-organizing? Put another way, how do women reach this understanding of their position as victims or of their marginal status in the society? And finally, what rouses them to do something about it?

There is no single or model explanation that can answer these questions.

Rather, individual women construct solutions, fashion a *raison d'être* out of a complex fabric of events and historical context. Rose's, Zola's, and Evelyn's narratives show that one way this process of cognition or political epiphany occurs is through specific circumstances or experiences that take place in the individual's life. If such events emerge in the form of a crisis, they may push the individual to recognize her position as a marginal person, compelling her to take action—as in the case of Zola. For many women, however, crisis can be such a commonplace occurrence that they are desensitized and learn to adapt themselves to fit the situation. For them, women's groups serve as environments that breed changing visions of how women should be treated and that encourage transformation to take place at the personal level as well as in both the community and individual homes. Safa reaches a similar conclusion in her discussion of women's social movements in Latin America: "Women's participation in social movements has produced changes in Latin American women's self-definition."[6]

This interpretation is consistent with other recent research on women's groups in Latin America and other parts of the world. In the context of Latin America, Teresa Pires de Rio Caldeira contends that women's groups serve as multifaceted sites of negotiation and resistance. One of the most important contributions such groups make, she finds, is to provide women with "new forms of socializing" "These movements, while generating new forms of external confrontation, are internally creating new forms of socializing and changing the patterns of interpersonal relations and social roles, especially of gender roles."[7] Brenner and Laslett support the view that women's groups create anew or strengthen existing "information networks, social solidarities, and self-definitions."[8] They go further in asserting that these aspects are essential elements that facilitate women's political mobilization.

Drawing from this literature, I would argue that the significance of women's groups in Belize is their ability to transform matters of personal conflict into matters of political debate.[9] They accomplish this first by drawing upon women's concerns with issues related directly to social reproduction—that is, those "activities and attitudes, behaviors and emotions, and responsibilities and relationships directly involved in maintaining life on a daily basis and inter-generationally."[10] Women's groups work to circumvent these constraints of gender, which make women almost exclusively responsible for the management of social reproduction, through the use of specific strategies.

Not only do these strategies nurture the individual and collective identities of women, but in the process they challenge the culture of gender that surrounds them. Three strategies are most effective:

1. Breaking the social isolation and silence that separates women from one another;

2. Enhancing women's personal identities by developing their self-esteem, encouraging assertiveness, and building leadership skills; and
3. Creating a safe environment where women can learn about and gain greater understanding of their rights as individuals and citizens.

The outcome or "value" of these strategies can only be measured by the benefits women say they derive from their participation. In the following responses to my question, "How does being in a women's group make you feel?" women talk about the importance of their involvement.

[I feel] that women are no longer in the background; that I am not the only one with a particular problem.

[It] makes me feel that women are important and play an important [part] in life and that we are special.

Well, it makes me feel like I have some people I can share my problem with; someone who will listen to my problems and give me suggestions. Well, makes me feel good!

I feel very confident that what we're doing is not in vain; [we] help ourselves, children, and the community. I learn a lot about people, their behavior—that teach me and I learn from that.

Makes you feel good. Helps you have a strong self-esteem to [talk] to women like yourself. When you talk to other women you get courage to solve your problem.

These comments affirm the far-reaching impact of women's groups on individual lives beyond the momentary existence of the organizations. As Rose, Zola, and Evelyn have all shown, participation in these groups enables women to forge bonds of solidarity, educate themselves, and gain a confidence in their own abilities that has been seriously eroded. These results suggest that the potential or impact of a women's group reaches beyond the boundaries of individual experiences to effectively challenge or change the larger community and its culture of gender.

There is nothing uniquely "Belizean" in these features of women's groups or the ramifications of their collective action. Rather, similar to women's organizations in the 1960s in the United States, Belizean women's groups have made "consciousness raising" their first order of business. Major differences, however, exist: in Belize, it is poor, often uneducated, women who are the primary impetus behind grass-roots organizations. Further, such groups rarely begin as a consequence of some explicit, confrontational political ideology; instead, they emerge out of what Sonia Alvarez, drawing upon Maxine Molyneux, terms "practical gender concerns."[11] This is not to say that such groups lack a clear understanding of their position as women; rather, their "political" demands are couched in the rhetoric of everyday life. Nonetheless, their concerns are as compelling as those who use explicitly political language and make ideological challenges, and the state's or community's response to their presence has the same political and social implications and ramifications.

Another major difference is the absence of the class/"race" critique leveled against the women's movement in the United States by poor (mostly nonwhite) women.[12] They have argued that the name "women's movement" has been a euphemism for "white, middle-class women's movement." This is not the case in Belize. Whatever differences may divide women there, they are not as rigidly related to social class and "race"/ethnicity as in the United States. However, most Belizean organizations emerge out of local or community contexts and thus display some degree of homogeneity in terms of class and ethnicity, primarily because residential districts tend to be ethnically concentrated. In these situations, the articulation of concerns is by those women who live in the communities. Although there are no specific data that describe the composition of women's groups, my own research suggests that where ethnic and class differences exist, groups with specific ethnic constituencies coexist side by side and some groups even manage to draw members from across these social barriers. It must be kept in mind that Belize has a relatively small number of women who might be considered middle class in terms of income, occupation, and education. The ability to mobilize across the existing social class barriers is especially evident in the membership of national nongovernmental organizations like BIB, BFLA, and BRWA, which make every attempt to be representative. They accomplish this most often by forming district (local) chapters, drawing on their members' knowledge of their own communities to mobilize neighbors.

The success of grass-roots organizing in Belize can be attributed to several variables, including the country's small size, a general absence of rigid institutional and economic ethnic stratification, and the seeming absence of a hierarchical prestige system based purely on socioeconomic status. Further systematic investigation is needed to determine the degree to which social class is a salient feature of Belizean culture. In Belize, status and prestige are determined by multiple factors that can vary depending on the ethnic group. Among Creoles, family name, ethnicity, family background, education, occupation, political affiliation, and economic status seem to be important indicators of social status. Yet no single factor among these seems to be absolute, thus allowing considerable room in the society for negotiation and social mobility. This is especially true in the political arena, where party loyalty is a much more salient qualification for political office than experience, education, or political savvy. Individuals who have held high office run the gamut from highly educated professionals to those with minimal formal education but strong political alliances. As a result of this open system, the strict class and racial barriers that have impeded effective organizing among women in the United States do not appear to present the same obstacles in this small country. In 1991 in Belize, only 7 percent of adult females earned at least $8,640BZ per year and 84 percent of all adult women earned less than $4,320BZ.[13] Those few women who are educated and rise above their modest origins often maintain strong ties to the communities into which they were born while keeping a foot on the ladder upward to the social class to which they aspire. According to the *Belize Report for the Fourth World Conference on Women*, the most stark differences in economic status are those between urban and rural women.[14]

Alternative Approaches to Explaining Women's Agency

In trying to understand what compels women to come together in groups, it is useful to review some of the literature on women's collective activities.[15] I have relied mostly on the research pertaining to Latin America, not only because of its geographic proximity to Belize and its sociocultural relevance, but also because I believe Alvarez and Caldeira, who focus on this region, have made major contributions toward diffusing the tensions that are inherent when researchers attempt to compare so-called Third World women's collective behavior with that of so-called First World women's behavior.[16]

The problem the literature poses is one of categories, meanings, and values. Specifically, women's behavior that does not conform to the standards prescribed by the white Western-centric feminist movement is sometimes interpreted as nonfeminist and regarded as reactionary. The result has been that the actions taken by women who lacked an explicitly political rhetoric or a clear feminist ideology have been viewed as "less than" the behavior of "real" feminists, who are generally represented in the literature as white, Western, middle class, and from developed countries.[17] Although much of this approach has been critiqued and altered, there are lingering tendencies to try to "find" feminism in whatever activities women are engaged.

Alvarez diffuses this conflict by expanding the categories available to us for describing, understanding, and critically evaluating women's collective activities. Her examination of the multiplicity of women's collective behavior in Brazil enables us to understand that there is no *single* cause to which we can attribute women's agency. Indeed, she allows for what might be termed "nonfeminist" female agency, which she sees as directed toward improving women's situation, but *within* the boundaries of the culture of gender in a particular society. According to Alvarez, these diverse approaches by women's groups to alleviating the problems women face may have a twin genesis.

Drawing upon Molyneux's work, she argues that some women are motivated by what she terms "strategic gender concerns," which are directly linked to feminist ideology and praxis, while others may act out of "practical gender concerns."[18] These latter actions tend to be organized around issues pertaining to family, self, and survival, or what Brenner and Laslett term "social reproduction" and what Sylvia Walby defines as "gender politics," a term she sees as encompassing "[women's] economic position and participation in collective action around the issues of equality in employment and education; child-care facilities; the provisions of contraception and abortion; women's financial and legal independence; sexual oppression and male violence against women."[19]

Thus matters related to the daily struggles of life such as garbage collection, access to adequate water supplies, affordable housing, sufficient medical care, or roads become the content of social agendas to be negotiated between individuals and communities or between communities and the state. Such issues are not women specific or "women centered," of course, because they affect all members of the community to varying degrees. One can argue, however, that women are more adversely affected by inadequate policies or resources related to the sustenance of daily life.

Alvarez argues that the difference between the two approaches to women's self-organization is a matter of ideology, style, and strategies. According to her analysis, "women-centered" or feminist women's groups start out in an oppositional mode. Women who operate from this standpoint intentionally seek to challenge the existing gender system because they question the way women are currently inserted into it.[20] In contrast, women who organize around "practical gender concerns" or from a "female" or "feminine" perspective do not necessarily begin with the idea of changing the existing gender system. This stance "grows out of and accepts prevailing feminine roles and asserts rights on the basis of those roles. . . . [F]eminine groups mobilize women around *gender-related* issues and concerns. The cost of living, for example, is one such issue. The sexual division of labor in most societies holds women responsible for managing family budgets and allocating family incomes to provide for basic necessities. Women, then, may organize to protest the rising cost of living because inflation undermines their ability to adequately feed, clothe, or house their family."[21] If change occurs, it is often unintentional, something Susan Hyatt labels "accidental activism."[22]

These models, which Alvarez presents as parallel rather than antagonistic ways to explain women's activism, demonstrate that women articulate their agency as a result of different personal or collective agendas.[23] Her models also help us to avoid privileging feminist social action over nonfeminist social action.

Finally, women's activism is also shaped by the meaning they attribute to their relationship to the culture of gender. As the literature points out, this meaning may complement the existing gender system or conflict with it. To better understand the other variables beyond women's personal experiences that shape collective action in Belize, it is important to examine the historical antecedents that might account for the large number of women's groups distributed throughout the country.

Women in the Footsteps of a Tradition

Pat Ellis has documented in her book *Women of the Caribbean* the long history of volunteer church and community organizations in the region.[24] She attributes to these groups the development of the leadership skills requisite for women's involvement in political self-organizing. Ellis tells us that "by their involvement in such groups many woman have gained valuable experiences and have developed skills in planning, organization, and leadership; others have improved their skills in child care, nutrition, and interpersonal relationships."[25]

In these groups, and through the social networks they created, she traces the origins of modern-day women's groups. Her findings are relevant to the case of Belize, which also has a long tradition of volunteer women's groups dating back to the early 1900s. Groups such as the Black Cross Nurses, founded in 1920 and revived in 1988 after a long hiatus, and the Wesley Women's League, affiliated with Wesley Church and founded in 1926, not only were social organizations but also provided ways for women of similar backgrounds (professional or religious) to meet without suspicion at a time when women's social interaction beyond the home was severely restricted.

My consultants tell me that in the early 1900s and to some extent today, it was thought inappropriate in Belize for women simply to "walk about." Given this, women's groups may have given women the means to do just that—walk about—thereby challenging the constraints on their mobility, yet in an acceptable fashion.

Another tradition that may also help to account for the growing number of women's groups in Belize today is women's involvement in party politics. Examples from Cuba, Nicaragua, and many African countries fighting for independence indicate that once the struggle for national liberation ceases, people begin to focus on other forms of oppression, such as class, gender, and ethnicity or other forms of difference used to stratify societies. Although no published scholarly account of a suffrage or equal rights movement among Belizean women currently exists, I have been told by consultants that the country has a long tradition of women's political activism. But it is a muted one that so far has been ignored by social historians and political scientists, who construct Belizean history as essentially androcentric. For example, a reading of Belize's political history by Assad Shoman gives little indication that women made any significant contributions to either the nationalist movement that emerged in the 1940s and led to the country's self-rule or the independence movement that led to Belize's constitutional independence in 1981.[26] Shoman provides an excellent history of party politics in Belize, but any insights he may have into the workings and minds of women as political figures are not included.

Unfortunately, though not surprisingly, the only evidence to be found of women's contributions to mainstream politics is in the pages of fiction. Zee Edgell's *Beka Lamb* is an account of women's participation in the two critical moments in Belize's political history: nationalism and independence. In an interview in 1991, Edgell spoke vividly of the active involvement of her grandmother, Inez Lamb Webster, and women like her. In the novel, the character Granny Ivey represents a composite of the women whom Edgell remembers from childhood. She recalls that it was the women who were in the street canvassing and getting men out of jail in the period between 1950 and 1981 during which Belize transformed itself from the British Honduras, a colony, to Belize, an independent nation. In a more recent interview, Edgell laments this muted history: "I think more women than men were in the streets supporting early leaders. They contributed money and labor. But apart from very token acknowledgment of their contributions, the women were not part of the dialogue. They weren't part of the discourse."[27]

In more contemporary times, women have yet to gain any but small accommodations in the political arena. Kathy Esquivel, wife of the former prime minister for the United Democratic Party and founder and first president of the National Women's Commission, explains this continuing marginalization by noting that political parties have not been aggressive in taking actions to encourage women. Parties lack motivation to do so because "they won't take any actions where they won't win. It is the nature of political parties to win." According to Esquivel, women have a better opportunity for political involvement at the local level on town boards and city councils. One problem women encounter when trying to establish themselves in the political arena, she says, is the entrenched notion of women as subordinate. Even when they do hold an office, they are not necessarily perceived as "in charge." Esquivel explains: "Other problems [women candidates might encounter] is marital status. Widow status or single is best. When married, [the husband] is seen as the one running it. It is not the same about men whose wives may not be liked, . . . it doesn't affect [the men in the same way]."[28] Safa comments further that women are excluded from traditional party politics not only as a result of how men view them but also as a result of how women themselves view the political arena: "The other reason women's social movements took place largely outside the realm of traditional political parties is that politics is seen as men's sphere, particularly by poor women. Latin American political parties traditionally have been dominated by men and have been seen as engaged in struggles for power in which the poor are essentially clients."[29]

One barrier to women's involvement in the political processes has to do with style and access to resources. According to Esquivel, male-dominated politics are individualistic and adversarial by design and run counter to the collective and participatory style of women. If women follow their own style of politics, their efforts are devalued as ineffective. Women also do not have sufficient resources with which to barter in a system where favors can determine the outcome of political decisions.

In Belize, where political power is regulated through a system of client patronage,[30] the system excludes women because, as Esquivel puts it, "women are never the people to whom political favors are owed." When being in a position to repay a political favor is crucial, women who lack the resources to do so begin at a severe disadvantage and never recover. The irony behind their exclusion from leadership positions is that women are often the bulwark of political parties during elections. Women's importance at this grass-roots level of voting has been well documented in a study by Myrtle Palacio.[31] Women, she finds, are the most active voters in both political parties. Leading politicians vigorously court them, without, however, having to relinquish any political space at the top level of their party to women or owing them political favors.

Although the PUP established both the "United Women's Group" and the "Women's Marshals" in its 1975 constitution, only since the late 1980s, perhaps in response to the increasing demands made by women within their political parties, has either the PUP or the UDP organized a women's component with the aim of involving women more as district candidates. There has been no research to evaluate if such (add-on or revitalized) components facilitate greater integration of women into the mainstream of the party process or if they are merely a strategy for placating the most vocal female elements in the political party. Women are becoming more visible as active participants in local village and town political processes, however, whether the women's units are singularly responsible or not. In 1993 the mayor of Dangriga, who was the first woman to hold such a position, was reelected to a second term. Examples like hers suggest some progress, though at times it is barely discernible.

Belize Women and the World of Global Feminism

The worldwide acceptance of the perspective that throughout much of the world women have been economically, politically, and socially subordinate was slow in taking hold. The difficult task of educating the world about the status of women fell to the United Nations, longtime defender of human rights issues, though women's rights did not become part of its agenda until 1975. For the next ten years the United Nations Decade for Women worked to convince the world's nations that women were a valuable resource.

Hilkka Pietila and Jeanne Vickers, in their study of this period, claim that the Decade was used as a vehicle by women throughout the world to mobilize around issues that encompassed not just equality with men and equal participation in society but also reproductive rights, equality in parenting responsibilities, recognition of women's domestic labor as a valuable contribution to state economies, and the eradication of cultural behavior and attitudes that suppressed women and often supported violence against them.[32] This made the Decade important not only as a source of information but as a catalyst for challenging long-held views on the role of women in their societies. Another important outcome of the Decade was the emergence of women's groups in urban and rural areas globally. The groups, often formed outside of mainstream political structures, became the incubators for ideas and activities related to the growth and development of women's self-esteem, women's economic autonomy, and greater participation by women in traditional political processes.

Although 1985 marked the formal end of the Decade for Women internationally, at the nation-state level this culmination was just the beginning. Drawing on the Decade's momentum, women around the world, often perceived by their communities as passive observers, were suddenly and persistently making demands about matters directly related to their subordinate status as women. A. Lynne Bolles describes this global phenomenon: "All over the world, the global movement of women has drawn many into the ranks of activism. Women are there on the front line because of their politics or their personal convictions to improve the quality of life for all in their homelands."[33]

Many of the demands and much of the activism and discussion took place under the auspices of women's groups. Women, in their frustration and disenchantment with traditional political parties, where they were barred from leadership levels, turned to one another for practical solutions to their dilemma. They drew upon the unique social bonds generated by what some have described as "women's culture"—and which I take to mean the common experiences and value system generated by women's involvement in social reproduction—to forge these political networks.[34] Temma Kaplan explains how this unified vision was possible:

> A sense of community that emerges from shared routines binds women to one another with their class and within their neighborhoods. The degree to which women carry out their work in community settings that bring them into contact with each other also influences what and how they think. Physical proximity—such as occurs in plazas, wash houses, markets, church entries, beauty parlors, and even female jails—contributes to the power of female communities. These loose networks facilitate the tight bonds that exhibit their strength in times of collective action.[35]

In Belize today, twenty years after the initial launching of the Decade for Women, at least forty-five local women's groups are currently active in the country according to a survey conducted in 1992.[36] Many seemed to have come into existence during these pivotal moments of the Decade or immediately thereafter. A few of these organizations owe their support to development projects, mostly funded by external sources, designed to integrate women socially and economically into their societies. The contemporary women's groups in Belize thus owe their origins not only to the traditions of volunteer, community service–oriented women's groups and women's muted involvement in the country's nationalist and independence movements but also to the globalization of women's issues that occurred in the United Nations Decade for Women and the emergence of women in development (WID) programs. A tangible example of the relationship between the Decade, Women in Development (WID) programs, and women's collective action in Belize is the birth of what is today called the Department of Women's Affairs, a government agency that was started in 1978.[37]

The Department of Women's Affairs

From 1981 to 1993, a woman served as the governor general of Belize. This figurehead position is more noted for its symbolism than its actual power, but her tenure was important nonetheless as the most obvious manifestation of women's increased visibility in the public, political arena. Prior to this time, few women held important positions. Between 1975 and 1993, there were only three women in government serving as heads of departments (two under both UDP and PUP governments and one under PUP).[38] In 1995 seven women were heads of departments, while two women held the prestigious and powerful posts of permanent secretary, positions that are some of the most prestigious in the Civil Service and that traditionally have been held exclusively by men.

The most up-to-date report on women's status, *The Belize Report for the Fourth World Conference on Women,* published by the government in 1994 for the 1995 international conference on women held in Bejing, provides the most complete summary of Belizean women's access to and participation in power and decision making. These two factors are viewed in the report as true "indicators" of women's integration into the country's social fabric. Examining Belize at three crucial points (1980, 1985, and 1994), the report concludes that "women continue to be heavily underrepresented in key decision-making positions within the public sector." [39] For example:

> At the parliamentary level, there was one woman in the House of Representatives in only the latter of those years. Over the same period, growth in the size of the House meant that the numbers of men grew from 17, to 27, and to 28 by 1994. In the 9-person Senate, to which members are appointed, there was one woman in each of 1980 and 1985, and 3 women in 1994, with the number of men correspondingly declining from 8 to 6. In 1994, the one female member of the lower house was also a Minister. At the same time, one of the six Ambassadorial posts is occupied by a female.

The report goes on to state that women are the largest clientele in family court but represent a very tiny fraction of those involved in "such areas as land dealings, investment matters, and business interests." These data support the conclusion that women have relatively little access to economic power. [40]

The slow but emerging presence of women in decision-making structures like the national government and village councils is not accidental but can be viewed as the direct result of efforts made over the last decade. It is a small number of women, however, who have access to education and/or professional training; they benefit the most. They represent an elite able to compete with men for the lucrative jobs in law and government. The majority of women in Belize, however, working within the government and outside, hold positions that require little or no training. According to the 1993 Labor Force Survey Report, 1,408 men were employed as professionals as opposed to 542 women. An almost equal number of women (1,815) were trained as technicians as men (1,653), but almost three times as many women (1,433) were trained as clerks as men (332) while six times as many men (6,440) were trained in crafts as women (1,058). These figures indicate that women are at a disadvantage from the moment they enter the work force. [41] This conclusion is echoed by the *Belize Report for the Fourth World Conference.* Similarly, it concludes that "women are more likely to occupy lower-paid jobs and that there is a greater labour market segmentation for women, between low-paid semi- and unskilled jobs and higher-paid professional and clerical occupations, than for men, thus dooming many women to no upward mobility in employment and, more importantly, few prospects for economic independence."[42]

In the late 1970s there was only one female department head in the Belizean government, and women more often found themselves relegated to clerical or semiprofessional positions. That period in the civil service was described by one professional woman in the following way: "Women in the country have always been the movers and shakers but were not given recognition. Things done at home like child rearing, making preserves, and arts and crafts were not recognized. Women could not go any further; they . . . [often] hit a glass ceiling." Interestingly, many of the women struggling to become part of the government establishment at that time did not begin as enlightened advocates of women's issues. For many, action preceded any inkling of what might be called "feminist consciousness" or "women-centered" ideology. A few women I spoke with traced their growing awareness of the need to make women's concerns a primary goal directly to the United Nations Decade for Women. Through seminars sponsored by the Decade, some of them became personally aware of the global dimensions of their specific concerns as women. A few were motivated to strive to create concrete programs.

The rest, as they say, is history. The first women's conference in Belize was held sometime in 1976. There are no newspaper articles or notices heralding the event—an indication of the minor significance ascribed to women's collective action at the time—nor are there any government archival records. Trying to reconstruct a history of the Department of Women's Affairs is difficult, because most of its archival files have been lost or discarded. Much of what I learned came through oral histories from individuals directly involved in the department's formation, current staff, and women in various communities who have worked with the department or participated in its programs over the years.

Asking women to speak about past attitudes today, however, is a sensitive issue. Although many recognize the value of documenting the history of women's struggle in the country, they express a reluctance to be overly critical given the progress they feel has been made. Despite this current ambivalence, there is no denying that the barriers women faced in government in the late 1970s and early 1980s were real and formidable. One woman recalls: "We had an uphill fight with the males in government and male politicians who felt threatened. We had to work hard to assure men that we were not a power movement, that we did not want to destroy their male ego, but wanted to work with them." Despite such obstacles, women inside the government as well as those actively involved in the political parties persevered. The Department of Women's Affairs is the tangible result of their efforts.[43]

Much has happened since the initiatives (first a Women's Desk in 1978, later a Women's Bureau in 1981) to create the department began. Today the director of the department is no longer subject to the whims of political parties; the post became pensioned (eligible for retirement benefits) sometime after 1991, lending it legitimacy and stability within a system that ebbs and flows on the basis of political alliances.[44]

A comprehensive and critical study of the Department of Women's Affairs is sorely needed. Even my brief interaction with the department and its staff between 1991 and 1992, however, suggested that some of the more recent changes that directly affect women's place in Belize's society can be attributed to the department's unique mission as a sort of government watchdog. Yet this very role also places it in an ambiguous position. Political parties in Belize, as is often true elsewhere, are very sensitive to criticism. By definition, the department's role is one of being critical of the status quo, as it adversely affects women. Attempting to accomplish this goal without alienating colleagues and politicians is a delicate task. Maintaining this tenuous balance may be precisely the reason why the department has not forged a stronger leadership role in seriously challenging the way in which women have been systematically excluded from positions of power in government and within the political parties—it is hard to bite the hand that feeds you.

Nor has the department been in a position to lobby for funds or support for new policies or programs that might radically alter women's limited access to economic and political power. The department emphasizes traditional training, child-care training, nutrition, and health education programs.[45] Programs that seek to educate women toward greater political participation seem to be, at the moment, outside the department's domain. This leaves its future wide open in terms of what it might be able to accomplish. Despite the obvious political and administrative constraints, the support the department gives and the legitimacy it lends to the numerous activities sponsored by the many nongovernmental women's groups throughout the country must be seen as a significant achievement.

The tactics utilized by nongovernmental groups to change women's position are often more confrontational than those of the department. Both approaches, in the context of Belize, seem to have their place, providing opportunities for those who wish to work within existing structures and those who choose to work outside of the mainstream to erode the continuing barriers of attitude, behavior, and institutional policies and practices that hamper women's access to key positions of power. For now, Belizean women seem to be more visible on all fronts, including in the government. The significance or import of their integration into the economic and political mainstream of Belizean society needs to be critically assessed.

A Tale of Two Local Women's Groups

Change of any kind is slowest at the national level. Yet as one Creole saying goes, "dis heah time no like befo' time"—women in Belize do think differently than their forebears, and some have put their ideas into action. This activism is more discernible in local women's groups, in which women operate without the constraints imposed by political parties. Where such groups are most effective is in their impact on the behaviors and attitudes of the communities in which members live, as both Zola and Evelyn suggest in their narratives.

The Orange Walk Community Group

Orange Walk is one of the fastest-growing towns in the north of Belize. With Mestizos (Spanish-speaking) making up well over half of the town's population, which stood at 11,014 in the 1991 census, it is culturally and linguistically homogeneous.

In 1992 the Orange Walk Community Group (OWCG) listed its membership at thirty women with a working core of ten women. In addition, some of the women had persuaded their husbands to participate, although the organization is still a women-centered group. The group meets on a fairly regular basis in Maria Rodriguez' home. Rodriguez recognizes certain basic features as essential to the "success" of her group. She says: "You have to have a core to be able to function. [My] house is very central to members. This is a secret to groups. You have to have a central location to meet, and have to know each other."

Consistent with Caldeira's theory, Rodriguez says she formed the group in 1985 initially to "socialize." She was able to bring women together primarily because of the stable character of her community. In response to my question about why the group has persisted for almost seven years, she responds: "This community is stable. Change is minimum. People own their own homes. All our members are in the neighborhood. The group has expanded a bit, but this has worked perfectly. It is perfect for getting information out." Since its inception, the group has broadened beyond its initial goal of socializing, which entailed planning trips to different parts of Belize for members and their friends and relatives and putting on a cultural show for the community.

Now, according to Rodriguez, the group's central aim is to develop women's leadership skills and community awareness. She is careful to distinguish her group and its objectives from the many women's groups throughout most of Belize: "My group has never been to teach [women] arts and crafts. Our goal was to become community-minded. Women can do arts and crafts if they want. Our goal is to educate women to become leaders in the community, give them basic training; nothing to frighten anyone [meaning men]. We educated women in speech training, encouraged them to get out of their shells, that they are leaders, that they have power." Here Rodriguez touches upon a crucial point about women's groups. Many tend to emphasize traditional domestic skills such as sewing, cooking, and child rearing as the primary aim of skill development. In doing so, they lock women into employment opportunities, such as domestic work, waitressing, or retail positions, that are historically undervalued, underpaid, and limited in their opportunity for future job mobility. This is one of the contradictions in focusing development projects on what women already know. Because women often perform domestic tasks as part of their responsibilities in social reproduction, focusing on such skills does not distract women from their daily chores and, thus, is less disruptive to their lives than other nondomestic activities. In fact, emphasizing homemaking skills is part of the subterfuge some groups use so that members' participation is condoned and they can escape the confines of their homes with the least amount of repercussions or reprisals.

What the OWCG illustrates is that "success" for a women's group must be internally defined. In this instance, Rodriguez uses fairly traditional criteria. She views the group's persistence, the regularity of meetings, and the relevance of its activities to the needs of the community as indicators of its success. But she also incorporates some of the standards of what Caldeira calls the "new politics" in making her assessment.[46] In Rodriguez' view, the group is successful because her members are more involved in other organizations as leaders, and some have become more active in party politics and the village council, although the OWCG intentionally divorces itself from any political party affiliation. In this respect, intentionally or not, this organization and others in Belize have become a bridge for women into the arena of public political participation. What Rodriguez sees as the main agenda for the group—creating leaders, women leaders—therefore assumes even greater significance: "Most women's groups are these that do things with their hands, but this group isn't. Our women have become leaders in other women's groups. They were trained that they are leaders." In this respect, the OWCG has successfully negotiated the difficult boundaries between women's groups and local political processes. Her members train themselves in how to make their issues the concern of the larger community. Rodriguez might argue that because they have selected issues that affect all members of the community, they are able to be heard.

Beyond this successful broadening of the group's concern into community concerns, one other indicator of a group's success is the degree to which it influences individual members' lives. Marta, a long-term member of the OWCG, talks about how she has personally gained from her participation:

I have changed; I gained more friends and can talk more freely. It is nice to be among people and see what you have in common. I've learned to share and cooperate. [I have] worked as secretary and treasurer in the group [and I like] to "put up" [save] money. When I say I will do things I will do them. [In my] other women's group, The Homemakers, [I have] been president and treasurer. [My] skills in [OWCG] helped [me] with The Homemakers. In [OWCG] we try to understand each other's problems. I like [OWCG] more [than The Homemakers] because we help others—I like that. The money we make is not for us but for others.

The history of the OWCG and Marta's personal testimony both seem to validate Caldeira's thesis that women's groups facilitate change within individuals, in interpersonal relations, and in gender roles. The OWCG has also challenged the culture of gender in Belize by inviting men to participate alongside them. In doing so, the group seeks to alter the typical male attitudes and behaviors that are automatically suspicious of and hostile toward women's groups and those activities where women come together.

Maria Rodriguez has a specific strategy she employs to break through this attitude. She says that by having couples socialize with each other, the group has managed to diffuse the typical male attitude of suspicion that surrounds women who do not stay at home in isolation. The result is a bond of common interests between each husband and wife, who often find themselves in opposition to each other in other aspects of their lives. In the context of these groups, men and women now work toward common goals that benefit their community.

To elicit how widespread the group's impact was in the community, I asked: "Do you think your group has changed what people think about women?" Rodriguez responds:

Definitely! You used to have problems where husband and wives never go anywhere together. Now they go as couples. The macho thing is not as strong. [We] have had problems when women talk about meetings with men in it, but we have managed to overcome that. . . . Through joking [in the meetings] women have their own way of getting across [their point] and they have straightened some lives. [Also] meeting with other couples and seeing how they live, and [we] have learned for women to talk to men and know nothing going on. People can see that now.

The OWCG represents a solid example of grass-roots achievement; it manages to combine traditional organizational forms with new styles of interaction. The group's activities center on issues that relate to women's everyday lives and that enhance the collective life of the community.

One of the most crucial dimensions of this group is its emphasis on self-reliance. The OWCG insists on fiscal autonomy and has not sought funding from Belize's national women's organizations. Indeed, the group is sometimes critical of those larger organizations, which it perceives as spendthrift. The group does not totally reject financial assistance, but it is eager to avoid relying on outside "handouts" to solve the community's needs.

The group is adamant in its rejection of the dependency syndrome for itself. Therefore, even when it receives external assistance, as was the case in a garden project funded by a Canadian organization, the group insists that those who participate in the activity also make a contribution, no matter how small. People had to pay a few dollars for the soil and seeds they received as part of the garden project, a feature Rodriguez firmly believes fosters self-respect and nurtures independence.

The Roaring Creek Women's Group

The Roaring Creek Women's Group (RCWG) is a study in contrasts. It is located in a small village of 842 people situated just over the bridge from Guanacaste Park and about five miles outside of the capital of Belize, Belmopan. The village of Roaring Creek is in the Cayo District, which is predominantly Mestizo (58 percent), although this western Cayo region as a whole has the third largest concentration of Creoles outside of Belize City and Stann Creek. The composition of community groups often parallels the ethnic composition of the communities within which they are located. Membership reflects either the homogenity of a neighborhood or its diversity, depending upon where the group is located. Most often, women's groups tend to be ethnically homogeneous. The RCWG was a Creole women's organization, founded in 1988 in a particular neighborhood. According to Lilly Waters, its Jamaican-born Belizean founder, the group came into existence because "a group of women decided that there was work to do in their village. They felt that the youth needed help and perhaps they could help feed and visit the elderly." By the time I interviewed Waters, the group's formal structure had dissolved. Several reasons may account for the group's demise. Similar to the Orange Walk Community Group, the RCWG also aimed to focus on community issues as the core of the group's vision; however, in this instance, that vision was not shared by all of the group's members. According to Waters: "What I tried to do is to do things that will interest them. It is sad to say they are not interested. They would do catering to make some money but [the women] were not interested in handicraft or sewing. Dis make me discouraged."

Although when the group started out, all agreed that "as women working together we could do things for betterment of ourselves," there were tremendous differences in the strategies various members felt should be used to accomplish this goal. And, over time, as in many organizations, it became increasingly apparent that members interpreted the goal differently as well. For example, some women were much more interested in working on projects that would advance them personally; others were directed toward projects that served the entire community.

Unlike Orange Walk, the village of Roaring Creek does not have the geographic features that contribute to a cohesive sense of community; it is divided by a major highway and the women are scattered throughout a rather large area. This physical separation made it difficult for women to meet with one another and was the most obvious impediment to organizing.

The RCWG illustrates that the problems a women's organization can encounter range from disjuncture between the leader's vision and the members' visions of a goal to certain characteristics of the community that make arranging meetings an awkward process. Yet these features that make the RCWG a transient rather than a stable group should not be unequivocally viewed as resulting in failure. The Roaring Creek Women's Group in fact accomplished much of what the Orange Walk group did but in a different way. Waters told me that all the women who had been involved in the group were now working, while those women who did not join continued to stay at home. In this respect, the "success" of this particular group may be measured more meaningfully by looking at the individual growth experienced by the women in it. Through their involvement, they strengthened existing bonds and created new networks of interpersonal relationships, an aspect which the literature on women's groups identifies as most significant. This achievement means that organizing women for a future activity will be less difficult. Further, it would appear that many of the women acquired a greater sense of self-esteem and confidence in their abilities, evidenced by the fact that many of them ventured outside the normal parameters of the domestic domain to seek employment—something they had not done before their participation in the group.

In this tale of two women's groups, it is important to emphasize the residual impact of the RCWG as its most significant achievement, in contrast to the highly formal and organized group structure, the contestation of gender boundaries, and the acquisition of leadership skills that were the primary accomplishments of the OWCG. The differences in the ways in which the women organize themselves and the ways in which their achievements reflect local constraints suggest that one of the most important evaluations of the success of a women's group must emanate from within the boundaries of the group and the community it purports to serve.[47]

With an Eye toward Tomorrow

As we have seen, women's groups in Belize grew out of a combination of traditions such as women's volunteer service and church groups and historical events such as Belize's struggle to self-rule and the globalization of women's issues during the United Nations Decade for Women. The style of organizing seems to be regional, fitting into the forms found among women's groups in the Caribbean and Latin America. Some Belizean women's organizations exhibit the characteristics of what Caldeira calls the "new politics," because as a collective they reject the practices of traditional political parties. Instead, women turn to women's groups to advance their cause as women, although some individuals remain actively involved in political parties and work to insert their perspective into the parties' political platforms. In contrast to traditional politics, where women form a loyal constituency but rarely hold positions of importance, women's organizations tend to be egalitarian and emphasize the distribution of power and the development of all female members as potential leaders. In addition, these groups set as a priority those demands and goals oriented toward survival or practical issues that are gender-related, though not always gender-specific. Despite the fade-away qualities of some groups, they have a lasting residual effect that is far more significant than their actual existence and that makes future organizing among women an easier process.

Although I was in touch with many of the national organizations, they were not my central focus. Nonetheless, the limited contact I had with national groups in relation to their local chapters suggests that women's overall attempts to collectively challenge social institutions and issues such as marriage, motherhood, and women's economic insecurity, all of which perpetuate and maintain the problematic and oppressive culture of gender in Belize, can be described as implicit challenges to the state or national government.

This larger impact is already apparent in areas such as child support, where women's demands that men be accountable to the children they have fathered outside of marriage have resulted in changes to national laws on child support and were the impetus for the creation of a more proactive Family Court system and procedures. The activities of women's groups have also aggressively challenged the state in the arena of domestic violence. By advocating for specific legislation, women's groups publicly resist the cultural legitimatization of domestic violence as a private matter and thereby an acceptable dimension of heterosexual relationships.

Their efforts came to fruition in March 1993 with the passage of the Domestic Violence Bill. They accomplished their goal through public education in the form of workshops, posters, radio talk shows, and consciousness raising among the various women's groups. This success symbolized a new phase for women's rights and certainly confirmed the ability of women's groups to step beyond the boundaries of their community organizations to reach the ears of the state. Although the implementation of this bill needs to be monitored over the next few years to see if it can deliver on its inherent promise of eroding the institutionalization of domestic violence, the new law is a tangible result to which women's groups can point in order to persuade potential members of the power of women's collective action to instigate social transformation.

These are small examples of the way in which women's agency at the personal and community level, spearheaded by women's groups, has broader social implications, and can challenge, modify, and even alter the culture of gender in Belize, Central America. In the years to come, much more evidence of women's increasing empowerment is likely to emerge.[48] Without women's groups as organized forums within which women are supported in their protests and contestation of the culture of gender, change in Belize would occur at a much slower pace.

Chapter 10　　*"Dis Heah Time No Stand Like Befo' Time"*

Today, all women do not have the possibility to choose
their roles—their roles are assigned to them.
　　　　　　　—Nafis Sadik, "Women Empowered," 1994

A few Belizean women are challenging the seeming in-
evitability of their destinies. They are facing and creating change; as the Creole proverb suggests, time does not stand still, the present is not like the past.
The narratives of Rose, Zola, and Evelyn actively posit not only the availability
of such change but their discovery of alternatives within the framework of
everyday life. These stories illustrate the varied challenges that women face as
they seek to create possibilities other than their prescribed social roles—the
road each traverses is not the same. Under one set of circumstances that are
generated by social contexts joined with specific life events, a woman may
choose to modify her social role as wife or mother; under another set of circumstances, she may choose to challenge either or both of these roles. Regardless of which road she takes, women's groups can be instrumental in giving her the tools and support with which to make such choices. Women's
groups are one of the many mechanisms that make such choices possible. Between 1975 and 1985, the United Nations placed women's needs on the
global agenda by designating that period "The Decade for Women"; in 1994
the Cairo Summit reiterated the belief that women hold a central place in
most societies and must be integral and full partners in any nation's planning

for population control and economic development. The Cairo Summit, intentionally or not, helped to publicize "gender equality, equity and empowerment of women. Women are half the population of the world, half the population of every country. . . . Indeed, if we are to be successful . . . the needs of women should be addressed in consultation with them, not as a prescription to them and imposed on them."[1]

Belizeans, like the rest of the world, must accept the fact that women are here to stay on the global agenda. More than that, Belizeans and others must accept that women have become more visible and more vocal, especially regarding issues directly related to their needs. As nations adapt to or learn to manage the forces of transnationalization and globalization—economic migration and immigration, advertising, television, export-processing zones, tourism—they must also contend with the fact that women are influenced by what is happening in the world around them. As the Decade for Women demonstrated, social transformation in the arena of gender derives from strategies wrought out of both the specific events of women's lives and what they learn by watching other women. Global linkages through all forms of media connect the struggles of women in the most remote areas of the world to those of women in the most technologically advanced nations. Belizean women's collective action and their changing attitudes about their social roles and place in society embrace and resonate with women's collective agency that is translating itself globally into banking cooperatives in India, feminist groups in the United States, cultural groups such as Sistren in Jamaica, mothers' clubs in Lima, the Health Movement of the Jardim Nordeste area in Sao Paulo, and the Mothers of the Playa de Mayo in Argentina. Belizean women are learning, as are their global counterparts, that the outcome of this activism, especially when channeled collectively through women's groups, not only has personal ramifications but can have an impact on the broader social fabric of their communities and their nation. In Belize, the expressed transformation of some women's attitudes and their behavior has already begun to affect the way in which national and local institutions respond.

The development of a Family Court, for example, signaled an end to an era where only the mother was held responsible for the maintenance of her children, especially those born outside of marriage. Male parental responsibility is now institutionalized—men must help support the children they father or go to jail; and although the amounts are not large, they legitimize the right of women, whether married to the fathers or not, to make demands on behalf of their children. As we have seen, the Domestic Violence Bill was written into law in 1993. The plan accomplishing this was engineered by Women Against Violence. This legislation will have far-reaching implications for the way in which men and women interact with each other. It is currently unclear how effective enforcement of the bill will be, and some men are defensive about the fact that matters which were once private are now public and subject to close scrutiny. But the bill remains a legal forum within which women can publicly proclaim their discontent with the societal view of them as minors, property, and sex objects.

To illuminate the struggle over the meaning of gender, this work presents not *the* definitive statement about the nature of gender in Belize but one example of the many kinds of questions prevalent in the society and the variety of solutions women have fashioned to meet their needs. This microlevel or individual perspective is a crucial component in the study of cultures and societies. As part of this approach, I assume that people are not just victims continuously adapting to the whims or events of the world in which they live, but human agents in constant negotiation and mediation with their environment, both cultural and physical. The result is change.

In an interview about the significance of the 1994 Cairo Summit for women and the implications for change, Nafis Sadik, the secretary-general of the United Nations Population Fund, observed: "Changing gender roles is threatening. Men and women are afraid of how these changes are going to affect them. Will they really be able to cope with the new circumstances? Women are also worried about a new role expected of them to be independent and fend for themselves. Change is always worrisome."[2] Indeed, change is uncomfortable, though inevitable and, if we believe the narratives of Rose, Zola, and Evelyn, very often necessary. Their stories provide a window onto the complexity and changing nature of Belize's culture of gender, rendering it more accessible to us. It is through their experiences that we are able to encounter and study the diversity of the human condition.

I have sought to provide the historical context of the lives of these three women while illuminating the fact that they are individuals and members of communities whose ideas and behaviors with regard to gender are deeply enmeshed with the ideologies and practices generated by social institutions. In this respect, I have tried to avoid the weaknesses of ethnographies that provide only narrative texts with little analysis or interpretation, or those that are simply structural analyses of institutions and economic and political processes. Life stories without social and historical context are meaningless, while structural models of society devoid of the individual perspective provide only partial insights into the workings of a particular society. Gender is not just a set of institutional practices and processes but an all-encompassing social phenomenon that implicates institutions, people, beliefs, behaviors, symbols, and meaning—in a word, culture. Any useful analysis must necessarily take a multi-faceted approach if it intends to document, describe, and interpret human variation with any degree of accuracy.

My goal, then, has been to point out not only the similarities in the way women's experiences are shaped by gender ideologies but also the differences that make Belize unique. Most important, Rose, Zola, and Evelyn reveal to us the way in which individuals learn to cope with their daily stresses and both the unforeseen and the predictable events that present themselves in the course of a single lifetime. But beyond viewing these efforts as merely examples of coping or adaptive strategies, I have emphasized how these women have channeled their responses to life events and crisis into agency.

Each of the women who speaks in this ethnography has seized control over some aspect—and sometimes every aspect—of her life. The process of doing so has inevitably altered the way in which she sees the world, sometimes rendering her discontent and eager to do something about her life, and sometimes leaving her reflective about her circumstances, but inactive. Women's groups aid the process of personal transformation by providing the necessary venue for this searching, questioning, and synthesis of self-discovery to take place, safely and without harsh criticism or fear of reprisal.

I do not claim that these three women are representative of all the women of Belize. In fact, I am convinced that I have begun to understand only a small segment of the cultural and social complex that constitutes Belizean society. But every project must begin somewhere; this is where I choose to start.

Scholarly inquiry inevitably generates more questions than it answers. The analysis of gender in Belize suggests many further avenues of inquiry. What are the sources or catalysts of social transformation at the individual level? How do individuals become politicized? Is the process magical, circumstantial, or is there a clear, easily definable progression toward the goal of personal change? And how does this get transferred into social transformation at the community level? These and other specific and interrelated questions concerning gender remain open, but the stories explored here may provide clues about where we should search for further understanding and knowledge.

The study of gender has also provoked in me a growing awareness that any future discussions on the topic anywhere in the world must attend to how men are socially situated and enculturated as well. We must document and analyze how men learn to rationalize their strategies of control and coercion over women. If we can shed greater illumination on the cultural and social forces that motivate all of us as social actors in our world and that create the conditions for women's subordination, we can begin to construct new ways of thinking about gender and gender enculturation. A research approach that asserts anything less runs the risk of masking the symptoms of gender inequality while leaving its sources still intact.

The overarching aim of anthropology has been and continues to be the expansion of the boundaries of our knowledge of modern humans. Though unique in many ways, Belize provides a mirror in which I hope we may yet catch a glimpse of ourselves.

Notes

Prologue

1. Central Statistical Office, *Population Census: Major Findings* (Belmopan: Ministry of Finance, 1991). For specific figures and a description of the population, see chapter 2.
2. The territorial dispute, between Guatemala and Britain, dates back to 1859 and is based on the Guatemala's alleged claim to the colony of British Honduras. Irma McClaurin, "A Writer's Life, a Country's Transition," *Américas* 46, 4 (1994): 38–43.
3. I thank Douglas Caulkins for the term "consultant." It reflects my recognition that the people I conferred with were in fact experts in their culture. The idea of "consultants" also confers a degree of autonomy and directedness to people's participation that is not dependent upon the researcher. Conversely, "informant" is an anthropological term that suggests people who exist only in relation to the presence of the anthropologist. As Webster defines it, an informant is "one who supplied cultural or linguistic data in response to interrogation by an investigator." In this context, the sense that people have independent, valid knowledge is obscured by the perspective that they are repositories of "data" that only comes into existence in response to anthropological or scholarly interrogations.
4. How Belizean women define these is discussed in chapter 1.
5. Belize Organization for Women and Development, "BOWAND'S Minimum Wage Campaign," *SPEAR's Studies on Belize*, Belize City, 1993, and Debra Lewis and Sandra Carr, "Noh bout wi rites: A Look at Women and Domestic Workers' Rights," BOWAND and UNICEF, Belize City, 1994. For a brief description of BOWAND's efforts, see chapter 7.
6. Family Court was established in 1989. See Government of Belize, *Belize Report for the Fourth World Conference on Women (Beijing 1995): Action for Equality, Development, and Peace*, Social Planning Unit and Department of Women's Affairs, Ministry of Human Resources, Youth, Women and Culture, 1994.
7. For specific figures on the number of women in government, see ibid. and chapter 9.

Chapter 1. Women of Belize

1. Conrad Kottak, *Anthropology: The Exploration of Human Diversity*, 6th ed. (New York: McGraw-Hill, 1994), 367.

2. "Lemongrass" is the pseudonym I adopted for the town where I conducted my main research. It is located in the southern district of Toledo.

3. Helen I. Safa, "Economic Restructuring and Gender Subordination," *Latin American Perspectives,* Issue 85 22, 2 (1995): 32–50.

4. For a discussion of patron-client relationships, see Carlene J. Edie, "The Persistence of Clientelist Politics in Jamaica," *Social and Economic Studies* 38, 1 (1989): 1–35.

5. Lila Abu-Lughod, "Writing against Culture," in *Recapturing Anthropology: Working in the Present,* ed. Richard G. Fox (Sante Fe: School of American Research Press, 1991).

6. Sherna Berger Gluck and Daphne Patai, eds., *Women's Words: The Feminist Practice of Oral History* (New York: Routledge, 1991), 2.

7. For an example of one of the earlier attempts to challenge this model, see Kevin Dwyer, *Moroccan Dialogues: Anthropology in Question* (Prospect Heights, Ill.: Waveland Press, 1982).

8. Lila Abu-Lughod, *Veiled Sentiments: Honor and Poetry in a Bedouin Society* (Berkeley: University of California Press, 1988); Sally Cole, *Women of the Praia: Work and Lives in a Portuguese Coastal Community* (Princeton: Princeton University Press, 1991); and Sally Price, *Co-wives and Calabashes* (Ann Arbor: University of Michigan Press, 1984).

9. Joseph G. Jorgensen, "On Ethics and Anthropology," in *To See Ourselves: Anthropology and Modern Social Issues,* ed. Thomas Weaver (Glenview, Ill.: Scott, Foresman, 1973).

10. Sondra Hale, "Women's Culture / Men's Culture: Gender, Separation, and Space in Africa and North America," *American Behavioral Scientist* 31, 1 (1987): 115–134.

11. In most Latin American and Caribbean countries, blackness is sometimes romanticized. Venezuela, for example, publicly acknowledges the influence of African culture while simultaneously exposing a policy of social "whitening." In Brazil, however, despite an extensive vocabulary of terms to describe ranges of skin color, class and color are interconnected and darker skin is most often affiliated with poverty. Moreover, people may be perceived as darker as a consequence of their lower class status. See Richard Graham, ed., *The Idea of Race in Latin America, 1870–1940* (Austin: University of Texas Press, 1990); H. Hoetink, "'Race' and Color in the Caribbean," in *Caribbean Contours,* ed. Sidney W. Mintz and Sally Price (Baltimore: Johns Hopkins University Press, 1985); and Winthrop R. Wright, *Café Con Leche: Race, Class, and National Image in Venezuela* (Austin: University of Texas Press, 1990).

12. Although I was absolutely confident that I would be viewed as a member of the Creole ethnic group, in actuality my friends surprised me by referring to me as "coolie girl," noting a resemblance to people with East Indian ancestry. When I asked for an explanation, I was given a meticulous description that detailed the way in which my hair texture and the "blackish" tone of my dark skin contrasted with the hair texture and "reddish" tone of Creole skin color. At the same time my daughter, who has reddish-brown skin, was seen as unequivocally Creole. That we were related, while perceived to be members of different ethnic groups, did not seem to pose any contradiction to those doing the classification.

13. Michael Cutler Stone has laid a good historical foundation for analyzing this very

issue. See "Caribbean Nation, Central American State: Ethnicity, Race, and National Formation in Belize, 1798–1990" (Ph.D. dissertation, University of Texas at Austin, 1994).

14. Such outbursts give voice to that subordinate partner in the touristic relationship from whom we hear very little. For a discussion of this perspective, see Jamaica Kincaid, *A Small Place* (New York: Plume Books, 1981), and Dean MacCannell, "Staged Authenticity," in *The Tourist: A New Theory of the Leisure Class*, ed. Dean MacCannell (1976; New York: Schocken Books, 1989).

15. Charles A. Valentine, *Black Studies and Anthropology: Scholarly and Political Interests in Afro-American Culture*, Addison-Wesley Modular Publications (Reading, Mass.: Addison-Wesley, 1972), 1–4.

16. W.E.B. Du Bois, *The Souls of Black Folk* (1903; New York: New American Library, 1969).

17. For further discussion of the significance of race, class, gender, and marital status in the fieldwork setting, see Nancie (Solien) González, "The Anthropologist as Female Head of Household," in *Self, Sex, and Gender in Cross-Cultural Fieldwork*, ed. Tony Larry Whitehead and Mary Ellen Conaway (Urbana: University of Illinois Press, 1986); Faye V. Harrison, "Ethnography as Politics," in *Decolonizing Anthropology: Moving Further toward an Anthropology for Liberation*, ed. Faye V. Harrison (Washington, D.C.: American Anthropological Association, 1991); Tony Whitehead, "Identity, Subjectivity, and Cultural Bias in Fieldwork," *Black Scholar* (September–October 1980); and Whitehead and Conaway, eds., *Self, Sex, and Gender in Cross-Cultural Fieldwork*.

18. I am particularly engaged by the way in which Faye Harrison blends both the personal and the theoretical when she writes about the complexity of the fieldwork experience. Her reflections on the way in which identity, selfhood, and fieldwork are all entangled strikes a chord of empathy within me, not only because she invokes Du Bois's metaphor of double-consciousness as I do, but also because she identifies the constructive role fieldwork plays in illuminating one's understanding of self in becoming an instrument of change. Harrison, "Ethnography as Politics."

19. Cf. Soraya Altorki and Camillia Fawzi El-Solh, eds., *Arab Women in the Field: Studying Your Own Society* (Syracuse: Syracuse University Press, 1988), and John Langston Gwaltney, *Drylongso: A Self-Portrait of Black America* (New York: Random House, 1980). For more general discussions of the fieldwork experience, see also Joan Cassell, ed., *Children in the Field: Anthropological Experiences* (Philadelphia: Temple University Press, 1987); Sherry Gorelick, "Contradictions of Feminist Methodology," *Gender and Society* 5, 4 (1991): 459–477; and Robert Lawless, Vinson H. Sutlive, Jr., and Mario D. Zamora, eds., *Fieldwork: The Human Experience* (New York: Gordon and Breach Science Publishers, 1983).

20. Cf. Marjorie Shostak, *Nisa: The Life and Words of a !Kung Woman* (New York: Vintage Books, 1981), and Dwyer, *Moroccan Dialogues*.

21. Direct quotes from my field notes are placed in italics throughout this book.

22. In a 1991 analysis of Belize laws and their fairness with regard to women, Lisa Shoman indicated that current laws, including those on property ownership, ensured equity for women. In fact, "from 1953, all the rights, powers and authorities of the husband existing at common law over and in relation to the property of a wife acquired before or after marriage shall cease to exist, and the husband shall not be liable in respect of any debt or obligation of the wife whenever incurred and

every married woman shall be entitled to sue and be liable to be sued in all courts of law in her own name without the intervention of her husband" (Lisa Shoman, "Women and the Law in Belize," Society for the Promotion of Education and Research [SPEAR], 1991, 24). What the analysis does not examine are actual practices with regard to the disposition of property attained during marriage or under a common-law union. In addition, even though the law, as stated, protects married women, cultural practices still assume the husband to be responsible for a wife's property. Because most women in Belize are not knowledgeable about the law and are too intimidated or embarrassed to ask for explanations, they often concede to cultural practices that are unfair and rob them of access to resources and their legal rights. The *Belize Report for the Fourth World Conference on Women* cites inheritance as one area where there is no specific legislation that takes into account gender (68).

23. Cf. Emecheta Buchi, *The Joys of Motherhood* (New York: George Braziller, 1979).
24. Cf. Claude Meillassoux, *Maidens, Meal, and Money: Capitalism and the Domestic Community* (New York: Cambridge University Press, 1981).
25. Frances Henry and Pamela Wilson, "The Status of Women in Caribbean Societies: An Overview of their Social, Economic, and Sexual Roles," *Social and Economic Studies* 24, 2 (1975): 165–198.
26. Susan C. Bourque and Kay Barbara Warren, *Women of the Andes: Patriarchy and Social Change in Two Peruvian Towns* (Ann Arbor: University of Michigan Press, 1981).
27. Kesho Scott, *The Habit of Surviving* (New Brunswick, N.J.: Rutgers University Press, 1991), 7.
28. Scott, *The Habit of Surviving*.
29. Sacks talks about the concept of women as minors in her discussion of Engels's theory. This characterization is a crucial component of Belize's gender ideology. Sacks asserts that this concept and women's subordination are strongly linked to the rise of private property and the creation of the family as an isolated unit in which women's behavior and movements are rigidly controlled. Karen Sacks, "Engels Revisited: Women, the Organization of Production, and Private Property," in *Toward an Anthropology of Women*, ed. Rayna R. Reiter (New York: Monthly Review Press, 1974).
30. As an African American woman in the United States, I have also felt the constraints of gender, as part of a structural triad that includes race and class, as an active influence on the choices I make and how I feel about them.
31. Epigraph: quoted in Hortense Powdermaker, *Stranger and Friend: The Way of an Anthropologist* (New York: W. W. Norton and Company, 1966). For a good overview of the development of feminist anthropology, see the introductions to the following books: Karen Sacks, *Sisters and Wives: The Past and Future of Sexual Equality* (Urbana: University of Illinois Press, 1982); Sandra Morgen, ed., *Gender and Anthropology: Critical Reviews for Research and Teaching* (Washington, D.C.: American Anthropological Association, 1989); Faye Ginsburg and Anna Tsing, eds., *Uncertain Terms: Negotiating Gender in American Culture* (Boston: Beacon, 1990); and Michaela di Leonardo, *Gender at the Crossroads* (Berkeley: University of California, 1992).
32. Jane Monnig Atkinson and Shelly Errington, *Power and Difference: Gender in Is-*

land Southeast Asia (Stanford: Stanford University Press, 1990), 3 (emphasis added).

33. Nafis Sadik, "Women Empowered: The Earth's Last Hope," *New Perspectives Quarterly* 11, 4 (Fall 1994). The conclusions reached at the summit are not new. Back in 1990, Carmen Deere et al. reported that "IMF, World Bank, and AID-supported structural adjustment policies have exacerbated poverty, with the costs falling unduly on the poor women of the [Caribbean] region, who increasingly are the main economic support of their families" (Carmen Diana Deere, Peggy Antrobus, Lynn Bolles, Edwin Meléndez, Peter Phillips, Marcia River, and Helen Safa, *In the Shadow of the Sun: Caribbean Development Alternatives and U.S. Policy* [Boulder and London: Westview Press, 1990], 13). Other assessments on the ways in which development policies have disadvantaged women can be found in the following reports: Economic Commission for Latin America and the Caribbean (ECLAC), *The Decade for Women in Latin America and the Caribbean: Background and Prospects* (Santiago: United Nations, 1988), and Commonwealth Secretariat, *Engendering Adjustment for the 1990s: Report of a Commonwealth Expert Group on Women and Structural Adjustment* (London: Commonwealth Secretariat, 1989).

34. Discussions of women as victims of historical forces and economic policies as well as the public/private or public/domestic theoretical model originally articulated by Michelle Zimbalist Rosaldo often obscure women's roles as active participants in community, regional, and national issues. See Rosaldo, "Woman, Culture, and Society: A Theoretical Overview," in *Woman, Culture, and Society*, ed. Michele Zimbalist Rosaldo and Louise Lamphere (Stanford: Stanford University Press, 1974).

35. My research was confined to a study of heterosexual relationships; while homosexuality may exist in Belize, it is not condoned, and none of the women discussed the subject.

36. For a discussion of women's activism in the Latin American context, see Sarah A. Radcliffe and Sallie Westwood, eds., *"Viva": Women and Popular Protest in Latin America* (London: Routledge, 1993); Sonia Alvarez, *Engendering Democracy in Brazil* (Princeton: Princeton University Press, 1990); Elizabeth Jelin, ed., *Women and Social Change in Latin America* (London: Zed Books, 1990); and Helen I. Safa, "Women's Social Movements in Latin America," *Gender and Society* 4, 3 (1990). For a discussion of women's activism in the Afro-Caribbean context, see Pat Ellis, ed., *Women of the Caribbean* (London: Zed Books, 1986), and Patricia Mohammed, "Reflections on the Women's Movement in Trinidad: Calypsos, Changes, and Sexual Violence," *Feminist Review*, no. 38 (Summer 1991): 33–47.

Chapter 2. So Where the Hell Is Belize?

1. Few sources on Central America go beyond a footnote in giving attention to Belize; see Clifford Krauss, *Inside Central America: Its People, Politics, and History* (New York: Simon and Schuster, 1991). The same is true for those works that seek to define the Caribbean as a sociocultural, geopolitical area. Although Belize may be mentioned, rarely is there any detailed description of its contributions to the region. See Franklin Knight, *The Caribbean: The Genesis of a Fragmented Nation-*

alism (New York: Oxford University Press, 1978); Gordon K. Lewis, *Main Currents in Caribbean Thoughts: The Historical Evolution of Caribbean Society in Its Ideological Aspects, 1492–1900* (Baltimore: Johns Hopkins University Press, 1983); and Bonham C. Richardson, *The Caribbean in the Wider World, 1492–1992* (Cambridge: Cambridge University Press, 1992).

2. Government of Belize, *Fact Sheet Belize*, Belize Information Service Publication, 1994.

3. Assad Shoman, "The Making of Belize's Foreign Policy: From Colony to Independent State," *SPEAReports* 8 (Independence Ten Years After), Fifth Annual Studies on Belize Conference, 1992, 13.

4. Meb Cutlack, *Ecotourism in Action* (London: Macmillan Press, 1993).

5. William Arlington Donohoe, *A History of British Honduras* (Montreal: Provincial Publishing Co., 1946), 28.

6. Cubola, *Atlas of Belize* (Benque Viejo del Carmen: Cubola Productions, 1990).

7. The government is engaged in a huge infrastructure plan to cover the canals over the next few years.

8. The legacy of Baron Bliss is evident throughout Belize. He is another one of the country's factual "myths." Bliss was an Englishman with a Portuguese title who used to anchor his yacht in the waters of Belize. When he died, he left a perpetual trust fund for cultural activities to the people whom he had admired from a distance and the tiny country whose shores he had never touched. The Bliss Institute, formerly the location of the National Library, is part of this legacy.

9. Cutlack, *Ecotourism in Action*, 13.

10. Elizabeth Boo, *Ecotourism: The Potentials and Pitfalls*, vol. 2, *Country Case Studies* (Washington, D.C.: World Wildlife Fund, 1990).

11. The Belizean intellectual Assad Shoman pinpoints this historically unequal relationship as one of Belize's key problems. He argues that the conditions of underdevelopment in Belize and in the modern world can be traced directly to historical trends of monopolization at the end of the nineteenth century that were the precursors to modern-day transnational corporations. According to Shoman, this emerging new world economy consisted of "the industrialized capitalist countries (mainly in Europe and North America) as the 'centre' of the system and most of the rest of the world as the 'periphery,' or satellites of the metropolitan countries." Assad Shoman, *Party Politics in Belize* (Belize: Cubola Productions, 1987), 7.

12. O. Nigel Bolland, *The Formation of a Colonial Society: Belize from Conquest to Crown Colony* (Baltimore: Johns Hopkins University Press, 1977), 2.

13. Even today Belize's land resources are greatly underutilized. Moreover, fewer and fewer Belizean youth, especially Creole men, view agricultural production as a viable occupation. In the recent past British administrators inferred from this disinterest evidence of innate laziness. The reasons are more complex, however, and lie partly in the cultural socialization. Early in Belize's colonial history, male slaves were oriented toward timber extraction, work that required strength and mobility. Such patterns lent themselves to a lifestyle that was more nomadic than sedentary. Although slave women occasionally had gardens, the conditions of the British presence in the British Honduras under numerous treaties precluded permanent settlements of any sort. Bolland points out: "Such seasonal or shifting cultivation was compatible with the economy of timber extraction—indeed, it is more accurate to say that agriculture was largely restricted to this form by the predominant

economy—but it did not encourage the development of a settled agricultural system" (see Bolland, *The Formation of a Colonial Society*, 71–72). Today Belize produces both sugar and citrus for export. Agricultural production is largely monopolized by factory-owned estates, with foreign capital controlling the processing (Mark Moberg, *Citrus, Strategy, and Class: The Politics of Development in Southern Belize* [Iowa City: University of Iowa Press, 1992], 31). Small-scale farming is left to the Mennonites, Mestizos, Maya,—in particular the Ketchi, whom Bolland characterizes as "the most traditional and self-sufficient people in Belize today" (O. Nigel Bolland, *Belize: A New Nation in Central America* [Boulder and London: Westview Press, 1986], 27)—and increasingly to Central American refugees. In the past and today, people in the more rural towns and villages, whether Creole, Maya, East Indian, or Garifuna, often have a small plot of land called a "plantation," used to produce just enough for household consumption and occasionally for local markets.

14. Deere et al., *In The Shadow of the Sun*, 13
15. See Government of Belize, *Fact Sheet*, 1994; for an in-depth description of the history of Belize's political structure, see Shoman, *Party Politics in Belize*.
16. See Kathleen Levy Esquivel, *Under the Shade*, self-publication, 1994, for a popular description of "the interplay between different ethnic groups."
17. Fredrik Barth, ed., *Ethnic Groups and Boundaries: The Social Organization of Culture Difference* (Boston: Little, Brown, 1969).
18. Richard Mahler and Steele Wotkyns, *Belize: A Natural Destination*, 2nd ed. (Sante Fe: John Muir Publications, 1993).
19. Bolland, *Belize: A New Nation in Central America*, 45.
20. For an excellent history and analysis of the various ethnic and cultural identities in Belize today, see Stone, "Caribbean Nation, Central American State."

Chapter 3. From the Marketplace to Lemongrass

1. For a description of the role of the traditional healer in Belizean culture, see Rosita Arvigo, *Sastun* (New York: Harper and Row, 1994).
2. A new market, in an impressive, modern building called the Commercial Center, was completed in 1992. Some vendors have moved in; others, like Auntie Barbara, prefer to stay in the poorly lit and poorly ventilated, but familiar, space of the old market. It still attracts a number of shoppers because the major fish market is located there.
3. It is unusual for a Belizean woman to have only one child, especially a woman of Auntie Barbara's generation; on fertility rates, see chapter 7. Tragically, in 1994 Auntie Barbara's daughter died of natural causes; the grandchildren continue to reside with her and assist her in the market when not attending school.
4. Negrito (*Simarouba glauco*), also known as "Dysentery bark," is from the plant family simaroubaceae. The bark and roots have a variety of uses and are known to affect "dysentery, diarrhea, hemorrhage, excessive menstruation, and internal bleeding" (Rosita Arvigo and Michael Balick, *Rainforest Remedies: One Hundred Healing Herbs of Belize* [Twin Lakes, Wisc.: Lotus Press, 1993], 121). Talla walla or Callawalla (*Polypodium areum*) is a fungus that is cooked in water and used to treat stomach ulcers (Barbara Fernandez, *Medicine Woman: The Herbal Tradition of Belize* [Belize City: National Library Service, 1990]). I could find no reference

to "young girl bubby" in either Arvigo and Balick or Fernandez. This does not invalidate Auntie Barbara's claims but highlights the fact that many of Belize's medicinal plants have local names for which the scientific genus has not been documented.

5. Valeriano (*Valeriana officinales*), also spelled Valerian, is a root used as a tranquilizer and for "body spasms, rheumatic or painful joints, [and] flatulent indigestion." Fernandez, *Medicine Woman*, 50.

6. Auntie Barbara once told me that whenever you visit an unfamiliar place, you need to find only two things: the market and the church.

7. The exchange rate is $2BZ to $1US.

8. There was no overt evidence of formalized prostitution in any of these establishments. But it was not uncommon for a man to have a wife or a common-law wife as well as a girlfriend, and the latter he might take to a bar, restaurant, or dance.

9. The Social Service Office has since relocated to a different building that it shares with the women's development officer of the Department of Women's Affairs. Other changes to the town include the construction of a stadium near the airstrip in 1993.

10. The Toledo District, where Lemongrass is located, is made up of a predominantly rural Maya population: Mopan (21.9 percent) and Ketchi (40.7 percent). It also has one of the largest communities of East Indians (7.9 percent), who seem to be one of the most marginalized groups in the entire country. Lemongrass and the Toledo District in many ways reflect the heterogeneity that attracts many anthropologists to Belize: other ethnic groups represented in the district are Creole (5.7 percent), Garifuna (10.0 percent), and Mestizo (11.9 percent). Central Statistical Office, *Population Census*, 1991.

11. In "college" students attend Forms 1–4 (see chapter 4, note 1, for a description of school levels). Those who wish to go beyond this may enroll in either a technical or general school for what is called Sixth Form; there is no separate fifth form. The program for the general Sixth Form is a liberal arts curriculum that covers two years. It is the equivalent of American junior college and upon completion, students may transfer to a four-year institution in the United States or in another country, if they have the financial means or are fortunate enough to obtain one of the coveted scholarship for study abroad.

12. The United Democratic Party won the 1993 elections with the promise of free education. School fees have been eliminated, although books are still costly.

13. Mary Lindsay Elmendorf, *Nine Mayan Women: A Village Faces Change* (Rochester: Schenkman Books, 1985). Although Elmendorf's ethnography is based on data collected almost thirty years ago, it does confirm the presence of certain attitudes. More recent studies of the Yucatan would have to be consulted to see if such attitudes still persist.

14. Elmendorf, *Nine Mayan Women*, 73.

15. This figure for the price of chicken is based upon the price I paid in Lemongrass in 1991. The figure is somewhat higher than those published in the 1994 poverty report on Belize. The price for chicken used to "value the basic needs food basket" ranged from a high of $2.41 in San Pedro to a low of $1.75 in Toledo Rural (all prices in Belize dollars). The figures used were based on 1990 prices. In addition, the report shows that pork and beef tend to be outside the price range of most people, with pork ranging from a high of $5.57 in San Pedro ($5.22 in Belize City)

to a low of $1.81 in Toledo Rural and beef from a high of $4.76 in Belize City to a low of $2.69 in Cayo Rural. The sharp contrasts between the figures may be explained by the fact that in the rural area, people are more likely to raise animals for their own and local consumption. Diane D. Lewis, *A Poverty Profile for Belize: Final Report, October 1994*, USAID/Belize Contract no. CO-505-0000.01-C-00-4024, Central Statistical Office, Ministry of Finance, Government of Belize.

16. Alcoholism among men from other ethnic groups also appears high. In isolated communities like Lemongrass, drinking is the main form of socializing and begins among young males at a very early age. In contrast, women do not socialize in bars. They may go with their male partners for a drink, and on occasion with a girlfriend, but drinking problems are not as prevalent among women. I did notice that alcohol is not kept as a matter of course in people's homes. It is brought in for special occasions, but is mostly something consumed outside the home.

Chapter 4. Rose's Story

1. Schools in Belize are divided into several levels. Children may attend a preschool, but mandatory education begins with primary school and includes Infant 1 and 2 (equivalent to the first and second grade in the United States) and Standard 1 (third grade). The middle division of primary school encompasses Standard 2 and 3 (fourth and fifth grade). The upper division of primary school goes from Standard 4 to 6 (sixth, seventh, and eighth grade equivalents). High school is Forms 1–4, which is the same as grades 9–12. Sixth Form is a two-year program and is the equivalent of junior college. Although Rose says she completed only Standard 2, I believe she is confusing terms and is actually referring to high school, meaning Form 2, which would be the second year of high school. This level of schooling would be consistent with the age she assigns herself in the narrative and would explain some of the academic skills she displays. Her telling people she completed "Standard 6" would be a reference to Sixth Form. My thanks to Wilma Wright for her careful explanation.

2. According to Diane Lewis's report on poverty in Belize, based on figures from 1990, households headed by women make up 24.7 percent of the total population. The *Belize Report for the Fourth World Conference on Women*, using 1991 census data, indicates that "21.8% of households are female-headed, although the rate in Belize District is 33.3%." Lewis, *A Poverty Profile for Belize*, 1994, 18.

3. Virginia Kerns, *Women and the Ancestors: Black Carib Kinship and Ritual* (Urbana: University of Illinois Press, 1983).

4. Cf. Aihwa Ong, *Spirits of Resistance and Capitalist Discipline: Factory Women in Malaysia* (New York: State University of New York Press, 1987), 2–3.

5. Patricia Hill Collins, *Black Feminist Thought* (New York: Routledge, 1991). Cf. Linda Alcoff, "Cultural Feminism versus Post-Structuralism: The Identity Crisis in Feminist Theory," *Signs* 13 (3), 405–436.

6. Like many couples in Belize, Rose and her husband are living apart. Legal separations are difficult to achieve; the courts see their role as maintaining the institution of marriage, and formal divorce is the exception rather than the rule. This is partly due to the fact that a couple must reside separately for three years before becoming eligible to file for no-fault divorce. The limited resources of men and women, and often the ambivalence of the separation as well, make this an unlikely option. Men

may leave and reside in another woman's household, but they keep open the possibility of return by visiting their first home periodically.

7. Katherine Borland, "'That's Not What I Said': Interpretive Conflict in Oral Narrative Research," in *Women's Words: The Feminist Practice of Oral History*, ed. Sherna Berger Gluck and Daphne Patai (New York: Routledge, 1991), 74.

Chapter 5. To Be a Girl

1. Harriet Whitehead, "The Bow and the Burden Strap: A New Look at Institutionalized Homosexuality in Native North America," in *Sexual Meanings*, ed. Sherry B. Ortner and Harriet Whitehead (Cambridge: Cambridge University Press, 1981).

2. Abraham Rosman and Paula G. Rubel, *The Tapestry of Culture: An Introduction to Cultural Anthropology*, 4th ed. (New York: McGraw-Hill, 1992), 6.

3. See Nancy Lundgren, "Socialization of Children in Belize: Identity, Race, and Power within the World Political Economy" (Ph.d. dissertation, University of Massachusetts, Amherst, 1987), and Zee Edgell, *Beka Lamb*, 5th ed. (London: Heinemann Educational Books, 1982).

4. Edgell, *Beka Lamb*, 18, 21, 51.

5. Brenda Rosenbaum, *With Our Heads Bowed: The Dynamics of Gender in a Maya Community* (Austin: Institute for Meso-american Studies, University of Texas, 1993), 45.

6. See Kerns, *Women and the Ancestors*, and Peta Henderson and Ann Bryn Houghton, eds., *Rising Up: Life Stories of Belizean Women* (Toronto: Sister Vision, 1993).

7. Lundgren, "Socialization of Children in Belize," 256.

8. Nancy Chodorow, *The Reproduction of Mothering: Psychoanalysis and the Sociology of Gender* (Berkeley: University of California, 1978).

9. Ruth Bleier, "The Brain and Human Nature," in *Science and Gender: A Critique of Biology and Its Theories on Women* (New York: Pergamon Press, 1984), 68.

10. Elmendorf, *Nine Mayan Women*, 35 (emphasis added).

11. Toledo Small Farmers Development Project (TSFDP), "Toledo Small Farmers Development Project: Baseline Survey Report (Draft)," 1989. I am grateful to Joseph Cayetano and Ludwig Palacio of the Toledo Small Farmers Development Project in Blue Creek for making this draft available to me. It is one of the few documents that give a detailed description of the daily life of Maya women in Belize.

12. Cf. Price, *Co-wives and Calabashes*.

13. Cf. Maurice Godelier, *The Making of Great Men: Male Domination and Power among the New Guinea Baruya* (New York: Cambridge University Press, 1990), and Sherry B. Ortner, "Is Female to Male as Nature Is to Culture?" in *Woman, Culture, and Society*, ed. Michelle Zimbalist Rosaldo and Louise Lamphere (Stanford: Stanford University Press, 1974).

14. Susannah Hoffman, Richard Cowan, and Paul Aratow, "Kypseli: Women and Men Apart—A Divided Reality," 1974 (film).

15. Elmendorf, *Nine Mayan Women*, 7.

16. M. Kenyon Bullard, "Hide and Secrete: Women's Sexual Magic in Belize," *Journal of Sex Research* 10, 4 (1974): 259–265, at 261.

17. Ibid., 264.

18. Ibid., 265.

19. UNICEF, *Children First: A Situational Analysis of Women and Children* (Belize:

UNICEF, 1991), 56. The total fertility rate for women in general is 4.5 children; the preferred number of births indicated by women is 3.4 children. Central Statistical Office, Ministry of Finance, Belize Family Life Association, Ministry of Health, and Division of Reproductive Health, Centers for Disease Control, *1991 Belize Family Health Survey* (Atlanta: U.S. Department of Health and Human Services, Public Health Services, Centers for Disease Control, 1992.)

20. Bullard notes that Belize is a society "where men prefer very young girls as wives and sexual partners" (Bullard, "Hide and Secrete," 261). This coincides with what one older woman told me occurred when she was coming of age. She stated that a young girl was married off early, often to older men who could provide her with security. She feels that young women are more vulnerable today, however, because the culture no longer demands that a man marry a young woman.

23. UNICEF, *Children First: A Situational Analysis of Women and Children,* 54.

22. In her study of Maroon women in Suriname, Price notes that maturation begins early in a young girl's life: "Around this time, the girl's father's lineage determines (in theory by watching the development of her nipples, which should have begun to protrude slightly) that she is ready to be socially recognized as an "apron girl" . . . , and a simple, brief ceremony is held in which one of them presents her with an unsewn piece of cloth that she will sew into an adolescent apron." Price, *Co-wives and Calabashes,* 15.

23. For an explanation of grade levels in Belize educational systems, see chapter 4, note 1.

24. Several laws in Belize apply to this situation. The Illegitimate Persons Act allows an unmarried woman to obtain child maintenance support from a man through an "affiliation order" with the local magistrate. Also relevant is the Family Maintenance Act, which provides recourse for unmarried women. Young girls are somewhat protected by the law that defines intercourse with a girl under age sixteen as "carnal knowledge"; this is punishable by imprisonment. For further information, see Belize's Criminal Code (CAP 84 of the Laws of Belize, R.E. 1980). Specifically, Section 46 imposes automatic jail terms of that range from two years to life, for "carnal knowledge of: female child; girl under 16 years; 'female idiot,' or imbecile girl." Although these laws are on the books, they do not seem to serve as major obstacles to what is a pervasive pattern. Shoman, "Women and the Law," 8, 17.

25. See also Irma McClaurin, "Women and the Culture of Gender in Belize, Central America" (Ph.D. dissertation, University of Massachusetts, Amherst, 1993).

26. The Belize Catholic Institute for Human Life, "Youth and Chastity: Essays on the Subject of Sex Education in Schools," BRC Printing, Benque Viejo Del Carmen, 1995.

27. Central Statistical Office et al., *1991 Belize Family Health Survey,* 1–2.

28. The Belize Family Life Association is affiliated with Planned Parenthood and the Caribbean Planned Parenthood organizations. Most of their funding is externally based. In the past, they have come under attack for dispensing Depo-Provera, a contraceptive given by injection every three months. It has been prescribed in Lemongrass mostly to rural women like the Maya who cannot get to town on a monthly basis for oral contraceptives and whose husbands will not use condoms.

29. BFLA has noted that Belizean women seem to have a high incidence of cervical cancer, but no research on this is available to date.

30. Government of Belize, *Belize Report for the Fourth World Conference on Women,* 27.

Chapter 6. Zola's Story

1. On March 1, 1993, two years after my interview with Zola, the Domestic Violence Bill was signed into law. It focused on providing immediate intervention in order to ensure the safety of the party at risk, who may be a spouse or a child. The bill provides a protection order to restrain the abuser from "being on the premises," "engaging in conduct of an offensive or harassing nature," "speaking or sending unwelcome messages," "taking possession of specified personal property," and other acts intended to intimidate or otherwise disrupt the life of the at-risk person (Domestic Violence Act, 1992, 10–11). This goal is affirmed in the bill's opening statement: "An Act to afford protection in cases involving domestic violence by the granting of a protection order; to provide the police with powers of arrest where a domestic offense occurs and for matters connected therewith or incidental thereto" (Gazette, June 20, 1992, 1). Of central concern to women's groups like BOWAND and WAV is the hope that this bill, which clearly delineates the role of the police in domestic violence, will move law enforcement agencies away from their current role of complicity toward a new one of prevention and intervention.

2. Belize Women Against Violence, "Domestic Violence, Woman Abuse, Wife Assault, Spouse Abuse, Battering," information brochure, Belize City, n.d.

3. Zola did not reveal how her husband financed his medical trip to the United States, but relatives often take up a collection for such emergencies. Many Belizeans also have relatives in the States who may be able to assist them while they seek treatment.

4. Belize Women Against Violence, "Domestic Violence, Woman Abuse."

5. The National Women's Commission's "origins lie in the Women's Bureau, established in August 1981, 'to upgrade the situation of Belizean women.' The Women's Bureau recommended in 1982 that a Cabinet-appointed National Women's Commission on the Status of Women in Belize be established" (National Women's Commission, "Objectives and Structure," March 1991). In November 1982, the fourteen-member group was appointed. All members are volunteers who represent the country's regional and ethnic/cultural diversity. They are appointed by the Cabinet and serve five-year terms. Between the formation of the commission and 1993, four women served as president: Jane Usher, Kathy Esquivel, Martha Marin, and Dorla Bowman.

6. Julie L. Stiles and Douglas Caulkins, "Prisoners in Their Own Home: A Structural and Cognitive Interpretation of the Problems of Battered Women," paper presented to the Iowa Academy of Sciences (1989).

7. Ibid., 8. Cf. Lewis Okun, *Woman Abuse: Facts Replacing Myths* (Albany: State University of New York Press, 1986).

8. Stiles and Caulkins, "Prisoners in Their Own Home," 8.

9. Cf. Ann Bookman and Sandra Morgan, eds., *Women and the Politics of Empowerment* (Philadelphia: Temple University Press, 1988); Teresa Pires de Rio Caldeira, "Women, Daily Life, and Politics," in *Women and Social Change in Latin America*, ed. Elizabeth Jelin (London: Zed Books, 1990); and Jelin, ed., *Women and Social Change in Latin America*.

10. Emphasis added.

11. Zola indicated that she was "adopted out" at the age of five.

12. Rina Benmayor, "Testimony, Action Research, and Empowerment: Puerto Rican Women and Popular Education," in *Women's Words: The Feminist Practice of Oral*

History, ed. Sherna Berger Gluck and Daphne Patai (New York: Routledge, 1991), 168.

13. Kerns, *Women and the Ancestors.*
14. Sacks, *Sisters and Wives.*
15. Lynn Bolles, "Kitchens Hit by Priorities: Employed Working-Class Jamaican Women Confront the IMF," 138–160, in *Women, Men, and the International Division of Labor,* ed. June Nash and María Patricia Fernández-Kelly (Albany: State University of New York, 1983).
16. Bolles, "Kitchens Hit by Priorities," and Deere et al., eds., *In the Shadow of the Sun.*
17. See Lila Abu-Lughod, "The Romance of Resistance: Tracing Transformation of Power through Bedouin Women," *American Ethnologist* 17 (1990): 41–55.
18. Alvarez. *Engendering Democracy in Brazil.*
19. Cf. Safa, "Women's Social Movements in Latin America."

Chapter 7. Women's Subordination in Modern Belize

1. Maya and Black.
2. Ministry of Labour and Social Services, "Policy Statement on Women in Belize," Government of Belize, 1988, 2.
3. Ibid., 3.
4. Kerns, *Women and the Ancestors,* 47.
5. Olga Stavrakis and Marion Louise Marshall, "Women, Agriculture, and Development in the Maya Lowlands: Profit or Progress?" *Belizean Studies* 8, 5 (1980): 20–28, at 24.
6. Government of Belize, *Belize Report for the Fourth World Conference on Women,* 9.
7. Ibid., 21–22.
8. Ibid., 21.
9. Ibid.
10. Lewis, *A Poverty Profile for Belize,* 23
11. It appears that Women's Workers Union disbanded in 1992; however, there seems to be a clear relationship between their activities, the labor hearings held about their case, and the subsequent establishment of a minimum wage of $2.25BZ for manual workers (who are usually male) and $2.00BZ for workers in agriculture and export industries (see Government of Belize, *Belize Report for the Fourth World Conference on Women,* 16, for a summary of the sequence of events). Ironically, women workers were initially excluded from the benefits of the minimum wage law. It was not until BOWAND waged its "Minimum Wage Campaign" in July 1992 on behalf of women, who are employed primarily as domestic workers and shop assistants, that new rates were extended to cover women's jobs. According to the BOWAND report, "In September, 1992, the Minimum Wage Council made their preliminary recommendation: $2.25BZ for shop assistants where liquor is sold; $1.75BZ for other shop assistants; and just $1.50BZ per hour for domestic workers." Although the lower rates are still less than the lowest rate for jobs traditionally held by men, they are an improvement. But as the report noted, "The outmoded beliefs about women's economic reality continue to be very strong, despite the evidence to the contrary we see every day. . . . Women . . . have little clout, little money and little power (in the usual sense of the word). Our only power is in

our collective voices, and the willingness to stand for our rights." "BOWAND's Minimum Wage Campaign," presentation for *SPEAR's Studies on Belize,* Belize City, October 21, 1993, 3–6.

12. For a discussion of gender inequality in export-processing zones, see June Nash and María Patricia Fernández-Kelly, eds., *Women, Men, and the International Division of Labor* (Albany: State University of New York Press, 1983), and Deere et al., eds., *In The Shadow of the Sun.*

13. SPEAR (Society for the Promotion of Education and Research) is one of Belize's most valuable nongovernmental organizations. It maintains the most comprehensive database on issues pertaining to contemporary Belizean life. SPEAR also produces a talk show, which is both televised and broadcast, and a newsletter. It sponsors an annual conference on Belize in Belize City in early fall; *SpeaReport* publishes the papers from the conference.

14. Adele Kalzim, "*Study Session on the Women's Worker's Union,*" report prepared for SPEAR, 1991.

15. For a discussion of how primarily women are targeted for exploitation by by multinational corporations and transnational factories as part of an international work force, see Annette Fuentes and Barbara Ehrenreich, *Women in the Global Factory,* 5th ed. (Boston: South End Press, 1988); Eva E. Abraham–Van Der Mark, "The Impact of Industrialization on Women: A Caribbean Case," in *Men, Women, and the International Division of Labor,* ed. June Nash and María Patricia Fernández-Kelly (Albany: State University of New York, 1983); Helen I. Safa, *The Myth of the Male Breadwinner: Women and Industrialization in the Caribbean* (Boulder: Westview Press, 1995); and María Patricia Fernández-Kelly, *For We Are Sold, I and My People: Women and Industry in Mexico's Frontier* (Albany: State University of New York Press, 1983).

16. At the time of the strike, the PUP (People's United Party) was in office. In 1993, the UDP won the elections for the second time in Belize's political history.

17. Safa, "Women's Social Movements in Latin America," 360.

18. "BOWAND's Minimum Wage Campaign." and Lewis and Carr, "Noh bout wi rites."

19. Government of Belize, *Belize Report for the Fourth World Conference on Women,* 21.

20. There are no figures available on the ethnic composition of this work force; such data would be extremely helpful in analyzing differences in the experiences of women across the various ethnic groups. It is possible to extrapolate from some of the reports. For example, a newly completed poverty report indicates that "poverty is most widespread among the Garifuna and Mayan ethnic groups, both of whom have an estimated incidence greater than the national average." Lewis, *A Poverty Profile for Belize,* 26. This would suggest that women from these ethnic groups might face greater disparities than their Creole, Mestizo, or East Indian counterparts. Further, an examination of the economic position of Chinese women might reveal differences related to the absolute status of their ethnic group. These are issues for future researchers.

21. Government of Belize, *Belize Report for the Fourth World Conference on Women,* 18; see also UNICEF, *UNICEF-Belize Country Programme 1992–1996: Final Report,* Belize City, 2. Rural women are particularly vulnerable, according to a proposal prepared by the Belize Rural Women's Association, which states that "in general rural women in Belize seem to have lost their resource base and have be-

come more economically dependent upon their men." Belize Rural Women's Association, "Role of Women in Agriculture and Rural Development in Belize," 1991, 22.

22. O. Nigel Bolland, in his research on colonial Belize, analyzes the myth surrounding Belize's seeming lack of incentive for increased agricultural production. He traces it back to the original treaty between the Spanish and British, which stipulated that Belize was not to be settled. Compliance with these terms and the nature of logwood extraction did not encourage farming at any level. Belize's participation in the world market and its close links to the United States also created a consumer preference for imported goods at a time when they were inexpensive. Although imported goods are now among the most expensive on the market, this combination of historical circumstances and consumer tastes provides little incentive for people to grow their own produce. Further, the government does little to discourage imports of foods and other items that could be locally produced, because it derives a large revenue from import taxes (O. Nigel Bolland, *Colonialism and Resistance in Belize* [Belize City: Cubola Productions, Iser, and SPEAR, 1988]).

23. Ester Boserup, *Woman's Role in Economic Development* (New York: St. Martin's Press, 1970), and Sidney Mintz, "Economic Role and Cultural Tradition," in *The Black Woman Cross-Culturally*, ed. Filomena Chioma Steady (Cambridge, Mass.: Schenkman Publishing Company, 1981).

24. In the 1983–84 Labour Force Survey, 10.1 percent of women were indicated as involved in agriculture. The 1991 UNICEF report, *Children First: A Situational Analysis of Children and Women*, states: "The labour force survey of 1983 indicates that 10 percent of working women in Belize are involved in agriculture. This figure is undoubtedly an underestimation as it does not reflect the number of women (and children) who perform unpaid labour on family farms or engage in subsistence farming. The Agriculture Census of 1984–85 showed that women represented 23 percent of all agricultural workers. Women account for 55 percent of small scale, landless peasants engaged in (presumably) 'milpa' farming. With the introduction of the larger scale, mechanized, cash crop farms many women lost their traditional farming activities. About 27 percent of rural women are unemployed, and an even greater number are under-employed" (18–19). The exclusion of women from agricultural sector is an important point. Much of the literature on women and the Caribbean or women and development has emphasized the importance of women's participation in subsistence agriculture in order to facilitate their own economic independence and as an important contribution to their communities. What must also be emphasized is the survival strategies women employ such as trading and bartering, supplying their communities with other types of consumer goods. For a discussion of agricultural development in Belize, see Mark Moberg, "Citrus and the State: Factions and Class Formation in Rural Belize," *American Ethnologist* 18, 2 (1991): 215–233; Moberg, *Citrus, Strategy, and Class;* and Stavrakis and Marshall, "Women, Agriculture, and Development in the Maya Lowlands."

25. This figure may appear low, because domestic work is often paid for under the table so that the employer avoids having to pay social security and other benefits. Domestic workers in the formal sector have a minimum wage scale and are entitled to social security and some holidays. These minimum benefits make their position somewhat better than that of their sisters who work in the manufacturing industry. There are no studies of women who work in the hotel and restaurant industry,

although this is a rapidly growing occupation. And I have heard women who work in wholesale and retail jobs complain of low wages and the arbitrary way they can be fired.

26. The government's emphasis upon tourism, which demands an increase in occupations in the service industry, threatens to exacerbate women's predicament by creating an increased demand for low-paid service workers. It is women who will bear the brunt of unskilled or low-skilled employment that is seasonal and subject to the ebbs and flows of an industry based on leisure and available disposable income.

27. Cf. Bullard, "Hide and Secrete."

28. Examples include Melville J. Herskovits, *Life in a Haitian Valley* (New York: Alfred A. Knopf, 1937); Edith Clarke, *My Mother Who Fathered Me: A Study of the Family in Three Selected Communities in Jamaica*, 1st ed. (London: George Allen & Unwin, 1957); Raymond T. Smith, "The Family in the Caribbean," in *The Caribbean: A Symposium*, ed. Vera Rubin, 1st ed. (Seattle: University of Washington Press, 1957); Nancie (Solien) González, *Black Carib Household Structure: A Study of Migration and Modernization* (Seattle: University of Washington Press, 1969); Nancie (Solien) González, "Toward a Definition of Matrifocality," in *Afro-American Anthropology: Contemporary Perspectives*, ed. Norman E. Whitten, Jr., and John F. Szwed (New York: Free Press, 1970); Nancie González Solien, "Household and Family in the Caribbean: Some Definitions and Concepts," in *Peoples and Cultures of the Caribbean*, ed. Michael M. Horowitz (Garden City: Natural History Press, 1971); Constance Sutton and Susan Makiesky-Barrow, "Social Inequality and Sexual Status in Barbados," in *The Black Woman Cross-Culturally*, ed. Filomena Chioma Steady (Cambridge, Mass.: Schenkman Publishing Company, 1981); Joycelin Massiah, "Women in the Caribbean (Parts I & II)," *Social and Economic Studies* 35, 1 and 2 (1986a); and Joycelin Massiah, "Women in the Caribbean Project: An Overview," *Social and Economic Studies* 35, 2 (1986b.)

29. Anne Sutherland and Laurie Kroshus, "Kinship and Family Structure on Caye Caulker," *Belizean Studies* 13, 5 and 6 (1985).

30. Ibid., 22.

31. Central Statistical Office, *Population Census*, 181.

32. Ibid.

33. Bullard, "Hide and Secrete," 260.

34. Government of Belize, *Belize Report for the Fourth World Conference on Women*, 30.

35. They state: "Most marital unions now begin when a couple decides to live together, establishing an independent household into which children are born. Most women begin their first union at about nineteen years of age and have their first child shortly thereafter. Young women agree that having children any younger causes the mother to suffer. While most marriages begin as consensual unions, there is a tendency for most to be legally formalized through civil marriage in later years. Some women, however, find themselves in a pattern of cyclical consensual unions, never marrying legally. . . . The disadvantages of consensual unions for women are several. First, there is always the possibility that a woman will be abandoned with the added responsibility of children." Bourque and Warren, *Women of the Andes*, 100.

36. Edgell, *Beka Lamb*, 108–109.

37. Ibid., 120.

38. In Belize, such pregnancies are referred to as "one drop pickni," because they often are the result of only a single sexual encounter.
39. Central Statistical Office, *Population Census*, 22.
40. Published in 1993.
41. Ruth Borker has argued that gossip is one example of women's power, which they use to regulate male behavior or to shape community attitudes. Certainly men fear being the topic of women's gossip and characterize women's talking as trivial and unproductive. She states: "Researchers have been especially interested in women's gossip because it is seen as an important source of social power for women in these communities. Researchers in southern Europe have seen women's gossip as an important mechanism for social control and for asserting social values, supporting the general anthropological view of the functions of gossip." Ruth Borker, "Anthropology: Social and Cultural Perspectives," in *Women and Language in Literature and Society*, ed. Sally McConnell-Ginet, Ruth Borker, and Nelly Furman (New York: Praeger, 1980), 34.
42. Bullard, "Hide and Secrete," 261.
43. Helen Safa describes similar attitudes among women in Latin America. Safa, *The Myth of the Male Breadwinner*.
44. See Mohammed, "Reflections on the Women's Movement in Trinidad."
45. This song was popular in Belize during 1991; I have translated the Creole words to the best of my ability. I thank Linden Lewis, who informed me that this was a calypso (not reggae) song sung by Marcie from Bardados.
46. At the time of my fieldwork (1991–92) there were two evening schools in Belize where young mothers could finish their education. One was located in Belize City and the other was located in Punta Gorda, the southernmost town in the country. The fees for evening school in 1991 were approximately $35BZ per month, somewhat higher than regular school fees ($30BZ per month). In addition to paying fees, students must also buy their own books. Although economic opportunities for everyone in small rural towns and villages like Lemongrass are limited, women with small children appear to have even fewer options that would enable them to acquire the funds needed to support themselves and pay school fees. This lack of resources is a source of discouragement above and beyond the negative attitudes they may encounter.
47. Belize has recently opened a new office specifically concerned with child rights and abuse, funded in part by UNICEF; UNICEF, *Children First: A Situational Analysis of Women and Children*, 54.
48. UNICEF, *Children First: A Situational Analysis of Women and Children*, 44.
49. Government of Belize, *Belize Report for the Fourth World Conference on Women*, 22.
50. I am not suggesting that women are more likely to abuse children than men. The few studies available on the issue in Belize tend to speak of "parents" as perpetrators and generally do not separate the frequency of abuse by gender. However, as Zola suggests in her narrative, women, who are usually in greater contact with children, often may take out their own frustrations with their conjugal relationship, itself often abusive, on their offspring. This issue requires further study and analysis, not only to document the frequency of abuse, but also to define what constitutes the appropriate exercise of parental authority in the Belizean context and what constitutes abusive behavior in a country with tremendous ethnic diversity and a range of cultural norms. This is a critical matter for governments given the pressure

by international agencies to create policies on the subject. Belize, while forging ahead in this area with the financial support of UNICEF (which has its own cultural notions of abuse, as defined in the United States), has yet to complete the extensive data collection needed to compare parenting styles among the various ethnic groups, examine the differences in understandings of what constitutes inappropriate child behavior, and evaluate children's responses to various disciplinary styles. Data on these areas are needed prior to any policy formulation. For an etic (insider's) analysis, see Joseph O. Palacio, *A Survey of Child Abuse and Neglect in Belize City: A Preliminary Report* (Belize City: National Council on Child Abuse and Neglect, 1985). UNICEF's position has been clearly delineated; see UNICEF, *Children First: A Situational Analysis of Women and Children.*

Chapter 8. Evelyn's Story

1. Cf. Jorgensen, "On Ethics and Anthropology."
2. O. Nigel Bolland, Belize's definitive historiographer, has written several books on the country, cited in Chapter 2. See, for example, *Belize: A New Nation in Central America.*
3. Kerns, *Women and the Ancestors.*
4. (Cf. Clarke, *My Mother Who Fathered Me;* Carol B. Stack, *All Our Kin: Strategies for Survival in a Black Community* (New York: Harper & Row, 1974); and González, *Black Carib Household Structure.*
5. "White" and "clear" are terms used in Belize in reference to light-skinned Creoles. They do not refer to ancestry so much as to skin color.
6. Louise Lamphere, ed., *Structuring Diversity: Ethnographic Perspectives on the New Immigration* (Chicago: University of Chicago Press, 1992).
7. Cf. Jacqueline Jones, *Labor of Love, Labor of Sorrow: Black Women, Work, and the Family from Slavery to the Present* (New York: Random House, 1986).
8. Throughout my initial stay in Lemongrass and thereafter, I never observed Alan involved in a job that required him to adhere to a schedule. He was always around and would periodically leave for a few days at a time. Despite the absence of any regularly scheduled job, he always seem to have money to invest in one scheme after another or to put toward his medical bills. Often he played the role of "cultural broker" for American businessmen, serving as a liaison between the visitors and Belizean culture. In many ways he was an entrepreneur, whom Richard Bee defines as an individual "who tend[s] to push the constraints harder than others or to circumvent some of them, so as to create new alternatives." Alan tended "to be more willing to take risks than others in . . . [his community]" and was more inclined to "be the first to try out new techniques of business, politics, or other social action." Robert L. Bee, *Patterns and Processes: An Introduction to Anthropological Strategies for the Study of Sociocultural Change* (New York: Free Press, 1974), 199–200.
9. For information about emigration in Belize, see Joseph O. Palacio, "Garifuna Immigrants in Los Angeles: Attempts at Self-Improvement," *Belizean Studies* 20, 3 (1992): 17–26, and Dylan Vernon, "Belizean Exodus to the United States: For Better or for Worse," *SpeaReports* 4 (1990): 7–25.
10. Cf. Fuentes and Ehrenreich, *Women in the Global Factory,* and Deere et al., eds., *In the Shadow of the Sun.*

11. It is not unusual for people in Belize to meet tourists or those on business trips who invite them to come to the States and work. This is especially true for women, who have no difficulty in finding live-in jobs as domestic workers.

12. In 1993 Evelyn sold the stock of her store and began building an extension on her house to house a "mini-market." Without the overhead cost of rent, she hopes to make this venture more economically productive. Her children and neighborhood kids assist her. Although Evelyn has a very strong business sense, she does not profit as much as she might if she stopped extending credit to neighbors and relatives.

13. Safa, "Women's Social Movements in Latin America," 363; see also Jelin, ed., *Women and Social Change in Latin America.*

14. Much has changed in Belize in recent years. Police have become much more aware of domestic violence as a specific form of harassment. In addition, the passage of the Domestic Violence Bill has given them an explicit mechanism for intervention.

15. Religion plays an important role in the lives of many Belizeans. "About 58% of the population are Roman Catholics, the other 34% are Protestants (this includes Anglican, Methodists, Seventh Day Adventists, Mennonites, Nazarenes, Jehovah's Witnesses, Pentecostal and Baptists). There are also small groups of Bahai's and Musims. The remaining 8% are other denominations." Government of Belize, *Fact Sheet Belize*, Belize Information Service Publication, 1994.

16. Peter J. Wilson, *Crab Antics: The Social Anthropology of English-Speaking Negro Societies of the Caribbean* (New Haven: Yale University Press, 1973).

Chapter 9. The Quest for Female Autonomy

1. As noted in chapter 6, to "get upstart" is a Creole phrase used to refer to children who attempt to act like adults; when applied to women, the phrase is meant to admonish them for acting assertive, independent, and beyond the boundaries of what men believe to be women's proper role—submissive and subordinate.

2. For a list of women's groups in Belize, see McClaurin, "Women and the Culture of Gender in Belize, Central America," appendix.

3. For more information on women's groups (both grass-roots and mainstream) in different societies, see Ellis, ed., *Women of the Caribbean;* Sally Yudelman, *Hopeful Openings* (West Hartford, Conn.: Kumarian Press, 1987); Ann Bookman and Sandra Morgen, eds., *Women and the Politics of Empowerment* (Philadelphia: Temple University Press, 1988); Susan Hyatt, "Accidental Activists: Women and Politics on a Council Estate," paper presented at the annual meeting of the American Anthropological Association in Chicago, Illinois, 1991; Ibrahima Bakhoum et al., *Banking the Unbankable: Bringing Credit to the Poor* (London: Panos Publications, 1989); Sacks, *Engels Revisited;* and Safa, "Women's Social Movements in Latin America."

4. Johanna Brenner and Barbara Laslett, "Gender, Social Reproduction, and Women's Self-Organization: Considering the U.S. Welfare State," *Gender and Society* 5, 3 (1991): 321–322.

5. Ibid., 313.

6. Safa, "Women's Social Movements in Latin America," 363.

7. Caldeira, "Women, Daily Life, and Politics," 49.

8. Brenner and Laslett, "Gender, Social Reproduction, and Women's Self-Organization," 323.

9. Cf. Alvarez, *Engendering Democracy in Brazil*; Caldeira, "Women, Daily Life,and Politics"; and Brenner and Laslett, "Gender, Social Reproduction, and Women's Self-Organization."

10. Brenner and Laslett, "Gender, Social Reproduction, and Women's Self-Organization," 314.

11. Cf. Alvarez, *Engendering Democracy in Brazil,* and Maxine Molyneux, "Mobilization without Emancipation? Women's Interests, State, and Revolution," in *Transitions and Development: Problems of Third World Socialism,* ed. R. Fagen, C. D. Deere, and J. L. Corragio (New York: Monthly Review Press, 1986).

12. Cf. Collins, *Black Feminist Thought,* and bell hooks, *Ain't I a Woman: Black Women and Feminism* (Boston: South End Press, 1981).

13. Government of Belize, *Belize Report for the Fourth World Conference on Women,* 23.

14. Ibid., 21.

15. Cf. Hyatt, "Accidental Activists"; Mohammed, "Reflections on the Women's Movement in Trinidad"; Caldeira, "Women, Daily Life, and Politics"; Sylvia Walby, "Gender, Class, and Stratification," in *Gender and Stratification,* ed. Rosemary Crompton and Michael Mann (Cambridge: Polity Press, 1986); Alvarez, *Engendering Democracy in Brazil*; Temma Kaplan, "Female Consciousness and Collective Action: The Case of Barcelona," 7 3 (1982): 545–566;

16. Cf. Alvarez, *Engendering Democracy in Brazil,* and Caldeira, "Women, Daily Life, and Politics."

17. Cf. Miranda Davies, ed., *Third World—Second Sex: Women's Struggles and National Liberation, Third World Women Speak Out* (London: Zed Books, 1983), and Elizabeth V. Spelman, *Inessential Woman: Problems of Exclusion in Feminist Thought* (Boston: Beacon Press, 1988).

18. See Molyneux, "Mobilization without emancipation?"

19. Walby, "Gender, Class, and Stratification," 33.

20. Alvarez, *Engendering Democracy in Brazil.*

21. Ibid., 24–25.

22. Hyatt, "Accidental Activists."

23. Cf. Faye D. Ginsburg, *Contested Lives: The Abortion Debate in an American Community* (Berkeley: University of California Press, 1989).

24. Ellis, ed., *Women of the Caribbean.*

25. Ibid., 11.

26. Shoman, *Party Politics in Belize,* 1987

27. McClaurin, "A Writer's Life, a Country's Transition," 40.

28. Interview with Kathy Esquivel, 1992.

29. Safa, "Women's Social Movements in Latin Amerca," 359.

30. Shoman, *Party Politics in Belize,* and Edie, "The Persistence of Clientelist Politics in Jamaica."

31. Myrtle Palacio,"Elections in Belize City—Who is Participating? A Critique of Our Voting System," in *SPEAR's Fourth Annual Studies on Belize,* Belize City, 1990.

32. Hilkka Pietila and Jeanne Vickers, *Making Women Matter: the Role of the United Nations* (London: Zed Books, 1990).

33. Cf. A. Lynn Bolles, "Doing It for Themselves: Women's Research and Action in the Commonwealth Caribbean," in *Perspectives and Resources: Integrating Latin American and Caribbean Women into the Curriculum and Research,* ed. Edna Acosta-Belén and Christine E. Bose (Albany: Center for Latin America and the Caribbean [CELAC] and Institute for Research on Women [IROW], 1991), 49.

34. Cf. Hale, "Women's Culture/Men's Culture." My thanks to Nina Glick Schiller for her comments on an earlier version of this chapter and in bringing to my attention the discussion of women's culture.

35. Kaplan, "Female Consciousness and Collective Action," 547.

36. I am indebted to Zee Edgell for sharing with me the survey data she collected for a "Directory and Inventory of Women's Organizations and Community Groups" in Belize commissioned by the Environment Liaison Centre International (ELCI) and scheduled for publication. I also wish to acknowledge the extensive and insightful discussion about women's groups I had with David Lopez, one of the field assistants for the project. See also *Integration for Development: A Resource Guide for Belize* (Belmopan: Ministry of Economic Development and UNICEF-Belize and United Nations Development Programme, 1991).

37. As a result of the Decade, Women in Development (WID) programs were often linked to development aid from USAID, the World Bank, and other sources as a way to integrate women into the development process at the national level.

38. I thank Louis Shaw, Central Statistical Office, Belize, for locating these data.

39. Government of Belize, *Belize Report for the Fourth World Conference on Women.*

40. Ibid., 12. For a discussion of women's economic status, see chapter 7.

41. Central Statistical Office, "1993 Labour Force Survey Report," vol. 1, Central Statistical Office, Ministry of Finance, 1993, 38.

42. Government of Belize, *Belize Report for the Fourth World Conference on Women,* 21.

43. For a fictionalized history of the formation of the Department of Women's Affairs, see Zee Edgell, *In Times Like These* (London: Heinneman, 1991).

44. The exact date for this change in the position was not available at the time of writing. For a discussion of political patronage, see Edie, "The Persistence of Clientelist Politics in Jamaica."

45. The Department of Women's Affairs' commitment to activities that reinforce or build upon traditional domestic skills may be explained by the fact that the impetus for it came from the Social Development Department (SDS), now known as the Department of Human Development. It was the SDS that initially sponsored conferences and organized workshops aimed at women. Moreover, the current district officers, known as women's development officers (WDO), who are responsible for program planning in their district, were originally called home economics officers. Thus, while the names have changed, the WDOs still concentrate their programming largely on activities related to the domestic area of women's lives.

46. Caldeira, "Women, Daily Life, and Politics."

47. Cf. Yudelman, *Hopeful Openings.*

48. Another example is the Women's Workers Union, discussed in chapter 7, which formed to protest wage and work conditions in the garment industry. Although no longer in existence, its efforts served to publicize women's low status in the labor force and the problem of minimum wage, which was recently increased. See BOWAND, "BOWAND'S Minimum Wage Campaign," and Lewis and Carr, "Noh bout wi rites."

Chapter 10. "Dis Heah Time No Stand Like Befo' Time"

1. Nafis Sadik, "Women Empowered: The Earth's Last Hope," *New Perspectives Quarterly* 11, 4 (1994).

2. Ibid., 13–15.

Index

About the Author

Irma McClaurin was born in Chicago, Illinois. An anthropologist and poet, she began writing poetry about her experiences as an African American when she was eight years old. She holds an M.F.A. in English and a Ph.D. in anthropology, both from the University of Massachusetts. She is the author of three books of poetry and her works have appeared in over 16 magazines and anthologies; her poetry has also been translated into Spanish and Swedish. She is currently associate professor of anthropology and an affiliate of the Centers for Latin American Studies, African Studies, and Women and Gender Studies at the University of Florida. She conducts research on domestic violence cross-culturally and is working on an intellectual biography of Zora Neale Hurston as an anthropologist.